Christian Nationalism in the United States

Special Issue Editor
Mark T. Edwards

MDPI • Basel • Beijing • Wuhan • Barcelona • Belgrade

MDPI

Special Issue Editor
Mark T. Edwards
Spring Arbor University
USA

Editorial Office
MDPI AG
St. Alban-Anlage 66
Basel, Switzerland

This edition is a reprint of the Special Issue published online in the open access journal *Religions* (ISSN 2077-1444) from 2016–2017 (available at: http://www.mdpi.com/journal/religions/special_issues/christian_nationalism).

For citation purposes, cite each article independently as indicated on the article page online and as indicated below:

Author 1; Author 2. Article title. *Journal Name* **Year**, *Article number*, page range.

First Edition 2017

ISBN 978-3-03842-438-3 (Pbk)
ISBN 978-3-03842-439-0 (PDF)

Table of Contents

About the Special Issue Editor

Mark Edwards is Associate Professor of US history and politics at Spring Arbor University in Michigan. His research centers on the intersection of American religion, culture, and politics. Mark has published articles in Religion and American Culture, Diplomatic History, Totalitarian Movements and Political Religions, Religions, the Journal of Religious History, and the Journal of Cold War Studies. His first book, The Right of the Protestant Left: God's Totalitarianism (Palgrave Macmillan, July 2012) offers a new view of Reinhold Niebuhr, Christian Realism, and the geopolitics of the ecumenical movement. Mark was also co-chair of the 2014 US Intellectual History conference in Indianapolis with Cara Burnidge. In the Spring of 2018, Mark will serve as Fulbright Scholar to Hankuk University of Foreign Studies in Seoul, Korea.

religions

MDPI

Editorial

Religions Series: "Christian Nationalism in the United States"—Ebook Introduction

Mark Edwards

Department of History, Political Economy, Geography, and Social Studies, Spring Arbor University, 106 E Main St, Spring Arbor, MI 49283, USA; mark.edwards@arbor.edu

Academic Editor: Victor Roudometof
Received: 9 May 2017; Accepted: 10 May 2017; Published: 13 May 2017

While Christianity in American history remains a vibrant subfield, the subject of Christian nationalism in the United States remains understudied. The best survey on the topic, Robert T. Handy's *A Christian America: Protestant Hopes and Historical Realities*, was lasted updated in 1984. The long absence of studies is particularly striking, given that related abstractions such as "civil religion" and "culture wars" receive regular updates. Recently, a number of historians have returned directly and indirectly to the subject of Christian nationalism, including John Fea (Fea 2016), Steven Green (Green 2015), Amanda Porterfield (Porterfield 2015), David Sehat (Sehat 2011), Emily Conroy-Krutz, (Conroy-Krutz 2015), Matthew Sutton (Sutton 2004), Kevin Kruse (Kruse 2015), Michael Thompson (Thompson 2015), and Sam Haselby (Haselby 2015), among others. Their scholarship teaches us several lessons. First, we should avoid "decline and revival" narratives and understand Christian nationalism as a construction (a "myth," as Green terms it) that has arisen at various times in various places to accomplish a myriad of work. Second, Christian nationalism has been advanced by a diversity of persons and groups favorable and hostile to the idea, not just by evangelical Protestants. Third, Christian nationalism can be operational even when its keywords "Christian nation" and "Christian America" are absent. Finally, and most importantly, "Christian nationalism" is a discursive site where politics and history meet—where assertions of identity and power are conjoined.

The essays in this Special Issue will assess and apply (or relate) those lessons to a number of new subjects, events, and time periods within American history. Our intent is not to document every instance of Christian nationalism from every possible perspective. Rather, our aim is to prove the utility of "Christian nationalism" as an analytical concept—like "civil religion" or "culture wars"—to understand continuity and disjuncture throughout U.S. politics, culture, and society. Our respective definitions, redefinitions, and reframing of Christian nationalism should spark further investigations into its multiple manifestations and impact.

Conflicts of Interest: The authors declare no conflict of interest.

References

Fea, John. 2016. *Was America Founded as a Christian Nation? Revised Edition: A Historical Introduction*. Louisville: Westminster John Knox.

Green, Steven. 2015. *Inventing a Christian America: The Myth of the Religious Founding*. New York: Oxford University Press.

Porterfield, Amanda. 2015. *Conceived in Doubt: Religion and Politics in the New American Nation*. Chicago: University of Chicago Press.

Sehat, David. 2011. *The Myth of American Religious Freedom*. New York: Oxford University Press.

Conroy-Krutz, Emily. 2015. *Christian Imperialism: Converting the World in the Early American Republic*. Ithaca: Cornell University Press.

Sutton, Matthew Avery. 2014. *American Apocalypse: A History of Modern Evangelicalism*. Cambridge: Belknap Press.

Kruse, Kevin. 2015. *One Nation under God: How Corporate America Invented Christian America*. New York: Basic.

Thompson, Michael. 2015. *For God and Globe: Christian Internationalism in the United States between the Great War and the Cold War*. Ithaca: Cornell University Press.

Haselby, Sam. 2015. The Origins of American Religious Nationalism. New York: Oxford University Press.

religions

MDPI

Article

Religion, the Federalists, and American Nationalism

Jonathan Den Hartog

Department of History, University of Northwestern—St. Paul, St. Paul, MN 55113, USA;
jdenhartog@unwsp.edu; Tel.: +1-651-628-3253

Academic Editor: Mark T. Edwards
Received: 30 September 2016; Accepted: 27 December 2016; Published: 5 January 2017

Abstract: It may seem a truism to assert that the Federalist Party in the Early American Republic possessed a nationalist emphasis, but the question remains as to the character of their nationalism. This article draws on categories from the historian John D. Wilsey to determine how "open" or "closed" Federalist nationalism was. It looks to public utterances of Federalist leaders to find that they attempted to hold up the nation as an ideal, but that they avoided expansionistic tendencies in foreign affairs. This allows the article to posit Federalist nationalism as "open." It then considers what role religion played in supporting this "open" Federalist nationalism. It finds that Federalist religious nationalism developed in three stages: "Republican," "Federalist," and "Voluntarist," as Federalists responded to needs within, and changes to, the new nation. The article concludes that religion (predominantly Protestant Christianity) thus operated creatively in support of an "open" Federalist nationalism.

Keywords: Christian Nationalism; civil religion; politics; Federalist Party; voluntarism; Protestantism; United States; Early American Republic; religion in America; religion and politics

1. Introduction

It seems an obvious assertion that in the early American Republic, the Federalists were nationalists. Whether discussing the coalition that rallied in favor of ratifying the Constitution or the political movement and nascent political party in the 1790s and early nineteenth century, the Federalists argued for an American nationalism. In the ratification debate, they supported a Constitution that created a national government, over and against the Anti-Federalists who defended the Articles of Confederation and the looser cooperation of sovereign states. Further, in the ratification debates the Federalists ironically seized the semantic high-ground, as the term "federal" had traditionally referred to dispersed and divided sovereign power, but now became applied to a nationalist movement.

In the 1790s, the Federalists became "Friends of Government," supporting the Washington and Adams administrations, in the face of challenges from Democratic-Republicans. Presidents Washington and Adams—with advice from nationalists such as Alexander Hamilton and John Jay—sought to build very real national political power [1]. Economically, Hamilton sought a national policy through assumption of state debts, a national bank, and federal encouragement of manufacturing [2]. Further, Henry Knox designed a small, but permanent, national army, and John Adams ordered construction of America's first navy. In the face of this political nationalism, Thomas Jefferson, James Madison, and other Republicans (or Democratic-Republicans) feared the centralizing power of the national government and sought ways to curb it. For Jefferson and Madison, this could lead to states negating and nullifying federal laws, as expressed in the Virginia and Kentucky Resolutions [3,4].

In his classic work *Imagined Communities*, Benedict Anderson rightfully demonstrated that nations and nationalism are about more than just power—though they are about that. Instead, they are about creating a sense of community and belonging that stretches far beyond the bounds of lived experience [5]. In fact, historical research of the past two decades has documented that Federalists took many steps to create a sense of nationalism in the new United States. The Revolution and its aftermath gave rise to public expressions of politics—parades, marches, and demonstrations helped Americans express their ideas about national issues, whether ratifying the Constitution or opposing French threats to American interests [6]. These celebrations could particularly be seen at times of national celebrations, whether for Washington's birthday (particularly important for the Federalists) or for Independence Day [7,8]. Further, print culture helped to unite the country and give written expression to a sense of the nation. Printing, reading, and writing helped bind the nation together [9,10]. Federalists used newspapers to advance their perspective, as well as magazines like Joseph Dennie's *Port Folio* [11]. In certain circumstances, even the spoken word could produce nationalistic sentiments [12].

Federalists sought a nationalism that was more robust than simply a vision of political unity. The Federalists realized that the Constitution had created "a roof without walls"—a political structure without a national identity, and they, therefore, worked to create a more extensive and well-developed national culture ([13], pp. 333–48). This cultural nationalism advanced on a number of fronts. Culture could mean literature and the culture of *belles lettres*, and the Federalists worked to craft reflective essays that could be read around the world [14,15]. The American language came under Federalist notice, as Noah Webster labored to create a national dictionary [16]. Law was necessary for national flourishing, an opinion shared not only by Chief Justice of the Supreme Court John Marshall but by many other Federalist jurists, like James Kent in New York or Theophilus Parsons in Massachusetts ([17], pp. 135–72; [18,19]). The art Americans produced and displayed carried national implications [20]. Even the topic of geography could take a nationalist turn, as the Federalist minister Jedidiah Morse demonstrated [21]. This article will suggest below that Federalists also deployed religion as another key component for creating a Federalist nationalism.

This overview has supported the initial claim that the Federalists were standing for nationalism in the new nation. The question remains, however—what *kind* of nationalists were the Federalists? Further, how was religion a part of Federalist nationalism, and how did it function to support a certain type of nationalism?

2. "Open" and "Closed" Nationalism

In assessing the Federalists, we first have to address the previous question of evaluating nationalism. For some writers on the topic, nationalism is problematic at best, and inherently evil at worst. Nationalism, it is true, does carry within itself a great capacity to do wrong—in previous centuries it has tended toward being exclusionary to minorities, oppressive to dissenters, and expansionistic both within its borders and beyond them. As a substitute type of religion—or perhaps a political commitment in the place of traditional religion—it finds ways to justify many wrongs. Thus, we have to admit that nationalism carries many implicit dangers. Without a doubt, the places where nationalism led Europe in World War I and World War II should give all scholars pause. If nationalism is dismissed out of hand, there is not much to say: nationalism's builders should be condemned briskly.

It will prove more useful, however, to consider nationalism historically and contextually. Rather than rejecting it out of hand, the roles and purposes of specific nationalisms deserve consideration. It thus matters how and why nationalism was deployed. This approach allows us to consider the particularities of the different times and places in which nationalism has operated. It also allows a more nuanced and historically accurate picture of the interaction between the Federalist concerns for religion and nationalism.

In evaluating the Federalists, a helpful strategy comes from John D. Wilsey, in his book *American Exceptionalism and Civil Religion*. The category of "civil religion" is conceptually related to a religious nationalism, although the two are not the same thing—one might see civil religion as reversing the order of priority from a nationalism colored by religion to a religion centered on nationalism. Still, Wilsey provides tools and definitions which we can adapt to our goal of understanding Federalist nationalism. Particularly helpful is Wilsey's ideas of "open" and "closed" versions of American exceptionalism. Wilsey observes, "In short, when American exceptionalism calls for a God-ordained empire, then it leads to idolatry and injustice. When American exceptionalism points to moral and civil example, then it leads to compassion, justice and general human flourishing" ([22], p. 19). To Wilsey, an idolatrous empire is the direction of a "closed" type of exceptionalism, while a nation affirming a moral and civil example is an "open" type of exceptionalism. This "open" version "can serve as a beacon pointing to justice, natural rights and the ethical well-being of the nation and the world" ([22], p. 19). Wilsey goes on to provide other helpful contrasts—"The closed side is exclusive; the open side is inclusive. The closed side limits freedom to some; the open side expands it to all. The closed side is self-satisfied, because it is based on determinism. The open side is never satisfied, because it is reaching for an ideal based on natural law and rights theory as well as historical contingency" ([22], p. 19). In his work, Wilsey concludes by endorsing and even encouraging an "open" exceptionalism as healthy and as a pathway for civic engagement.

This article, then, must address the question of whether the Federalists' view of nationalism was of more an "open" or "closed" variety. In taking on this question, Wilsey raises some important categories to consider, such as the place of the nation in the realm of ideals and ideas, the foreign policy of the nation (how imperial it is), and its treatment of minorities. With these questions in hand, we can turn to understand how the Federalists considered the nation in relation to other nations and how they defined a foreign policy toward the wider world. The best method for this investigation will be to consider the public expressions of leading Federalists, especially those made in prominent declarations. Once we understand the character of the Federalists' nationalism, we can then understand how religion either supported or tempered it.

3. Federalists and the National Example

We can start by examining how Federalists viewed their nation in its symbolic and theoretical relation to the rest of the world. Here, Federalists emphasized the American example for other nations and stressed the importance of a healthy nationalism that could be communicated to the world. This impulse was on display as early as Alexander Hamilton's fanfare to readers in his *Federalist Papers* essay #1:

> The subject speaks its own importance; comprehending in its consequences nothing less than the existence of the UNION, the safety and welfare of the parts of which it is composed, the fate of an empire in many respects the most interesting in the world. It has been frequently remarked that it seems to have been reserved to the people of this country, by their conduct and example, to decide the important question, whether societies of men are really capable or not of establishing good government from reflection and choice, or whether they are forever destined to depend for their political constitutions on accident and force [23].

Was self-government possible? Could an America in a national union be a pattern for other nations? Hamilton suggested the American example would be determinative, a living commentary on whether "reflection and choice" could triumph over force in self-government, and the answer would be delivered on the world stage.

Additionally, during the debates over ratifying the Constitution, John Jay raised a similar point. For him, nothing less than a world-historical issue, "the cause of freedom" was in the balance. In his stand-alone essay, the *Address to the Citizens of the State of New York*, Jay pointed to the negative consequences that would follow failing to create a self-governing nation:

> [I]f the event should prove, that the people of this country either cannot or will not govern themselves, who will hereafter be advocates for systems, which however charming in theory and prospect, are not reducible to practice[?] If the people of our nation, instead of consenting to be governed by laws of their own making and rulers of their own choosing, should let licentiousness, disorder and confusion reign over them, the minds of men everywhere, will insensibly become alienated from republican forms, and prepared to

prefer and acquiesce in Governments, which, though less friendly to liberty, afford more peace and security ([24], p. 19).

Americans could also offer a negative example, proving to the world that self-government was not possible. Observers would opt for "peace and security" over either "republican forms" or governments "friendly to liberty." Again, the American example mattered, but because American nationalism was, itself, uncertain, it could hardly be guaranteed as a panacea to other nations. Instead, Americans had to prove by their example the value of republican self-government.

Once the Constitution was ratified, Federalists continued to emphasize the stakes of the national endeavor. In his First Inaugural Address, President Washington illustrated how he saw the Federalist endeavor. "[T]he preservation of the sacred fire of liberty, and the destiny of the Republican model of Government," Washington insisted, "are justly considered as deeply, perhaps as finally staked, on the experiment entrusted to the hands of the American people" [25]. Phrases like this lent great moral weight to the journey upon which Washington and the new nation were embarking. The very "destiny" of republican self-government rested on American behavior. In this light, then, Federalists saw themselves as a model to other nations.

To serve as an example to other nations, the Federalists worked to cultivate patriotic nationalism. The Massachusetts Federalist Fisher Ames delineated this goal by asking, "What is Patriotism?" He answered, "It is an extended self-love, mingling with all the enjoyments o life ... It is thus we obey the laws of society, because they are the laws of virtue. In their authority we see ... the venerable image of our country's honor. Every good citizen makes that honor his own ... " ([26], p. 1170). Thus, the creation of nationalism would be an on-going project for Federalist leaders, and it sparked the varied endeavors identified in the introductions. Still, the pursuit was a valuable one to the Federalists, and its value would be expressed in a two-fold way: through the flourishing of the American people—with every man sitting under his own vine and fig tree (Micah 4:4)—and through the example it offered to other nations.

4. Federalists and Foreign Policy

Another way of assessing Federalist nationalism would be to observe their actual foreign policy. Although not in a position to function in a markedly expansionist way, still, the Federalists sought a different strategy out of both principle and prudence, one of neutrality. Instead of advocating for further conquest beyond the lands granted the country in the Treaty of Paris (1783), the Federalists sought positive relations with other nations, desiring to earn their good opinion and a proper reputation for the new nation. Generally, Federalist diplomacy aimed for peaceful cooperation and encouraging international trade. When confronted with the French Revolution and the brewing European war between France and England, Federalists under President Washington pursued a policy of armed neutrality. This course would prepare to defend the nation while doing everything in their power to avoid war. A strong example of this general impulse came with Washington's appointing John Jay as a special diplomat to Great Britain to avert war in 1794–1795. The result—Jay's Treaty—sought to create the best possible resolution of national differences, even as it passed silently over irreconcilable points. A Federalist attitude of cooperation was evident in Jay's strategy—to work out points open to multiple interpretation, a joint commission from both nations would work collaboratively to resolve difficulties [27].

President Washington reemphasized these commitments in his "Farewell Address," his political benediction. Washington instructed his countrymen and successors, "Observe good faith and justice towards all Nations. Cultivate peace and harmony with all. It is our true policy to steer clear of permanent alliances with any portion of the foreign world; so far, I mean, as we are now at liberty to do it ... Harmony, liberal intercourse with all nations, are recommended by policy, humanity, and interest" [28]. Positive and forthright interactions with other nations were justified by both good policy and humanitarian principle. Similarly, American diplomacy would work to uphold its national commitments made via treaty. In discussing his policy of neutrality, Washington insisted that it arose from both "duty and interest" for the American nation and that, once made, Washington was committed to following it with "moderation, perseverance, and firmness" [28]. This strategy of armed neutrality actively avoided foreign intervention. It did not set the country on a policy of advancing ideals of democracy and representative government by force of arms. If anything, it sought national defense as a means of protecting "the sacred fire of liberty" Washington had praised in his First Inaugural Address ([29], pp. 56–92).

Two decades later, this Federalist approach to foreign policy was re-echoed by Secretary of State John Quincy Adams. In his foreign policy, Adams was not only the biological heir of the Federalist John Adams but the ideological one, as well. John Quincy Adams sought to improve diplomatic relations through formal treaties that could be agreed upon and kept. He, thus, pursued the Transcontinental Treaty with Spain (also known as the Adams-Onís Treaty, 1819). More importantly, he directed American foreign policy when confronted with multiple revolutions in Latin America. In a famous public speech, he laid out a policy entirely consistent with Federalist approaches of earlier years. He began by placing American activities within the framework of relations with other nations:

> America, with the same voice which spoke herself into existence as a nation, proclaimed to mankind the inextinguishable rights of human nature, and the only lawful foundations of government. America, in the assembly of nations, since her admission among them, has invariably, though often fruitlessly, held forth to them the hand of honest friendship, of equal freedom, of generous reciprocity. She has uniformly spoken among them, though often to heedless and often to disdainful ears, the language of equal liberty, of equal justice, and of equal rights. She has, in the lapse of nearly half a century, without a single exception, respected the independence of other nations while asserting and maintaining her own. She has abstained from interference in the concerns of others, even when conflict has been for principles to which she clings, as to the last vital drop that visits the heart [30].

In this statement, Adams reiterates American desire for self-defense while holding up American self-government (founded on "the rights of human nature") in the international arena. While defending her own rights, though, Adams points out how America has "abstained from interference" in other countries' affairs. While loving principles, American foreign policy has been non-interventionist [31].

From this general principle, Adams went on to advance a specific application in his day. As much as Americans advocated for independence and self-government, they should not attempt to advance them abroad. He memorably asserted, "Wherever the standard of freedom and independence has been or shall be unfurled, there will her heart, her benedictions, and her prayers be. But she goes not abroad in search of monsters to destroy. She is the well-wisher to the freedom and independence of all. She is the champion and vindicator only of her own" [30]. While there would be plenty of monsters to combat, Adams drew the line between cheering for principles and actively fighting for them abroad. Adams advocated for this because of the danger posed by engaging in global battles: "The fundamental maxims of her policy would insensibly change from liberty to force. . . . She might become the dictatress of the world. She would be no longer the ruler of her own spirit" [30]. Respect for other nations' self-determination meant the United States had to refrain from an interventionist, expansionist policy. It served the world best by setting a principled example.

5. "Open" Federalist Nationalism

With these articulations of Federalist nationalism, I assert that the Federalist perspective, following Wilsey, was an "open" nationalism. It held up American ideals for the rest of the world, and it worked to make the nation an example to other nations. In its foreign policy, it sought constructive engagement with other nations and worked to maintain treaty obligations. In this view of mutual international cooperation, Federalists prioritized opening up trade and settling differences through compromise and collaborative commissions. Put together, this "open" nationalism offered a welcoming stance that sought to advance ideals through persuasion, not force. In the process, it posited a national community that, while still recognizing inequalities, could bring individuals together into a national identity.

In this "open" nationalism, Federalists created spaces for minority groups. Although not all Federalists were opposed to slavery, many leaders of the anti-slavery cause were Federalists or the sons of Federalists. For example, many of the members of the New York Manumission Society were Federalists, an effort typified by John Jay and his family [32]. Meanwhile, in New England, many religious Federalists were at the forefront of opposing slavery [33–35]. Further, the Federalists recognized a political role for women—even though those same women would be subject to a Democratic-Republican "backlash" to expel them from politics [36,37]. Federalists even conceptualized a place for Native Americans in the new republic [38]. Although Federalist ideals were still imperfectly held and practiced, they at least embodied an attempt at an "open" nationalism in the early republic.

This Federalist "open" nationalism developed through bringing multiple streams of thought and belief together. It harmonized beliefs rooted in both "reason" and "revelation." Put another way, it brought together Jewish and Christian concepts inspired by the Scriptures while also being informed by less religious descriptions of politics ([22], pp. 39–58). Following moderate elements of "enlightened" thinking in the era, Federalists described universal principles that could speak to humans across times and cultures. Such principles were rooted in a description of humans as carrying rights rooted in nature, but a nature designed by a Creator ([39], pp. 4–10, 131–46). Such a combination was evident even in the Declaration of Independence's claim that "We hold these truths to be self-evident, that all men are created equal, that they are endowed by their Creator with certain unalienable Rights" [40]. A belief in Rights rooted in Creation allowed for open engagement and cross-cultural application. It also enabled cooperation between classical political theory, moderate forms of enlightened political thought, and traditional Christianity. Although these streams of thought did not always align fully, they did provide enough common ground to support an "open" nationalism.

6. Religion and Federalist Nationalism

If the Federalists drew on religious beliefs to nurture an "open" nationalism, the next logical step would be to inquire what role religion played in developing that vision of nationalism. I describe this process at much greater length in the monograph *Patriotism and Piety: Federalist Politics and Religious Struggle in the New American Nation* [41].[1] For our purposes, the significant point is that religious outlooks evolved as Federalists' relationship to the new nation evolved. As Federalists worked to construct the nation, religion served a "republican" purpose. At this point, religious belief (usually, Protestant belief) was seen as naturally supporting the national, republican project. In the partisan battles of the 1790s and early 1800s, many Federalists turned to a "combative" stance. This "fighting" religious Federalism perceived that there was no guaranteed tie between the nation and Christian belief. Instead, a great deal of activity was required to preserve the religious element within the nation, and this was tied to active opposition to religious and political enemies, both foreign and domestic. Finally, as Federalists lost power, religious Federalists offered a "Voluntarist" formula for participating in the nation. This strategy aimed to preserve the nation through voluntary activity in the realm of civil society, rather than through politics. Further, it tended to make use of the nation, while simultaneously looking beyond the nation. That is, it helpfully relativized the nation and re-centered religious Federalists on distinctively Christian themes.

In the first, "republican," stage, Christian Federalists saw religion as endemic to the nation, bound up in the national project. In this language, Federalists perceived Providence itself working to create the American nation [42]. Several examples could be offered. For instance, Episcopal Federalist and First Chief Justice of the Supreme Court John Jay argued for a providential nationalism. This theme was prominent in the Grand Jury Charge he offered during his first year riding circuit. Here, Jay opened

---

[1] Note: Material from this section is drawn from the longer work.

with his belief in the Providential origins of the national government and the responsibilities incumbent on his hearers to preserve it:

> Providence has been pleased to bless the people of this country with more perfect opportunities of choosing and more effectual means of establishing their own government, than any other nation has hitherto enjoyed; and for the use we may make of these opportunities and these means, we shall be highly responsible to that Providence, as well as to mankind in general, and to our own posterity in particular ([43], p. 4).

Providential help implied a duty to that Providence, to posterity, and to the whole world, which would be watching the practice of republican government. Such a challenge laid the groundwork for Jay's description of the jury's duties as an expression of republican service. Jay called for his hearers to evince republican virtue through conscientious participation. Service was the appropriate response to a providentially-approved national government, because "our individual prosperity depends on our national prosperity; and how greatly our national prosperity depends on a well-organized, vigorous government, ruling by wise and equal laws, faithfully executed" ([43], pp. 13–14). The jury's service would, in a localized way, conduce to the good of the nation ([41], pp. 32–35).

Similarly, the New Jersey Presbyterian Federalist and U.S. Representative Elias Boudinot described a happy union of national and religious concerns. In a 1793 speech to the Society of the Cincinnati, Boudinot readily combined religious and political themes ([44], p. 10). In the new nation, he claimed, Christianity could endorse the republic and support it. The meeting of the Society of the Cincinnati itself illustrated this, with prayers offered and religious songs sung. In Boudinot's oration, religious and political ideas were intermixed. The dead soldiers being remembered were "martyrs to liberty," while independence from Great Britain was a "miraculous deliverance from a second Egypt"—another house of bondage. Boudinot even compared the fourth of July celebration to the annual Jewish Passover ([44], pp. 5, 7). Boudinot asserted the role of "Providence," "Divine Providence," and "a divine over-ruling hand" in bringing about American independence ([44], pp. 7, 9). Within the nation, Boudinot saw Christianity as inspiring patriotism. It challenged Americans not to be "careless, indolent, or inattentive in the exercise of any right of citizenship" ([44], p. 13). Further, it inspired the morality and virtue necessary in a republic, as a bulwark against the decay of republics: "if the moral character of a people once degenerate, their political character must soon follow" ([44], p. 14). Christian Americans could gladly support the republic and benefit from the liberty it protected ([41], pp. 99–101).

This cooperation was finally and famously evident in President Washington's "Farewell Address." In this address, Washington asserted:

> Of all the dispositions and habits which lead to political prosperity, religion and morality are indispensable supports. In vain would that man claim the tribute of patriotism, who should labor to subvert these great pillars of human happiness, these firmest props of the duties of men and citizens. . . . And let us with caution indulge the supposition that morality can be maintained without religion. Whatever may be conceded to the influence of refined education on minds of peculiar structure, reason and experience both forbid us to expect that national morality can prevail in exclusion of religious principle [28].

With news of the French Revolution arriving in America, Washington offered a defense of the need for religion and morality in the nation. Washington even insisted that morality was impossible without religion. It should be noted that Washington's "religion" was more vague than that of many Federalists—indeed it lacked the Christian specificity favored by many Protestant Federalists like Boudinot and Jay. Still, it suggests how even Washington viewed the necessity of public religiosity in the American republic. Thus, up to the mid-1790s, Federalists saw an easy agreement between the national identity and their religious commitments.

In the "combative" phase of Federalist religious nationalism, Federalists deployed religious beliefs to support the nation and actively fight off perceived threats. These threats came from external and internal enemies. The external threat came from the French Revolution. In particular, Federalists opposed French "Jacobins," whose beliefs were dangerous on both a religious level—supporting religious infidelity and unbelief—and a political level, encouraging national destabilization. Fear only increased as conflict grew between the United States and France in 1797–1798. Internally, Federalists grew concerned about Democratic-Republicans. When these political enemies championed the French Revolution, they appeared as a dangerous fifth column within the United States. Further, when some of them openly questioned tenets of Christian belief, the identification with French Jacobins seemed easy.

An excellent example of a strong, religiously-combative stance comes from Timothy Dwight, the Congregationalist minister and president of Yale College. Dwight used a 4 July Oration in 1798 to deliver a distinctive theo-political message. Confronted with the Quasi-War of naval conflict with France, the diplomatic insult of the XYZ Affair, and the perceived danger of a French declaration of war, along with the inroads of dangerous theological beliefs, Dwight urged his hearers to fulfill their religious "Duty" in defending the republic. For Dwight, "Religion and Liberty are the two great objects of defensive war. Conjoined, they unite all feelings, and call forth all the energies, of man. ...Religion and liberty are the meat and drink of the body politic. ...Here, eminently, they are inseparable" ([45], p. 1380). A courageous, combative public faith could beat off the threats to the nation ([41], pp. 125–29).

Even President John Adams developed a distinctively combative tone as he addressed the nation and responded to messages sent to him in 1798, when fear of a French war was at its height. In his public declarations, Adams pointed out the danger of French utopianism and claimed religion as a necessary bulwark for America. Adams insisted that reform could not be accomplished by the destructive power of the French Revolution. Improvements "will not be accomplished by the abolition of Christianity and the introduction of Grecian mythology, or the worship of modern heroes or heroines, by erecting statues of idolatry to reason or virtue, to beauty or to taste." Indeed, the French Revolution only demonstrated "the present reign of pretended philosophy in France" ([46]). Against this challenge, Adams also saw Christianity as a social and political good. Moreover, public morality and virtue, as bulwarks of the republic, could not be supported without religion. As Adams told the students of Princeton, "You may find that the moral principles, sanctified and sanctioned by religion, are the only bond of union, the only ground of confidence of the people in one another, of the people in the government, and the government in the people" ([47], p. 206). Finally, Adams insisted that free American government depended on the religious character of the nation. In a statement that would be quoted repeatedly in American history, Adams declared, "Our Constitution was made only for a moral and religious people. It is wholly inadequate to the government of any other" [48]. Thus, Adams joined Dwight in advocating for a combative Federalist mix of religious and political concerns ([41], pp. 125–29).

After the election of 1800, and increasingly as the nineteenth century wore on, Federalists confronted new questions about how they might support the nation when, electorally, the nation seemed to be rejecting their perspective [49,50]. Federalists, thus, faced the challenge of working for the nation, preserving the ideals of the nation, even if they seemed increasingly not to be the majority views. Just as New England felt marginalized in the nation, so religious Federalists felt disenfranchised from the wider society [51,52]. Federalists creatively responded to this dilemma by choosing to build the nation through voluntary societies in the cultural and religious realm, rather than in the political realm where they were having declining success. The voluntarist strategy would model and create a firmer national identity and foster national cooperation ([53]; [54], pp. 234–45, 452–58). Many of these societies were explicitly religious, with one of the best examples being the American Bible Society (ABS) [55]. In this society, with Federalist Elias Boudinot as its first president and William Jay (son of John Jay) as the drafter of its constitution, the organization was created as a Christian, nationalist endeavor. The ABS Constitution followed Federalist inspiration. It created a national superstructure of leadership with local auxiliaries [56]. The Society could, thus, possess, simultaneously, national direction and national identity, while drawing on local, grassroots activity.

One irony of this Voluntarist endeavor is that it ultimately led religious Federalists to look beyond the nation. In the process of establishing and building these voluntarist endeavors, they were forced to clarify that their ultimate loyalty was to a trans-national Christian identity. For Timothy Dwight, this led to a redoubling of efforts at ministerial training at Yale [57]. American missionaries wrestled with this dilemma of Christian and American identity on foreign fields [58]. The minimizing of nationalism can even be seen within the American Bible Society. Both Elias Boudinot and John Jay—the Society's first two presidents—ended up delivering messages that looked beyond the American nation. For Boudinot, the value of the ABS lay in its contribution to God's providential plan. "This then is the great object we have in view and which we would draw the attention of this Audience on this important day;" he declared, "for by disseminating the Bible, without Note or Comment, throughout the known World, we are bringing about the great, the eventful period" [59]. Boudinot hoped for Christ's return as a result of the work of the ABS ([41], pp. 111–15). Similarly, Jay in his presidential addresses only mentioned the United States once, and then in regard to the missions societies. "We have reason to rejoice," he observed, "that such institutions have been so greatly multiplied and cherished in the United States; especially as a kind Providence has blessed us, not only with peace and plenty, but also with the full and secure enjoyment of our civil and religious rights and privileges" [60]. This national situation opened the door to inter-denominational, and even international, Christian cooperation. Boudinot, Jay, and the ABS looked beyond the nation to other, greater, more spiritual goals.

7. Conclusions

In conclusion, then, we can describe the Federalist project as one that pushed not just for nationalism, but for an "open" nationalism. That "open" nationalism held, as a significant component, the importance of public religiosity. Further, Federalist religion, which was mostly Protestant Christianity, could support that "open" nationalist project.

As the country developed, this religion operated in various keys. It began in a "republican" key, where religion supported a Federalist nationalism without much conflict. In the second stage, a "combative" key, Federalists rallied to support a nation they felt was threatened in the 1790s. After 1800, Federalists supported a "Voluntarist" agenda which hoped for a voluntary remnant to support the nation. This fragmented, often sectional, nationalism would keep the nation on course, whether the nation realized it or not. It also looked beyond the nation to trans-national Christian endeavors.

In these ways, Federalist nationalism evinces a contrast with the competing nationalism on display in this period, that favored by the Democratic-Republicans, the followers of Thomas Jefferson, and then Andrew Jackson. This Democratic-Republican nationalism was of a more "closed" character. Although it favored enhanced equality of opportunity for those within the group—specifically adult, white males—it marginalized and minimized minority groups. It sought territorial conquest in the War of 1812 [61,62]. Later in the nineteenth century, the same attitude produced the attitude of Manifest Destiny and promoted the dispossession of Indian tribes from their lands [63,64]. The political battles of the early republic were, thus, not only about policy, they were about competing visions of nationalism, rival metaphysical notions of what the new nation should become.

The Federalist attempt to build an "open" nationalism informed by Christianity also speaks to on-going debates about religion and national identity. The Federalists are one part of a larger story documented throughout this volume of *Religions*. Further, they make their own contribution to present debates about the religious component of American nationalism. Their story acknowledges the constructed nature of that nationalism and that it developed historically ([65], pp. 3–56). Indeed, they were some of the first who set out to construct that national identity. On the other hand, their words and actions demonstrate the very real presence of religious motivation in both the creation of the nation and its early development. Thus, those who see public religiosity as an important component of American nationalism can find very real evidence among the Federalists. Such evidence would counter those who depict the idea of a religious founding primarily as an "invention" or a "myth" ([66], pp. 1–20). A historically nuanced view can recognize the significant influence of Christianity in the formation of American nationalism without describing it as the sole or even central element.

Thus, religion in the new nation for Federalists supported an "open" nationalism that pointed optimistically to what the nation could become. The fact that the nation of citizens, electorally, did not accept this vision suggests one cause for the problems which the nation developed after the Federalists. The Federalist view of an "open," religiously-inspired nationalism was a path largely not taken, and historians' appreciation of this fact leads to an understanding of the developments of "closed" nationalism in the early republic as nothing less than tragic.

Acknowledgments: The author would like to thank Mark T. Edwards for encouraging the writing of this article; John D. Wilsey for conversation and ideas; the participants at the 2016 Biennial Meeting of the Conference on Faith and History, where I presented a version of this paper, for their helpful feedback; Nathan Runke, student at the University of Northwestern-St. Paul, for his assistance in editing this article; and Jacqueline Den Hartog for her interest and support.

Conflicts of Interest: The author declares no conflict of interest.

References

1. For a perceptive assessment of this nationalism, see Rogers M. Smith. "Constructing American National Identity: Strategies of the Federalists." In *Federalists Reconsidered*. Edited by Doron Ben-Atar and Barbara Oberg. Charlottesville: University of Virginia Press, 1998, pp. 19–40.
2. On these debates, see Carson Holloway. *Hamilton versus Jefferson in the Washington Administration: Completing the Founding or Betraying the Founding?* New York: Cambridge University Press, 2015.
3. James Madison. "The Virginia Resolutions, 21 December 1798." *Founders Online, National Archives*, last modified 6 December 2016. Available online: http://founders.archives.gov/documents/Madison/01-17-02-0128 (accessed on 2 January 2017).
4. Thomas Jefferson. "The Kentucky Resolution—Alien and Sedition Acts." *The Avalon Project*, 2008. Available online: http://avalon.law.yale.edu/18th_century/kenres.asp (accessed on 2 January 2017).
5. Benedict Anderson. *Imagined Communities: Reflections on the Origin and Spread of Nationalism*. New York: Verso, 1991.
6. David Waldstreicher. *In the Midst of Perpetual Fetes: The Making of American Nationalism, 1776–1820*. Chapel Hill: University of North Carolina Press for the Omohundro Institute of Early American History and Culture, 1997.
7. Simon Newman. *Parades and the Politics of the Streets: Festive Culture in the Early American Republic*. Philadelphia: University of Pennsylvania Press, 1997.
8. Len Travers. *Celebrating the Fourth: Independence Day and the Rites of Nationalism in the Early Republic*. Amherst: University of Massachusetts Press, 1997.
9. Michael Warner. *The Letters of the Republic: Publication and the Public Sphere in Eighteenth-Century America*. Cambridge: Harvard University Press, 1990.
10. Trish Loughran. *The Republic in Print: Print Culture in the Age of U.S. Nation Building, 1770–1870*. New York: Columbia University Press, 2007.
11. William Dowling. *Literary Federalism in the Age of Jefferson: Joseph Dennie and the Port Folio, 1801–1812*. Columbia: University of South Carolina Press, 1999.
12. Sandra Gustafson. *Eloquence is Power: Oratory and Performance in Early America*. Chapel Hill: University of North Carolina Press for the Omohundro Institute of Early American History and Culture, 2000.
13. John Murrin. "A Roof without Walls." In *Beyond Confederation: Origins of the Constitution and American National Identity*. Edited by Richard Beeman, Stephen Botein and Edward Carter III. Chapel Hill: The University of North Carolina Press, 1987, pp. 333–48.
14. Catherine O'Donnell. *Men of Letters in the Early Republic: Cultivating Forms of Citizenship*. Chapel Hill: University of North Carolina Press for the Omohundro Institute of Early American History and Culture, 2008.
15. Lewis Simpson. *The Federalist Literary Mind: Selections from the Monthly Anthology and Boston Review, 1803–1811, Including Documents Relating to the Boston Athenaeum*. Baton Rouge: Louisiana State University Press, 1962.

16. K. Alan Snyder. *Defining Noah Webster: Mind and Morals in the Early Republic.* Lanham: University Press of America, 1990.
17. Linda Kerber. *Federalists in Dissent: Imagery and Ideology in Jeffersonian America.* Ithaca: Cornell University Press, 1980. First published in 1970.
18. James Simon. *What Kind of Nation: Thomas Jefferson, John Marshall, and the Epic Struggle to Create a United States.* New York: Simon & Schuster, 2002.
19. John Horton. *James Kent: A Study in Conservatism, 1763–1847.* New York: Appleton-Century Co., 1939.
20. Joseph Ellis. *After the Revolution: Profiles of Early American Culture.* New York: W.W. Norton & Co., 1979.
21. Amy De Rogatis. *Moral Geography: Maps, Missionaries, and the American Frontier.* New York: Columbia University Press, 2003.
22. John D. Wilsey. *American Exceptionalism and Civil Religion: Reassessing the History of an Idea.* Downers Grove: IVP Academic, 2015.
23. Alexander Hamilton. "The Federalist Papers: No. 1." *The Avalon Project,* 2008. Available online: http://avalon.law.yale.edu/18th_century/fed01.asp (accessed on 2 January 2017).
24. John Jay. *An Address to the People of the State of New-York, on the Subject of the Constitution, Agreed upon at Philadelphia, the 17th of September, 1787.* New York: Samuel and John Loudon, 1788.
25. George Washington. "First Inaugural Address of 1789." In *The National Archives.* Available online: http://www.archives.gov/exhibits/american_originals/inaugtxt.html (accessed on 2 January 2017).
26. Fisher Ames. *The Works of Fisher Ames.* Edited by William B. Allen. Indianapolis: Liberty Fund, 1983.
27. Samuel Flagg Bemis. *Jay's Treaty: A Study in Commerce and Diplomacy.* New Haven: Yale University Press, 1962.
28. George Washington. "Farewell Address." *The Avalon Project,* 2008. Available online: http://avalon.law.yale.edu/18th_century/washing.asp (accessed on 2 January 2017).
29. George Herring. *From Colony to Superpower: U.S. Foreign Relations since 1776.* New York: Oxford University Press, 2008.
30. John Quincy Adams. *An Address, Delivered at the Request of the Committee of Arrangement for Celebrating the Anniversary of Independence at Washington on the Fourth of July, 1821, upon the Occasion of Reading the Declaration of Independence.* Cambridge: University Press, 1821.
31. Charles Edel. *Nation Builder: John Quincy Adams and the Grand Strategy of the Republic.* Cambridge: Harvard University Press, 2014. Although John Quincy Adams was serving in the Monroe administration, his outlook continued to reflect Federalist themes.
32. Stephen Budney. *William Jay: Abolitionist and Anticolonialist.* Westport: Praeger, 2005.
33. Peter Hinks. "Timothy Dwight, Congregationalism, and Early Antislavery." In *The Problem of Evil: Slavery, Freedom, and the Ambiguities of American Reform.* Edited by Steven Mintz and John Stauffer. Amherst: University of Massachusetts Press, 2007, pp. 148–61.
34. Harry Stout, and Kenneth Minkema. "The Edwardsean Tradition and the Antislavery Debate, 1740–1865." *Journal of American History* 92 (2005): 47–74.
35. One specific example of the Federalist openness to African-American participation and opposition to slavery comes from Lemuel Haynes. See John Saillant. *Black Puritan, Black Republican: The Life and Thought of Lemuel Haynes, 1753–1833.* New York: Oxford University Press, 2002.
36. Rosemarie Zagarri. "Women and Party Conflict in the Early Republic." In *Beyond the Founders: New Approaches to the Political History of the Early American Republic.* Edited by Jeffrey Pasley, Andrew Robertson and David Waldstreicher. Chapel Hill: University of North Carolina Press, 2004, pp. 107–28.
37. Rosemarie Zagarri. *Revolutionary Backlash: Women and Politics in the Early American Republic.* Philadelphia: University of Pennsylvania Press, 2007.
38. Frederick Hoxie, Ronald Hoffman, and Peter Albert. *Native Americans and the Early Republic.* Charlottesville: University Press of Virginia for the United States Capitol Historical Society, 1999.
39. Thomas Kidd. *God of Liberty: A Religious History of the American Revolution.* New York: Basic Books, 2010.
40. The National Archives. "Declaration of Independence: A Transcription." *The National Archives.* Available online: https://www.archives.gov/founding-docs/declaration-transcript (accessed on 2 January 2017).
41. Jonathan Den Hartog. *Patriotism and Piety: Federalist Politics and Religious Struggle in the New American Nation.* Charlottesville: University of Virginia Press, 2015.

42. On political uses of Providence at this time, see Nicholas Guyatt. *Providence and the Invention of the United States, 1607–1876*. New York: Cambridge University Press, 2007.

43. John Jay. *The Charge of Chief Justice Jay to the Grand Juries on the Eastern Circuit: At the Circuit Courts held in the Districts of New-York, on the 4th, of Connecticut on the 22nd days of April; of Massachusetts on the 4th, and of New-Hampshire on the 20th days of May, 1790*. Portsmouth: George Jerry Osborne, Jr., 1790.

44. Elias Boudinot. *An Oration, Delivered at Elizabeth-Town, New Jersey, Agreeably to a Resolution of the State Society of Cincinnati, on the Fourth of July, M.DCC.XCIII*. Elizabeth-Town: Sheperd Kollock, 1793.

45. Timothy Dwight. "The Duty of Americans, at the Present Crisis, 1798." In *Political Sermons of the American Founding Era*. Edited by Ellis Sandoz. Indianapolis: Liberty Fund, 1991, pp. 1363–94.

46. John Adams. "To the Grand Jurors of the County of Hampshire, Massachusetts." In *The Works of John Adams, Second President of the United States*. Edited by Charles Francis Adams. Boston: Little, Brown and Company, 1854, vol. 9, p. 227.

47. John Adams. "To the Students of New Jersey College." In *The Works of John Adams, Second President of the United States*. Edited by Charles Francis Adams. Boston: Little, Brown and Company, 1854, vol. 9, pp. 205–207.

48. John Adams. "To the Officers of the First Brigade of the Third Division of the Militia of Massachusetts." In *The Works of John Adams, Second President of the United States*. Edited by Charles Francis Adams. Boston: Little, Brown and Company, 1854, vol. 9, pp. 228–29.

49. Edward Larson. *A Magnificent Catastrophe: The Tumultuous Election of 1800, America's First Presidential Campaign*. New York: Free Press, 2007.

50. James Horn, Jan Ellen Lewis, and Peter Onuf, eds. *The Revolution of 1800: Democracy, Race, and the New Republic*. Charlottesville: University of Virginia Press, 2002.

51. This marginalization eventually led to the Hartford Convention. James Banner. *To the Hartford Convention: The Federalists and the Origins of Party Politics in Massachusetts, 1789–1815*. New York: Alfred A. Knopf, 1970.

52. For the results of the Hartford Convention, see "The Report of the Hartford Convention." In *The American Republic: Primary Sources*. Edited by Bruce Frohnen. Indianapolis: Liberty Fund, 2002, pp. 447–57.

53. On voluntarism, see Johann Neem. *Creating a Nation of Joiners: Democracy and Civil Society in Early National Massachusetts*. Cambridge: Harvard University Press, 2008.

54. Also on voluntarism, John L. Brooke. *Columbia Rising: Civil Life on the Upper Hudson from the Revolution to the Age of Jackson*. Chapel Hill: University of North Carolina Press for the Omohundro Institute of Early American History and Culture, 2010.

55. For a broader interpretation of the American Bible Society, see John Fea. *The Bible Cause: A History of the American Bible Society*. New York: Oxford University Press, 2016.

56. American Bible Society. *Constitution of the American Bible Society, Formed by a Convention of Delegates, Held in the City of New York, May, 1816. Together with Their Address to the People of the United States; A Notice of Their Proceedings, and a List of Their Officers*. New York: Hopkins, 1816.

57. For Dwight at Yale, see John Fitzmeier. *New England's Moral Legislator: Timothy Dwight, 1752–1817*. Bloomington: Indiana University Press, 1998.

58. Emily Conroy-Krutz. *Christian Imperialism: Converting the World in the Early American Republic*. Ithaca: Cornell University Press, 2015.

59. Elias Boudinot. "Address to the American Bible Society May 1821." May 1821. Elias Boudinot Papers. American Bible Society, New York City. Folder 8.

60. Address to the Annual Meeting of the ABS. May 13, 1824. John Jay Papers. American Bible Society, New York City. Folder: Correspondence: Addresses, Individuals.

61. On the War of 1812, see John Charles Anderson Stagg. *Mr. Madison's War: Politics, Diplomacy, and Warfare in the Early American Republic 1783–1830*. Princeton: Princeton University Press, 1983.

62. Also see Donald Hickey. *The War of 1812: A Forgotten Conflict, Bicentennial Edition*. Urbana: University of Illinois Press, 2012.

63. Mary Hershberger. "Mobilizing Women, Anticipating Abolition: The Struggle against Indian Removal in the 1830s." *Journal of American History* 86 (1999): 15–40. [CrossRef]

64. Jeremiah Evarts. *Cherokee Removal: The "William Penn" Essays and Other Writings*. Edited by Francis Paul Prucha. Knoxville: University of Tennessee Press, 1981.

65. John Fea. *Was America Founded as a Christian Nation? A Historical Introduction.* Louisville: Westminster John Knox Press, 2011. Fea helpfully constructs a narrative about how the "Christian Nation" theme developed across the nineteenth century.
66. Steven Green. *Inventing a Christian America: The Myth of the Religious Founding.* New York: Oxford University Press, 2015.

religions MDPI

Article

William Apess, Pequot Pastor: A Native American Revisioning of Christian Nationalism in the Early Republic

Ethan Goodnight

Master of Arts Program in the Social Sciences, University of Chicago, Saieh 246, 5757 S. University Ave., Chicago, IL 60637, USA; egoodnight@uchicago.edu; Tel.: +1-425-495-5158

Academic Editor: Mark T. Edwards
Received: 29 September 2016; Accepted: 11 January 2017; Published: 27 January 2017

Abstract: Pequot Native and Methodist Minister William Apess has received growing recognition among historians as a unique voice for Native Americans—and minorities in general—during the early Republic. This essay began by inquiring into Apess's relationship with the Christian nationalism of his day. Extensive readings of Apess's works, scholarship on all aspects of Apess's life, and analyses of Christian nationalism during the early Republic initially revealed severe conflict. Apess is fiery in his critique of Anglo American society and religion; he questions the integrity of Christians who treat Native Americans with a double standard. Analyzing Apess's critiques and his proposed solutions in depth, however, shows that his main problem rests with faulty implementation of genuinely good ideals. Apess's solutions actually rest on revising and enforcing, not destroying, the main components of Christian nationalism. This essay concludes that Apess should be read as advancing his own revised form of Christian nationalism; his plan for the future of America and national unity embraced establishing a more perfect Christian union.

Keywords: Christian Nationalism; William Apess; Pilgrims; Puritans; Divine Providence; common law; Methodism; Jacksonian era

---

In the opening chapters of his monumental work *Democracy in America*, Alexis de Tocqueville observed how "the social condition of the Americans is eminently democratic; this was its character at the foundation of the colonies, and it is still more strongly marked at the present day" ([1], p. 47). Tocqueville identified the settlement of New England by the Pilgrims and Puritans in the 1620s as demarcating the beginning of a social trend toward democracy. By highlighting this democratic national heritage established in Protestant faith, Tocqueville illuminated one aspect of a greater early Republic campaign to reimagine colonial and revolutionary American history. As a cultural and political project emanating from the second Great Awakening, as well as the fears of political division, numbers of lettered men and women were "reinventing" the United States as a Christian nation [2][1]. Outspoken Christian nationalists like Justice Joseph Story joined Tocqueville in solidifying the Pilgrims and the Puritans as the foundation of religious and political liberty present in antebellum America ([2], pp. 187, 194; [3], pp. 220–21).

As historian Steven Green has recently explained, the establishment in the early Republic of the Pilgrims as American's religious forbearers forms the first of what may be termed the four key pillars of Christian nationalism. The second pillar was constructed by the Christian nationalist movement through the composition of countless hagiographies of the supposedly great Christian

---

[1] For American nationality as an unanswered question being debated instead of a solid entity being reinforced, see Haselby, *The Origins of American Religious Nationalism* [2].

leaders of the newly-founded nation, the Founding Fathers. Working their same interpretive magic on America's heritage of religious and political liberty, second-generation Americans identified the third pillar, American common law tradition, as having emerged from Christian principles. The success of these three pillars was credited to and codified in the fourth pillar: Divine Providence guiding the nation ([3], p. 201)[2]. Taken together, these four pillars form the backbone of Christian nationalism in the early Republic. Mark Noll, John Fea, George Marsden, George McKenna, and Nathan Hatch are a few historians who have revealed the building process behind America as a Christian nation. As Fea makes clear in his work, America was not founded as a Christian nation; the attempted construction of such a nation was advanced during the early Republic by evangelicals ([4], pp. 4–5).[3] Tocqueville's commentary on America demonstrates how this new history was gaining traction. He, a foreigner, was convinced of the veracity of this new national narrative. Nevertheless, there were some native born Americans who recognized the mythical portions of the new national history.

One such critic was the Methodist Reverend and Pequot native William Apess. In his most famous speech, "Eulogy on King Philip," presented on 8 January 1836, Apess added a darker side to the Christian nationalist narrative, specifically to the Pilgrims' noble settling of America.

> [In] December ... 1620, the Pilgrims landed at Plymouth, and without asking liberty from anyone they possessed themselves of a portion of the country, and built themselves houses, and then made a treaty, and commanded [the Natives] to accede to it. This, if now done, it would be called an insult, and every white man would be called to go out and act the part of a patriot, to defend their country's rights; and if every intruder were butchered, it would be sung upon every hilltop in the Union that victory and patriotism was the order of the day ([5], p. 280).

Apess here is concerned with highlighting the hypocrisy practiced by the Pilgrims. They would fight to destroy any perceived threat to their land or livelihood, but they did not grant this same right to their neighbors, the Native Americans. Moreover, by relating the historical incident to the potential reaction of his audience should such an event occur to them, Apess demonstrated that New Englanders would respond in the same manner as his Native American ancestors did. Clearly, Apess was highly skeptical of the narrative of a Puritan heritage of liberty.

This vocal criticism typifies the fiery Pequot preacher. Apess scholars have documented his wide-ranging assault upon the racist hierarchies and histories of his Christian contemporaries, like Justice Story.[4] To many of his contemporaries and to present-day scholars, Apess was the antithesis of Christian nationalists. They established the past as sacred; he labeled it a degrading myth. They used their authority to conduct missions, build churches, and educate; he deemed their authority morally bankrupt and exposed the failures behind their endeavors. While as a minister Apess championed spiritual revival through the Methodist church, he does not appear remotely fond of the nation-building portion of Christian nationalism. For these attacks, Apess has rightly been understood as an opponent of the Christian nationalist project.

Because of the jeremiad of Apess's preaching and lecturing it becomes tempting to read Apess as a strident voice for some sort of innovative Indian Nationalism. Apess, however, criticized the old project in order to offer up a revised one. Apess did fight to restore Native Americans to their place, both geographically and politically. In "Eulogy," Apess constructively reworked the contemporary historical understanding by proposing his own nation-building heritage. In *Indian Nullification*, he documented the fight of the Mashpee for their rights by appealing to the Declaration of Independence,

---

[2]   While Steven Green provides the framework for this essay, John Fea, Mark Noll, Nathan Hatch, and George Marsden also contribute heavily.

[3]   Christine Heyrman's work *Southern Cross* provides an excellent example of scholarship attempting to understand how evangelicals fought to build a certain nation and how those efforts changed the very format of evangelicalism itself.

[4]   For some striking examples see the following: [6–9].

the Constitution, and the broad common law tradition of the country. However, in both his written works and his political deeds, Apess advanced his nationalistic vision for America rooted still in Christianity. This essay contends that despite—or rather, because of—his vicious attacks on Christian nationalism, Apess should be understood as offering not a competing history of and for the United States but as reforming the Christian nationalist one.

Despite never explicitly using the term "Christian nationalism," Apess throughout his works incorporated each and every one of the four major pillars. Like his contemporaries, Apess was deeply worried about the current state of America and used a new history and his preaching as a salve to soothe the wounds of the country. Investigating Apess's relationship to Christian nationalism reveals numerous fundamental differences of interpretation, but it also illuminates a shared goal and similar means to accomplish said goal. Here, Linford Fisher's understand of the strategic affiliation of Natives with white Christian America cogently applies ([10], pp. 86, 88–89, 101, 106). While William Apess was blisteringly critical of white America and her sins, he nonetheless supported the emergent understanding of Christianity's role in America. By embracing a Christian vision for America and rooting that vision in a new history, Apess showed himself to be a sincere Christian nationalist concerned with advancing America as a Christian nation.

1. Understanding Christian Nationalism in the Early Republic

Before explicating Apess's stance on America as a Christian nation it is necessary to survey the landscape of Christian nationalism as established in the antebellum period. On a general level, the propagated idea of America as a Christian nation simply means that the majority population, Protestant evangelicals, defined America as such ([4], pp. 4–5). With their emphasis on personal conversion, "evangelicals specialized in ... providing rhetoric about the United States as a Christian nation where piety was free to grow" ([11], p. 77). On a deeper level, early American Christian nationalists were convinced that God had been and was still working in unique ways throughout America; only Divine Providence could adequately explain the awesome success of the Founding Fathers ([4], p. 5; [12], p. 108). Christian nationalism in the 1830s was at its most basic an outgrowth of the domination of popular culture by Protestant denominations, their influence in the present, and their ability to define the past ([11], p. 101).[5]

Why was there a press for national unity during the antebellum era? Why did this nationalizing project become essentially Christian? Barely fifty years old in the 1830s, the American nation was on shaky ground. Three main concerns haunted American politicians (and ministers): fear of national division; the shifting, unstable American demographic; and the breakup of the religious establishment ([12], pp. 110–11). Examining these concerns will contextualize Apess's work, reveal more clearly the nature and form of 1830s nationalism, and clarify the shifting makeup of Christianity in the early Republic.

The fear of national divide was fundamentally manifested as "mistrust of the other party." Admiration for the storied success of General Washington was matched in America by worry surrounding the current political climate. While the nation had survived the election of 1800, it emerged bitterly divided between Jefferson's Democratic-Republicans and Adams' Federalists. This conflict transformed politics as parties fought each other for support of various demographics, popularizing mass politics ([11], pp. 48, 76–77). After the collapse of the Federalists, the Whig party attempted in the 1830s and 1840s to secure the integrity of the nation "by lyrical invocation of America's origins" which were in turn mixed with their agenda to provide a hopeful vision for the future ([16], p. 110). The Whig agenda appealed to the common roots of Puritan heritage, championed connection through markets, and advocated for increased

---

[5] For a broad survey of Protestantism consider ([13], esp. Ch. 2: "A Complete Christian Commonwealth"); ([14], esp. Part IV, *Americanization*); ([15], esp. in conversation with Noll, *Princeton and the Republic*).

infrastructure development to bind the nation together ([4], p. 7; [16], pp. 114–15).[6] What made this Whiggish nationalism Christian was not only an appeal to the romantic religion of the Puritans but also a vision of American culture as fundamentally Protestant ([4], pp. 7–8; [16], p. 108).[7] This Whiggish Christian nationalism project was set in opposition to the Democratic version of a nation separated from the past by revolutionary ideas and destined (not divinely provisioned) for greatness through "democracy, equality, and individualism" ([16], pp. 106–9).

Adding to this political split, a shifting demographic, both ethnically and regionally, contributed to growing political instability as new states quickly gained power. Hearkening back to Washington and the Revolution as a glorious event that established America should therefore be seen as a response to the climate of political hostility and regional fracturing that threatened unity ([12], p. 111).

A final negative component underpinning the nation-building process was the denominationalizing of American Christianity. Evangelical Protestantism split in this period between more traditional Congregationalist and Presbyterian churches and the "upstart sects" of Baptist and Methodist movements intent on saving all of America ([16], pp. 79, 100; [17]). The rising diversity of American Christianity was stimulated by "the competing claims of old denominations, a host of new ones, and of supremely heterodox religious groups; people veering from one church to another; and the unbridled wrangling of competitors in what Joseph Smith called a 'war of words'" ([12], p. 112). While most states did have a declared Christian affiliation, the nation at large possessed no unifying idea of how religion should function in the United States in the early Republic ([4], p. 146). Protestant evangelicals were bitterly divided over the role of religion in America, with Christian nationalism forming only one movement [2].[8]

Despite the divisiveness of sectarian squabbles, the evangelical movement involved members of all denominations ([16], pp. 3, 81).[9] This unifying tide "helped to make irrelevant the theological differences" between Protestant sects. McKenna identifies significant people (Francis Asbury, Charles Finney, and Lyman Beecher) rather than specific denominations as driving forces behind theological, social, and political advancement ([16], pp. 81–83). The 1830s, then, becomes a tricky time for "American Christianity" as religious pluralism protected by the First Amendment diversified it while the evangelical movement of the Second Great Awakening unified it. For the purposes of this essay, "Christian nationalism" is Christian because of the belief that evangelizing the nation and establishing a country of church-going people (who are free to disagree about theological specifics but united under Protestantism) will provide needed stability and identity to America. Thus defined, Christian nationalism emerged in the first 40 years of the 19th century as Americans attempted to accurately understand the incredible events surrounding the birth of their nation, most notably the underdog victory of America over Britain in the Revolutionary War. The positive construction aspect of a specifically Christian vision for national identity was jumpstarted by the death of George Washington in 1799. Almost immediately, the beautification of General Washington began. He was compared to Moses, Joshua, and King David for his role in delivering America from Britain's grasp. His dedication to God, virtue, and his fellow man was lauded for years ([3], pp. 201, 205). While Washington's contemporaries—Thomas Jefferson in particular—wondered about the faith of this "quiet" man, second-generation Americans spared no mental expense in venerating their fallen hero as God's primary instrument. For many living in the 1830s, George Washington represented not only an exemplary American but also embodied the essence of the nation. Consequently, any religious motivation Washington experienced would have profoundly affected the birth of the nation ([4], pp. 171–75).

---

6 The idea was that farmers taking goods to market along new roads would begin to conceive of the world as more than their community, as a nation.
7 Fea and McKenna describes this Whiggish idea of Protestant culture as one "where slavery did not exist, alcohol use was under control, and Sunday was kept as a day of Sabbath rest" and where Divine Providence summons America to greatness.
8 Haselby's entire book is dedicated to exploring the contest of ideologies and denominations in the early Republic.
9 McKenna does believe Methodists deserve a place of honor in the movement, however.

Washington's role as God's instrument dovetailed nicely with the growing idea of America as God's tool to advance His Kingdom. God's implementation of America in His grand plan was reinforced by postmillennialism, forged by the Second Great Awakening. According to this understanding, a tactile "Kingdom of God on earth" would arise in America. This "Kingdom" would be a "golden age" of love, prosperity, and virtue ([16], p. 94). Before the Revolutionary War, America had been compared to Israel as a nation wandering listlessly in the desert. In the early 1800s, America was still being compared to Israel but now in reference to themselves as the chosen nation of God. The hope in God's utilization of America led to a renewed effort to instill morality and virtue in the American population at large. The most common method for accomplishing this moral regeneration was found in reform organizations and laws which would help God accomplish His will in the fledgling country ([3], pp. 211–19; [11], p. 77).

The reformers did not have to look far to find the material needed to bolster the morality of God's chosen people; they simply rededicated America's common law as primarily beholden to and mutually reinforcing Christian principles. Justice Joseph Story, for instance, contended that "the obligatory force of the law of nature upon man is derived from its presumed coincidence with the will of the Creator." Story's work in tying America's legal virtues to Christian influence in no small way shaped the understanding of America as a *fundamentally* Christian nation, especially in the legal and political sector ([3], pp. 220–21). Story and his contemporaries did not end their historical examination of the roots of America's legal system at the virtues of the Revolution, however. They reached further back to establish one of the greatest trademarks of American Christian nationalism: the righteous settlement of America by the blessed Pilgrims and Puritans ([3], p. 227).

Primarily originating in New England, the early nineteenth century movement to codify the Pilgrims and Puritans as the bedrock for future American societies enjoyed great success. Daniel Webster was a key ophthalmologist behind opening America's previously blind eyes to envision their influential Pilgrim ancestry. From 1820 onward, Webster sought to establish the Pilgrims as the forefathers of Americans. He traced the highly-held American values of self-governance, social compacts, republicanism, and religious liberty back to the Pilgrims. After delivering "The First Settlement of New England," Webster's idea of the Pilgrims as national progenitors was reiterated by John Quincy Adams and George Bancroft, among others, who further expanded the Pilgrim's national influence. Nathaniel Hawthorne took the rise of pro-Pilgrim sentiments and directed them to the Puritans as well, celebrating their hardiness and virtue. In this way, "the Puritan/Pilgrim saga became the cornerstone of the emerging national identity narrative" ([3], pp. 227–38).[10]

The Christian nationalism of the early Republic should be seen as originating from the base fears and motives of politicians who saw a fractured, not unified, state, religious leaders who worried about the shifting populace and denominations, and the intelligentsia who desperately desired a national heritage and myth on which to build a history of the United States. While Noll and his contemporaries have done justice to the various building blocks of the Christian nationalists, more recent works by Amanda Porterfield, Steven Green, and Sam Haselby have exposed the ruthlessness of the era. Porterfield illuminates the almost commercialization of doubt and worry by American churches in the early Republic. The political atmosphere was as much Christianized by denominational conflict and sectarian squabbles as it was by a noble Christian history. Green ruthlessly exposes the hidden aspirations and impulses behind the Christian nationalist movement. Haselby highlights the intense conflict between frontier revivalists and national evangelists, revealing how Christian nationalism was at times a tool for advancing particular denominational concerns over a general Protestant narrative. Operating within this sphere of New England evangelicalism, Apess's contribution to Christian nationalism in the early Republic further underscores the varieties and conflicts within this already contested area.

---

[10] It is of course necessary to note that Hawthorne also offered substantial critiques of the Puritans. His was not a blind endorsement, but it was nevertheless an endorsement.

However, despite the reality of conflict, the construction of this myth frequently takes a positive tone. Architects like Noah Webster and Daniel Webster are hopeful about what God has done and will continue to do in their nation. This optimistic bent is perhaps best represented by the recognition of America's Pilgrim heritage, which embodies the other three positive constructive forces discussed. As with Washington, Pilgrims and Puritans had hagiographies composed about them. Divine Providence features heavily in the narratives of the Pilgrims survival. Puritan moral codes were credited with ensuring a Christian common law and legal system. In this way, constructing the Puritan/Pilgrim myth encapsulates and represents the positive constructive force of Christian nationalism. This reality makes the brutal lambasting of the Puritans by Rev. William Apess even more astonishing.

2. Life and Letters of William Apess

Apess's attacks on this myth flowed from his childhood in New England and his experiences with the hypocrisy of Christian Anglo Americans. Born in Colrain, Massachusetts, in 1798, William Apess was of mixed descent: his paternal grandfather was white; his paternal grandmother was a Native descended from, Apess claimed, King Philip of the Pequot ([18], pp. 3–4).[11] After suffering abuse at the hands of his maternal Native grandmother, Apess was taken in by the white Furman family as an indentured servant where he received some education. After living with two other families (the Hillhouses and the Williams) as a servant, Apess ran away with his friend John, enlisting into the Army at the age of fifteen. One of the reasons for Apess leaving the families was his feeling of helplessness and enslavement. In his autobiography, Apess demonstrated the historical precedent for such action by claiming, "If my consent had been solicited as a matter of form, I should not have felt so bad. But to be sold to and treated unkindly by those who had got [sic] our fathers' lands for nothing was too much to bear" ([18], pp. 7, 15, 16, 25).[12] After serving during the War of 1812 and deserting—he was denied his pay and decided this breach of contract merited his desertion—Apess wandered around the Northeast region of America and into Canada, holding down odd jobs and struggling against alcoholism and other "degrading practices" ([18], pp. 30–33; [6], pp. 112–13).

After his post-war travels, Apess reunited with his family. He lived with his aunt for several months before travelling to see his father. While with his father Apess received two vocations. First, his father taught him how to make shoes. Second, and much more importantly, he received a call from God to "preach the Gospel of our Lord and Savior Jesus Christ." It was during a Methodist camp meeting in December 1818 that Apess felt the Spirit call him to ministry. Throughout his life, Apess had struggled with finding his voice; now, the Spirit gave him the eloquence he needed to preach. He was baptized soon thereafter, although the struggles to obtain a license to preach followed him for a few years ([19], pp. 31–33).[13] In addition to the fact that Methodism was one of the only denominations willing to license non-white men, Apess would have been drawn to the Methodist belief that grace and the power of the Spirit mattered more than learning and to their flexible, loosely regulated method of evangelizing in general ([17], pp. 22, 29, 71–73, 109–10).[14] From here until the time of the publication of his autobiography *A Son of the Forest* in 1831, Apess continued

---

11 In reality, Philip was sachem of the Pokanoket tribe in Rhode Island, not the Pequots as Philip Gura ([19], p. 45) and O'Connell ([20], fn. 2, p. 4).

12 By "treated unkindly" Apess is referring to the numerous accusations and beatings he received as a child. He was whipped in an attempt to drive the devil out of him. He was called a "dog" by his masters. He was punished for joining Methodist revivals by his more conservative Christian masters.

13 Apess would have been one of ~1 million Americans who attended camp meetings annually in 1818 ([17], p. 97; [15], p. 257, n. 1).

14 Curiously, Wigger ([17], p. 192) contends that Methodism possessed very little appeal among Native Americans, citing one article as an example of the problems Methodism faced among Natives. Apess's story shows that Wigger glanced over this relationship too quickly.

to travel and preach throughout New England, with or without the approval of denominational leadership ([18], pp. 40, 42, 43, 46, 47–52).[15]

Although Apess ended his autobiography at a relatively stable point in his story, his life was about to take a turbulent turn. While ministering in Boston, Apess encountered a few Mashpee tribal representatives who had come to the capital to protest their government. This protest was part of six-year legal battle between the tribe and Massachusetts over issues of Native sovereignty. By 1833, the tribe had made little headway ([19], pp. 71–73). When Apess heard about this contest, he "resolved to visit the people of Marshpee" in order to investigate their condition for himself.[16] After preaching one sermon in the official church, Apess found a vast majority of the Natives worshipping in another place and preached to them. After his message, Apess opened the floor for the Mashpee to share their grievances with him. Apess was incensed to learn that the governor and the state leadership had never allowed the Mashpee to officially file their complaints. After his speedy adoption by the Mashpee tribe, Apess helped them draft a series of resolutions which powerfully resolved "that we, as a tribe, will rule ourselves, and have the right to do so; for all men are born free and equal, says the Constitution of the country." After issuing the resolutions and believing them to be granted, the Mashpee issued their own Declaration of Independence which stated that "said resolutions will be enforced after the first day of July, 1833" ([21], pp. 169, 171–73, 175, 179–80).[17]

In the hailstorm of newspaper articles, court proceedings, imprisonments, and appeals that followed, Apess's bitter irony and scathing critiques of white Americans became more polished ([22], p. 121). In *Indian Nullification*, Apess's work that documents the "revolt" of the Mashpee and the "nearly hysterical reaction" it provoked, Apess at one point quotes an article from the *Boston Advocate* which examines the regulatory laws governing the Mashpee Natives: "a Board of five Overseers [exists] . . . vested with full power to regulate the police of the plantation; to establish rules for managing the affairs, interests and concerns of the Indians and inhabitants" ([20], p. 164; [21], pp. 206–11). The law even allowed the Overseers to "bind out [Mashpee] children to suitable persons" if they deemed it necessary. After observing the immense amount of power held by outside men over the Mashpee, Apess questions the New Englanders, asking "generally how their fathers bore laws, much less oppressive, when imposed upon them by a foreign government" ([21], pp. 208–11). This clear reference to the Revolutionary War, and the overthrowing of oppression that occurred in it, is representative of one of Apess's main tactics in *Indian Nullification* and his other works: ironic criticism. With this tactic, Apess sardonically highlights the double standards of white Americans, forcing them to confront their hypocrisy. In this instance, Apess boldly claims the ideals of the Declaration to justify the Mashpee revolt. By establishing Natives as equal to Anglo-Americans in this way, Apess confronts the Anglo-Americans with their "hypocritical observance of their proclaimed ideals" ([20], p. 164).

Eventually, as noted in the *Daily Advocate* and cited in *Indian Nullification*, the Massachusetts' state government agreed to begin a process of "restoring the rights of self-government, in part, to the Mashpee Indians, of which our legislation has deprived them for one hundred and forty years..." ([21], pp. 241–42). The Mashpee success is one of the few positive results of legislation between Natives and government in the Jacksonian era. In large part, the Mashpee owe their success to the effective public relations campaign led by Apess who used his talents to convince Massachusetts' citizens that if they truly detested the forced removal of the Cherokee by Jackson then they should also stand up for the Mashpee ([23], p. 3). Hence, in a petition sent to the Overseers of the tribe at Harvard

---

15 Apess's autobiography follows the general outline of a typical conversion experience narrative popular in these times ([20], p. 1). Porterfield notes that "evangelicals made admission of [religious doubt] a step in conversion that could be revisited to rekindle belief whenever trust in God faltered" ([11], p. 13). The fact that Apess's autobiography follows this pattern exactly serves to demonstrate his acceptance of standard Methodist religious practice.

16 Originally the tribe was known as Marshpee. Today, and in academic circles, they identify as the Mashpee tribe.

17 One of the sparks of controversy was that the Mashpee Indians had unknowingly been in contact with the lieutenant governor, not the actual governor. Thus the Mashpee had to endure court cases and hearings for months before their resolution was adopted.

and published in newspapers in the surrounding area, Apess and the Mashpee wonder if "perhaps you have heard of the oppression of the Cherokees and lamented over them much, and thought the Georgians were hard and cruel creatures; but did you ever hear of the poor, oppressed and degraded Marshpee Indians in Massachusetts, and lament over them? If not, you hear now" ([21], pp. 175–77).

After the success of the Mashpee Revolt, Apess fell out of favor with his adoptive tribe for unknown reasons.[18] This was one of the contributing factors that led to his decision to relocate to Boston and continue his ministry there. In early 1836, Apess delivered his "Eulogy on King Philip" at the Odeon Theater in Boston ([19], pp. 101–7). It was met with some acclaim, but more public interest originated from those who were enticed by the idea of witnessing a performance by the eloquent Native responsible for all the recent Mashpee commotion ([24], p. 50).[19] He repeated the address multiple times in several locations, culminating in his transcribing the speech as a short book. It would prove to be his final work. Apess spent the next two years until the end of 1837 traveling and speaking between New York and Boston. At the end of 1837, Apess disappears almost completely from the record, leading some to suggest he was debilitated, like many others, by the Panic of 1837. He died from "apoplexy" in 1839 at the age of 41 ([19], pp. 114–15, 132–33).

Despite his death in relative obscurity (a sprinkling of papers made mention of his passing), Apess in 1837 was "one of the country's most important Native American intellectuals, having published more than any other indigenous writer before the twentieth century..." ([19], p. xiii). In his comparatively voluminous writings, Apess was ultimately trying to challenge the current Anglo-centric historical and cultural narrative with his own "cross-cultural written history" ([25], p. 165). The rest of this essay will contend that Apess's unique history should be read as reforming and advancing a Christian nationalist position. An examination of his writings reveals that he addressed, explicitly or implicitly, every major plank of Christian nationalism, from George Washington to the splintering of denominational unity. Given Apess's goal to "articulate the presence and being of Native Americans as an active part of American society," this is to be expected from the era's most prolific Native voice ([20], p. lxi).

3. William Apess: Revisionary Christian Nationalist

Apess is most well-known for his bold irony and shameless appropriation and rededication of traditionally white images of cultural superiority. His utilization of the eminent George Washington, and the other three pillars of Christian nationalism, is no exception. From 1799 to the 1820s, General Washington had become immortalized in the pantheon of democratic heroes to the point that Whig politicians believed his legacy and reputation as the foremost mason of the Christian foundation of America secure. In the 1830s, interest in Washington reached fever pitch with the coming of his centennial. By 1835 when Apess delivered his "Eulogy," George Washington had become a ubiquitous reference point for any political speaker. Washington had also become a cultural icon. He represented the very best of the republican virtues responsible for founding the nation. He was also credited with driving Natives out of Northeast U.S. during his time in the British army and as President. Apess knew about Washington's actions, as is clear from his introduction to "Eulogy" ([24], pp. 52, 54, 58). Nevertheless, Apess decided to use Washington as a foil for Philip, King of the Pequots (Pokanokets). Apess described his subject Philip as "a noted warrior, whose natural abilities shone like those of the great and mighty Philip of Greece, or of Alexander the Great, or like those of Washington—whose virtues and patriotism are engraven on the hearts of my audience." A few lines later, Apess declared that Philip is held in the same esteem by Natives as Washington is by "every white in America" ([5], p. 277).

---

[18] Multiple sources including local newspapers mention this falling out. No known source has a definitive reason for it.

[19] The common belief at the time was that Natives could be eloquent but only in the way a child can be. The idea of a sophisticated, smart, engaging, and witty Native American would have seemed oxymoronic to many in Apess's audience. O'Connell notes that Apess threatens whites simply by knowing how to read and write! ([20], p. xlii).

Apess's usage of Washington incorporated his status as Christian nationalist icon while subtly chipping away at the mythological portions of his biography. What better way to establish King Philip as a noteworthy personage in North America than by comparing him to the most significant North American? As he recognized Washington's renown, however, Apess's very presence on the stage in Boston testified to the mythological components of Washington's legacy: Washington failed to completely erase the Native American presence in the northeast, like it had been supposed ([24], pp. 41, 49). By comparing Philip to Washington—and by his own heritage—Apess reinserted Native Americans into the history of the founding of America, where they belong.

On a deeper level, Apess was engaging throughout "Eulogy" in "mimicry," ascribing to "the hierarchical ranks of cultural conflict" for the purpose of "reproducing that rhetoric's assumptions" in order to slyly undercut them ([26], pp. 15, 46). At first glance, Apess was simply acknowledging the beloved place that Washington held in the hearts of all Americans. However, as he continued to exalt Philip, Washington was shunned to the wayside. "As a man of natural abilities, I shall pronounce [Philip] the greatest man that was ever in America" ([5], p. 308). By treating Philip as nobler than the great General George Washington, Apess set Philip's war of independence against encroaching Pilgrims equal with the Revolutionary War. In so doing, he ensconced Philip with Washington into America's pantheon of nationalist heroes ([24], p. 60).[20]

While Apess did laud Philip as a greater forefather than Washington, a fairly overt denigration of Washington from the perspective of his audience, nowhere did Apess explicitly attack Washington's reputation as founder of a Christian America. He used him as a foil, but he did not abuse him. Of course, Apess knew about Washington's record with Native Americans and no doubt saw it reflected in the ethnocide of Southeastern tribes by President Jackson's policies. However, Apess's main tactic in mentioning Washington was to argue that Native Americans deserve as much credit for the current shape of the nation as white settlers do ([21], p. 240). In this way, Apess attempted not to remove Washington as a pillar of Christian nationalism so much as to argue for inclusion of Philip as another key founder alongside Washington. Apess's utilization of Washington touched on a common theme within his writing: the inclusion of Natives into America as a sovereign people.

Historically, the relation of Native Americans to the dominant culture in the antebellum period has been defined as a dichotomy between assimilation and authenticity, authenticity here understood as a rejection of the dominant culture in favor of one's own minority culture ([27], p. 1).[21] Apess revealed how false this dichotomy is. Apess's status as a Methodist has led some scholars to question whether he could be authentically committed to the Natives he ostensibly represented ([27], pp. 5–6). However, at the same time, Apess's radical critiques of America have led other scholars to state that he in no way desired straight assimilation ([8], p. 147). Instead of authenticity or assimilation, Apess is better characterized by the ideas of "affiliation" and "religious engagement" as established by Fisher ([10], pp. 8, 63–64, 67, 190). Apess affiliated with the Methodist church in order to gain enough authority to preach and lecture ([17], pp. 104–10).[22] This manner of religious engagement, forming a symbiotic relationship with religion to advance a particular cause, is typical of Native American interaction with Christian religion throughout the history of the United States ([10], pp. 86, 88–89, 99, 101, 106, 211). By utilizing the dominant culture's idolization of Washington as the greatest American, Apess defied cultural assimilation into the American nation and remained allegiant to his heritage. However, by placing Philip with Washington as a key political influence, Apess reintroduced Natives into the history of the nation. By balancing this tension between assimilation and authenticity, Apess charted a third way of religious engagement and affiliation with the American nation that characterizes his collective works ([27], pp. 11–12).

---

[20] Vogel goes so far as to conclude that Apess credits Philip with inspiring the Revolution and Washington himself.
[21] Apess scholars Krupat and Brumble have proposed two such theories which fail to reject this dichotomy.
[22] In this section, Wigger discusses how and why Methodism granted authority to "unqualified" preachers.

While Apess's utilization of Washington introduced the tension he felt with regards to nationalism, his treatment of the Puritans and Pilgrims, a critical Christian nationalist pillar, reflected his unwillingness to accept its mythical components. In Apess's praise of Philip as the greatest "American," he ended with a comparison of Philip to the Pilgrims: "I shall pronounce [Philip] the greatest man that was ever in America; and so it will stand... to the everlasting disgrace of the Pilgrims' fathers" ([5], p. 308). The Puritans and Pilgrims constituted the main antagonists for Apess in his writing. Apess's disillusionment stemmed mostly from the false Christianity, as he saw it, of the Pilgrims: "For be it remembered, although the Gospel is said to be glad tidings to all people, yet we poor Indians never have found those who brought it as messengers of mercy, but contrariwise." He continued to assert that 22 December, the agreed upon date for the landing of the Pilgrims at Plymouth Rock, should be remembered with tears instead of joy ([5], p. 286). The Puritans and Pilgrims were frequently seen as stalwarts of prayer, appealing to their Lord for guidance and protection. Apess, however, revealed a much darker side of this virtue: "it was a common thing [during King Philip's War] for all the Pilgrims to curse the Indians. . . . It is also wonderful how they prayed, that they should pray the bullet through the Indians' heart and their souls down into hell. . . . If this is the way they pray . . . I hope they will not pray for me" ([5], p. 304).[23] By attacking the Puritan's prayer life and their other lauded traits, Apess attempted to redefine the core virtues (and historical understandings) of his audience. Based on historical misrepresentation, this pillar of Christian nationalism was an unacceptable heritage; in its place, "the Puritan legacy, as told by Apess, was one of intolerance, deceit, and conquest" ([9], p. 688).

Apess was familiar with Daniel Webster and Nathaniel Hawthorne and was therefore well-versed in the pro-Pilgrim and pro-Puritan Christian nationalist arguments espoused by them ([22], p. 112; [27], p. 4). While Apess disagreed markedly with Daniel Webster, Noah Webster, Samuel Gardner Drake, and other revisionist historians on the correct reputation of the Pilgrims, he did agree that current Americans and the nation they inhabit are a product of the Pilgrims' actions. Throughout "Eulogy," Apess addressed his audience as "sons of the Pilgrims" ([5], p. 306). However, Apess ensured that this moniker was not something to be desired. As he related the tale of his ancestor Apess made sure that the history he was constructing was not only his history; his white audience was intimately connected to it as well given the role their forebears played as the antagonists. Throughout his speech Apess wove past and present together in such a way that his audience was forced to confront their guilt in the Indian Removal under Jackson and the poor plight of the Mashpee. In *Indian Nullification* he challenged his sensible white readers to balance their disgust with Jackson's policies and the Georgians' actions with their disregard for the Mashpee living among them ([21], p. 177).

In engaging with the history of the nation to make claims about the current state of affairs, Apess fit perfectly into the ranks of other Christian nationalist authors like Webster. By using this history not to bolster national unity but rather as proof that America was built upon systematic exclusion and injustice, Apess challenged the common notion of the progress of liberty in America in much the same way as current scholars like Amanda Porterfield. America was not living in a golden age of religious freedom as established by the Puritan forefathers; instead, injustice and ethnocide were still very present in the land of liberty ([7], pp. 68–69). However, Apess did not just attack the actions of the Puritans, he attacked the conception of Divine Providence that undergirded much of the reasoning behind their success and subsequent establishment of God's chosen nation.

In "An Indian's Looking Glass for the White Man," Apess questioned a third main Christian nationalist pillar, the narrative of God's blessing of America. He inquired of his reader, "can you charge the Indians with robbing a nation almost of their whole continent, and murdering their women and children, and then depriving them the remainder of their lawful rights, that nature and God require

---

[23] Apess continues later on the page to quote a number of Scriptures that clearly show how Christians should pray for their enemies' forgiveness, not their damnation.

them to have?" ([28], p. 157). In this and many other similar refrains, Apess redefined the taming of the continent as rooted in human design and evil, not as any sort of manifest destiny.

In an even more pointed attack, Apess questioned his readers, "did you ever hear or read of Christ teaching his disciples that they ought to despise one because his skin was different from theirs?" A few paragraphs later he uttered perhaps his most controversial statement of all: "If the Lord Jesus Christ, who is counted by all to be a Jew—and it is well known that the Jews are a colored people . . . if he should appear among us, would he not be shut out of doors by many, very quickly?" ([28], pp. 159–60). Not only was God not responsible for the spread of the original settlers, but these devout Americans descended from the champions of Christian virtue, the Pilgrims, would completely fail to recognize the Lord Christ because of his skin color. Apess contended that neither Divine Providence nor Christ-likeness were on the side of Anglo-Americans because of their horrendous treatment of Natives.

In his remarks on General Washington, Apess wavered between criticism and idolization. In his criticism of Divine Providence and the Puritan Myth, he appeared Samson-like, knocking down two critical pillars supporting the Christian nationalist temple. Apess struck a different chord, however, with his treatment of the common law based upon Christian dogma. He was fully supportive of this notion, although he was skeptical of how successful Americans were in following the law they so proudly claimed as their own.

Similar to his affiliation with Washington, Apess did not attack the original law. In fact, he regarded the American common law, the final pillar of Christian nationalism, as the standard for how white Americans should treat Native Americans. Apess focused his critique on the political powers behind the law responsible for twisting it to serve their own purposes and oppress Native Americans. This failure to uphold the original law of God and country formed a key theme of *Indian Nullification*. Responding to the original Mashpee Declaration of Independence, the county Sherriff told the Mashpee that "merely declaring a law to be oppressive [can] not abrogate it." The Sherriff subsequently urged the Mashpee as "good citizens" to go through the normal channels of the law to resolve their dispute. In response, Apess noted "surely it was either insult or wrong to call the Marshpees citizens, for such they never were, from the Declaration of Independence up to the session of the Legislature in 1834" ([21], p. 183). What makes this simple recommendation even more insulting is the fact that the Mashpee had been trying to get a hearing with the governor for years to address their grievances, as good citizens should, but the governor had refused to meet with them ([21], p. 173). While Apess continued to relate the restrictive and unjust nature of the laws binding the Mashpee and document their struggle to overcome these laws, what is important for this essay is how Apess engaged with the law itself, especially the Constitution and Declaration of Independence.

In the early Republic, the Constitution and Declaration of Independence joined the Bible as the second and third members of the Christian nationalists' textual trinity. Apess's first reference to the Constitution was emblematic of his overall treatment: he claimed the Truth undergirding the Constitution firmly for himself and his tribe. This first reference occurred in the "Indian Declaration of Independence" which adopted three resolutions. When the first resolution declared the right of self-government for the Mashpee, it did so on the authority that "all men are born free and equal, says the Constitution of the country" ([20], p. xxxvi; [21], p. 175). After issuing this seminal proclamation forming their own independent government, Apess admitted that he mistakenly wrote to the lieutenant governor. Turning this error to his advantage, Apess asserted that "our mistake was not greater than many that have been made to pass current by the sophistry of the whites, and *we* acted in accordance with the spirit of the Constitution, unless that instrument be a device of utter deception" ([21], pp. 179–80, emphasis added). Here Apess boldly contended that the greater common law tradition supported himself and his allies over and against white Americans who were condemned for selectively enforcing it. Again, when the Mashpee's initial efforts were ignored by many of the well-to-do of society, Apess commented in response that the "governor, senators, and representatives were arrayed against us, . . . we Marshpees account all who opposed our freedom, as Tories, hostile to the Constitution and the liberties of the country" ([21], p. 204). Thus, when the state leadership opposed the cause of the Mashpee they were simultaneously opposing the essence of the Constitution.

Apess's adoption and adaptation of the Constitution paralleled his implementation of the Declaration of Independence. In addition to naming the document of revolt after the Declaration, Apess frequently alluded to the Revolutionary War and the overthrow of laws believed to be unjust by the Founding Fathers. After detailing the nature of many of the repressive laws instituted by the Massachusetts' government against the Mashpee, Apess addressed his readers directly. "I will ask [the reader] how, if he values his own liberty, he would or could rest quiet under such laws. I ask the inhabitants of New England generally how their fathers bore laws, much less oppressive, when imposed upon them by a foreign government" ([21], p. 211). While Apess's description of British laws as "much less oppressive" may have been insulting to some of his readers, his overall request to be judged by the same standard white Americans hold for themselves was apt.

Apess accomplished a number of goals by incorporating the Constitution and Declaration of Independence into his arguments for Mashpee self-governance. On a general level, he was appealing to the cultural icons of his audience. More specifically, he used America's common law tradition, one of the main planks in the Christian nationalists' platform, as justification for the Mashpee Revolt. On an even deeper level, however, Apess implicitly supported the events and reasoning behind the Revolution. In fact, he oftentimes asserted that the current generation of Americans had failed to merit the great gifts they received in the founding of America: religious liberty, a noble common law, and the chance to control one's own destiny. Apess did not request these gifts be taken away from white Americans; rather, he demanded that Native Americans be allowed to share in the spoils of Revolution. "The [Mashpee] Indian soldiers fought through the [Revolutionary] war; and as far as we have been able to ascertain the fact, from documents or tradition, all but one, fell martyrs to liberty, in the struggle for Independence." Moreover, what was their reward? "Often and often have our tribe been promised the liberty their fathers fought, and bled, and died for; and even now we have but a small share of it" ([21], pp. 238–40). While appealing back to the virtues of the Revolutionary War and the common law it engendered, Apess explicitly demanded inclusion for the Mashpee—and Native Americans at large—in the freeing post-Revolution atmosphere of America. With regards to the common law of America in the 1830s, Apess affiliated wholeheartedly: Native Americans deserved full protection under the law, and any unjust laws should be repealed and recompense made.

Apess's affiliation with the four constructive pillars of Christian nationalism was multifaceted. While he demanded full inclusion in the common law, the backbone of the nation, he derided the glorification of the Pilgrims, broached numerous problems with Divine Providence, and implemented General Washington and the Founding Fathers as a foil for King Philip. While it has been established that Apess belongs to the nation-building intellectuals of the 1830s, what needs further elucidation is the nature of the nation Apess is constructing: what future did Apess envision between Native Americans and Anglo Americans specifically and the nation of America in general? Leaving for a moment the firebrand political activist, we must unpack Apess the Methodist preacher and "precociously devout Christian" ([27], p. 6).

4. William Apess, Millennial Methodist Missionary

In *A Son of the Forest* and *The Experiences of Five Christian Indians*, Apess established his conversion to Methodism as the key event between his previous, debauched life of wandering and his current life of political activism with a spiritual bent.[24] As with other aspects of Apess's writings, he used his

---

24 Current scholars disagree as to the nationalizing effect of Methodism in the early Republic. Amanda Porterfield sees Methodism as having the most profound impact upon popular culture and as being the main solidifying force of the young nation ([11], pp. 101–6, 162–75). Sam Haselby acknowledges that Methodism did becoming nationalizing but contends that this development occurred after the early Republic. He points out that early Methodist doctrine, tracts, and sermons were largely devoid of nationalistic or patriotic language—he contrasts this absence to the nationalist movement of New England

spiritual autobiography as a way to subvert the current Christian establishment. Concerning genre, Apess was dancing to the tune of his time in composing a spiritual autobiography; he did not hold back in detailing his sinful life and many failings. He did break from convention, however, in his attribution of some of those fears and failures to historical Christian precedent. Apess's autobiography "ultimately becomes an account of the shortcomings of the church and of individual Christians, and a theological argument for an alternative." Apess's sincere Christianity and minority perspective led him to the conclusion that Anglo-American Christianity had failed in its task ([29], pp. 162–70). He explored the nature of this failure and charted a way forward in his later sermons and discourses.

Apess developed his voice in his autobiographies, realizing that he could imbue it with great power by drawing on the "strategic power of Christian rhetoric;" Apess's later writings offered testament to his success in this endeavor ([29], pp. 149–50). In his only published sermon, "The Increase of the Kingdom of Christ," Apess condemned the failures of white Christian America and offered a hopeful new vision for the future of the Christian faith and nation.[25] After explaining how God must judge the heathen and the sinner, a sentiment his audience would second, Apess quickly revealed his intent to strategically agree with their ideals in order to critique their actions when he asserted the following:

> [Has] not the great American nation reason to fear the swift judgments of heaven on them for nameless cruelties, extortions, and exterminations inflicted upon the poor natives of the forest? We fear the account of national sin, which lies at the doors of the American people, will be a terrible one to balance in the chancery of heaven. America has utterly failed to amalgamate the red man of the woods into the artificial, cultivated ranks of social life ([30], pp. 106–7).

Americans, Apess contended, will have to face God with blood on their hands for their treatments of the Natives.[26] Apess was dealing in double entendre when he mentioned the failure of Americans to integrate with the Natives. First, he was accusing them of not even making the effort but rather just focusing on "extermination." Second, he was contending that Americans should not actually try to fuse with Natives; instead, Americans should respect Natives' sovereignty.[27]

The authority for this barrage of criticism was found in two places. First and foremost, Apess was convinced that true Christian doctrine forbids such horrid treatment of one race by another; Christ died for all men equally, a truth that binds all races together ([32], p. 608). However, more vital (and curious) for his argument was the notion of Indians as descendants of the Ten Lost Tribes of Israel. Apess defended his belief in this notion simply by saying that "many eminent men with apparently high presumption, if not unquestionable evidence, believe [this dogma]" ([30], p. 106). Apess explained this theory more fully in the appendix to his autobiography. Some scholars believed Native Americans descended from the Ten Lost Tribes of Israel because of the similarities in custom, religious rituals and rites, appearance, and linguistics ([18], pp. 74–76). For Apess, linking Native Americans back to Israel accomplished a number of purposes. First, it meant that Natives should not be outright "amalgamated"

---

evangelicals of more Reformed background ([2], pp. 121–37). For Apess, I see Methodist doctrine inspiring first his political activity and attacks on Anglo American Christian hypocrisy which in turn birthed his concern with nationalism. Perhaps Apess can be read as a middle ground between the two scholars. To say Methodism gave him his nationalizing bent would be too simplistic. To say it was not a key influencing factor would be too extreme.

[25] Notwithstanding his considerable frustrations with Anglo American implementation of Divine Providence, Apess's hope comes from this Methodist belief which imparted confidence in the ultimate triumph of good. See ([11], pp. 143–46).

[26] This paper might benefit from a more detailed examination of the wrongs perpetuated upon the Native Americans. For such a treatment see [31].

[27] I do not want to oversimplify the incredibly complex history of Protestant missions to the Native Americans. Apess is in fact mistaken when he asserts that an effort was never made. The New England Protestants' missions movement, which kicked into high gear after the collapse of Federalism in the 1810s, began "with the best of intentions" to see Native American's fully nationalized into the country ([2], p. 297). This intention collapsed under the pressure from Andrew Jackson when New Englanders were forced to choose between nationalization and Native American missions as popular pressure and Jackson's rise made the two antonymous. For a detailed breakdown of this process see ([2], esp. chapter 7).

into the American nation. After Apess commented on the failure of white Americans to settle down well with Natives, he credited this failure to the Israelite blood in Native veins that demanded freedom. Second, if Natives were descended from Israel then they were even more connected to Christ: not only were they both people of color but they were also the same ethnicity. This connection ensured God's covenant protection and required Natives to take the initiative in fighting for the increase of the Kingdom of Christ ([30], p. 107).[28] Presenting Native Americans as the Ten Lost Tribes of Israel was a significant component of Apess's Christian nationalism because it explained why Natives should be allowed to govern themselves *within* the setting of Christian America.[29]

While Apess's sermon did highlight the failures of white Americans and discuss the true identity of Native Americans, its ultimate purpose was to shed light on how the Kingdom of God could be furthered in the world. As a Christian minister, this was not a surprising doctrine for him to promote. What matters for the purpose of this paper is that Apess deemed this process of Christianization as a thoroughly nationalistic one. He spoke in terms of nations, national sin, and national duty throughout the whole sermon. While Apess spent significant time criticizing the church, he concluded on a hopeful note: "There is a great light of glory descending upon the American church. Revivals follow revivals, and the deep brown wilderness is vocal with the shouting and songs of the delivered tribes, long slaves to error but now emancipated and brought out of the wilderness of sin into the Canaan of Gospel liberty." In addition to the continued utilization of Israelite language, Apess's hope for the future of the church was startling in its equivocation of "American church" and "delivered tribes." To even speak of an "American church" was surprising given the incredibly divisive time he inhabited ([2], p. 191). He had personally experienced the division when his masters forbid him from attending the unruly Methodist sermons ([18], pp. 12–21). His classification of the church as American therefore reflected his bent towards Christian nationalism. For Apess to declare that "tribes of the wilderness" would be the ones to "conquer the world for Christ" was as shocking as his hope that these tribes could constitute part of the American church ([30], pp. 108–11). As the Methodist revivals continued to spread across the country—specifically through and amidst Native tribes—the *American* church as a whole would be glorified ([30], p. 111; [33], pp. 33–34). In this way, Apess linked the virtues of Native Americans with the spreading of the Gospel and the revivification of the American church as a whole, allowing for the possibility of Christian Native Americans coexisting with Christian Anglo Americans ([33], p. 37).

This hopeful tone amidst the overall bleak representation of American Christianity in Apess's writings can be credited to his belief in Millennialism. Like many Christians (and Christian nationalists) of his time, Apess was convinced that the full establishment of the Kingdom of Heaven was imminent ([20], p. 99; [30], pp. 107–9). If Apess's religious convictions in this regard are sincere, his prescription for the path forward takes on not a fanciful or dreamy hue but a strident and urgent tone. The Kingdom is coming; white Christians need to repent. White and Native Christians alike need to work together to build Christ's Kingdom before his coming. With this in mind, the national language of Apess is compelling. He advocated openly for unity in America between Natives and whites as Christian sisters and brothers. Apess's religious request as a pastor, therefore, was for repentance of misdeeds by all followed by national unification around the preparatory building of a Christian house for Christ to inhabit.

---

[28] Of course, Apess does not think of Natives as being *Jewish* but only Jews. In other words, he connects them ethnically but not religiously; Apess is still a firm Christian believer. On another note, in *A Star in the West*, Elias Boudinot uses the Ten Tribes idea to argue that Natives should be sent to Palestine ([2], p. 218)! Apess implements his mimicry once again by drawing on this popular doctrine but completely reversing its intended purpose. He uses it to argue for inclusion and respect where it had previously been cited as another reason why Natives do not belong in America.

[29] As a Christian minister, Apess would have assumed that the "Jews" of America would accept the truth of Christianity when it was presented to them. He certainly was not a Zionist.

With the impetus for religious respect established, Apess's prescriptions for the political realm can be better understood. After critiquing the different planks of Christian nationalism and describing the wrongs of white Americans, Apess concluded that "justice demand[s] that the relationship between natives and newcomers be revived on an equal and honorable basis" ([6], p. 92). The foundation for this new relationship would be the construction of a "cross-cultural written history of the region ... to assert the vital presence of Native Americans." His history would provide the grounds for inter-ethnic respect and foster national unity ([25], p. 165). This essay has argued that the first piece of evidence supporting Apess as a Christian nationalist is his interaction with the four main pillars of the movement. The second critical support is Apess's incorporation of these pillars into his new cross-cultural history. Concerning Philip and Washington, Apess's version of history respected and honored both. He clearly believed Divine Providence to have been abused in the past, but the possibility of God's Divine Blessing still existed for present Christians. As for the hated Puritan myth and misuse of the common law, Apess magnanimously offered to "bury the hatchet and those unjust laws and Plymouth Rock together and become friends." He went on to ask "will the sons of the Pilgrims aid in putting out the fire and destroying the canker that will ruin all that their fathers left behind them to destroy?" If so, then "let us have principles that will give everyone his due ... Give the Indian his rights, and you may be assured war will cease" ([5], pp. 306–7). In this oft-quoted appeal, Apess offered friendship and the possibility of a mutually cooperative nation under "one general law" where Native and Anglo American alike can respect and live alongside each other by the grace of God ([5], p. 310).

If an American Christian nationalist is simply someone who believes that God will fuel their nation's growth and success, then Apess was certainly a Christian nationalist. However, many of the Christian nationalists of the 1830s believed not only in a bright Divinely-blessed future but in a Divinely purposed past, something Apess challenged. However, while Apess warned of potential damnation because of gross injustices, he did find God's blessing and providence in a few aspects of history, especially the general principles of the nation solidified in the Constitution. He credited rebellious, misguided people with the current state of affairs, not an absent God. In his sermons and autobiographies, Apess attempted to convict his audience of their faults, drive them to repentance, and restore their relationship with God. In his speeches and political tracts, he once again highlighted the injustices, but he also proffered a new future of friendship and cooperation. This new future was based on replacing the old mythical history with a new history, one that was not as comforting as his audience would prefer. It was a multi-ethnic history of fears, failures, massacres, and mutual hatred. Apess hoped that this bleak history would spark a desire for love and cooperation that had been absent. He trusted in God to accomplish this task of conviction, repentance, and renewal. Apess yearned for national conversion back to the ways of God, who had been there all along; it was this pursuit that made him a Christian nationalist.

Conflicts of Interest: The author declares no conflict of interest.

References

1. Tocqueville, Alexis de. *Democracy in America Volume I*. Translated by Esq Henry Reeve. New York: Alfred A Knopf, 1966.
2. Haselby, Sam. *The Origins of American Religious Nationalism*. Oxford: OUP, 2015.
3. Green, Steven K. *Inventing a Christian America: The Myth of the Religious Founding*. Oxford: OUP, 2015.
4. Fea, John. *Was America Founded as a Christian Nation?* Louisville: Westminster John Knox Press, 2011.
5. Apess, William. "Eulogy on King Philip, as Pronounced at the Odeon, in Federal Street, Boston." In *On Our Own Ground: The Complete Writings of William Apess, a Pequot*. Edited by Barry O'Connell. Amherst: University of Massachusetts Press, 1992, pp. 277–310.
6. Benn, Carl. *Native Memoirs from the War of 1812: Black Hawk and William Apess*. Baltimore: Johns Hopkins University Press, 2014.

7. Dannenberg, Anne Marie. "'Where, then, shall we place the hero of the wilderness?' William Apess's Eulogy on King Philip and Doctrines of Racial Destiny." In *Early Native American Writing: New Critical Essays*. Edited by Helen Jaskoski. Cambridge: Cambridge University Press, 1996, pp. 66–82.

8. Doolen, Andy. "William Apess and the Nullification of Empire." In *Fugitive Empire: Locating Early American Imperialism*. Minneapolis: University of Minnesota Press, 2005, pp. 145–83.

9. Lopenzina, Drew. "What to the American Indian is the Fourth of July? Moving beyond abolitionist rhetoric in William Apess's eulogy on King Philip." *American Literature* 82 (2007): 673–99. [CrossRef]

10. Fisher, Lin. *Indian Great Awakening: Religion and the Shaping of Native Cultures in Early America*. Oxford: OUP, 2012.

11. Porterfield, Amanda. *Conceived in Doubt: Religion and Politics in the New American Nation*. Chicago: University of Chicago Press, 2012.

12. Noll, Mark A., Nathan O. Hatch, and George M. Marsden. *The Search for Christian America*. Westchester: Crossway Books, 1983.

13. Handy, Robert T. "'A Complete Christian Commonwealth' (1800–1860)." In *A Christian America: Protestant Hopes and Historical Realities*. Oxford: OUP, 1984, pp. 24–56.

14. Noll, Mark A. *America's God: From Jonathan Edwards to Abraham Lincoln*. Oxford: OUP, 2002.

15. Hatch, Nathan. *The Democratization of American Christianity*. New Have: Yale University Press, 1989.

16. McKenna, George. *Puritan Origins of American Patriotism*. New Haven: Yale University Press, 2007.

17. Wigger, John H. *Taking Heaven by Storm: Methodism and the Rise of Popular Christianity in America*. Oxford: OUP, 1998.

18. Apess, William. "A Son of the Forest: The Experience of William Apess, a Native of the Forest." In *On Our Own Ground: The Complete Writings of William Apess, a Pequot*. Edited by Barry O'Connell. Amherst: University of Massachusetts Press, 1992, pp. 3–97.

19. Gura, Philip. *The Life of William Apess, Pequot*. Chapel Hill: The University of North Carolina Press, 2015.

20. O'Connell, Barry. *On Our Own Ground: The Complete Writings of William Apess, a Pequot*. Edited by Barry O'Connell. Amherst: University of Massachusetts Press, 1992.

21. Apess, William. "Indian Nullification of the Unconstitutional Laws of Massachusetts Relative to the Marshpee Tribe; or, The Pretended Riot Explained." In *On Our Own Ground: The Complete Writings of William Apess, a Pequot*. Edited by Barry O'Connell. Amherst: University of Massachusetts Press, 1992, pp. 166–274.

22. Bergland, Renée L. *The National Uncanny: Indian Ghosts and American Subjects*. Hanover: University Press of New England, 2000.

23. Vogel, Kerstin. *The Native American Declaration of Independence: William Apess's Reflections of Ethnic Consciousness*. Heidelberg: Winter, 2008.

24. Vogel, Todd. "William Apess's Theater and a 'Native' American History." In *ReWriting White: Race, Class, and Cultural Capital in Nineteenth-Century America*. New Brunswick: Rutgers University Press, 2004, pp. 40–61.

25. O'Connell, Barry. "'Once More Let Us Consider': William Apess in the Writing of New England Native American History." In *After King Philip's War: Presence and Persistence in Indian New England*. Edited by Colin G. Calloway. Hanover: University Press of New England, 1997, pp. 162–77.

26. Walker, Cheryl. *Indian Nation: Native American Literature and Nineteenth-Century Nationalisms*. Durham: Duke University Press, 1997.

27. Sayre, Gordon. "Defying Assimilation, Confounding Authenticity: The Case of William Apess." *Auto/biography Studies* 11 (1996): 1–18. [CrossRef]

28. Apess, William. "The Experiences of Five Christian Indians of the Pequot Tribe." In *On Our Own Ground: The Complete Writings of William Apess, a Pequot*. Edited by Barry O'Connell. Amherst: University of Massachusetts Press, 1992, pp. 119–61.

29. Elrod, Eileen Razzari. "Finding a Way in the Forest: The Religious Discourse of Race and Justice in the Autobiographies of William Apess." In *Piety and Dissent: Race, Gender, and Biblical Rhetoric in Early American Autobiography*. Amherst: University of Massachusetts Press, 2008, pp. 146–70.

30. Apess, William. "The Increase of the Kingdom of Christ: A Sermon." In *On Our Own Ground: The Complete Writings of William Apess, a Pequot*. Edited by Barry O'Connell. Amherst: University of Massachusetts Press, 1992, pp. 101–12.

31. Hia, Thomas. *Manifest Design: American Exceptionalism and Empire, Revised Edition*. Ithaca: Cornell University Press, 1985.

32. McQuaid, Kim. "William Apes, Pequot: An Indian Reformer in the Jackson Era." *New England Quarterly* 50 (1977): 605–25. [CrossRef]
33. Donaldson, Laura. "Making a Joyful Noise: William Apess and the Search for Postcolonial Method(ism)." In *Messy Beginnings: Postcoloniality and Early American Studies*. Edited by Malini Johar Schueller and Edward Watts. New Brunswick: Rutgers University Press, 2003, pp. 29–44.

religions ‖MDPI‖

Article

America's "Peculiar Children": Authority and Christian Nationalism at Antebellum West Point

Michael Graziano

Department of Philosophy and World Religions, University of Northern Iowa, Cedar Falls, IA 50614, USA;
michael.graziano@uni.edu; Tel.: +1-319-273-6221

Academic Editor: Mark T. Edwards
Received: 2 October 2016; Accepted: 29 December 2016; Published: 6 January 2017

Abstract: This essay examines how the United States Military Academy at West Point developed an explicitly "federal" Christianity to help train the antebellum officers of the United States Army. It begins by examining how the Episcopal Church was quietly "established" at West Point, and how the church allied with the federal government and US Army to encourage a potent Christian nationalism that collapsed the sovereignty of the United States into the sovereignty of God. The case of West Point illustrates how federal officials, Army leaders, and Academy administrators understood religion as a central component of national security.

Keywords: nationalism; military; Christianity; authority; education; antebellum; civil war

1. Introduction

This essay examines how the United States Military Academy at West Point developed an explicitly "federal" Christianity to help train the antebellum officers of the United States Army. It begins by examining how the Episcopal Church was quietly "established" at West Point, and how the church allied with the federal government and US Army to encourage a potent Christian nationalism that collapsed the sovereignty of the United States into the sovereignty of God. The case of West Point illustrates how federal officials, Army leaders, and Academy administrators understood religion as a central component of national security. The informal establishment of the Episcopal church and the subsequent revivals it spawned shaped the political and religious loyalties of a generation of US Army leaders.

West Point grappled with the task of molding an appropriately federal religious culture in an era of rapid and widespread religious disestablishment and political polarization. West Point cultivated a religious atmosphere which prized an unemotional, calculated Christianity informed by the demands of American nationalism. This uniform religious instruction complemented the Academy's larger mission of producing ideologically homogenized citizen-soldiers: men who, while "neutral" and "non-partisan," would also be sufficiently nationalist and ready to bear arms. To be a graduate of West Point was to be immersed in the developing Christian nationalism of the United States. The educational experience at antebellum West Point assumed that religion and national security were closely linked. West Point produced a curious product: military officers sworn to uphold the Constitution of a nascent federal government through service in a federal Army that existed largely on paper. Nevertheless, the Academy's conviction that what cadets believed influenced their ability to defend American interests motivated the Academy to provide exacting training in the political and religious aspects of American identity. The result, as one former student noted, was that West Point cadets were "the peculiar children of the nation." ([1], p. 15).

If scholars wish to understand how Christian nationalism and the US government interacted in the early republic, West Point is a good place to start. Along with the federal Congress and the

Naval Academy at Annapolis, West Point was one of the few existing federal institutions. Even the army for which it trained its graduates to lead was organized largely by the state. While newspapers, pamphlets, and travel diaries can give historians some perspective on regional interactions between budding nationalism and religion, West Point offers something different. Jeffrey L. Pasley argues in *The Tyranny of Printers* (2001) that decentralized newspaper networks in the early republic offered a way to "filter" news and opinions to suit local tastes while still contributing to a national political discourse ([2], p. 208). A study of antebellum West Point effectively reverses this process, opening a window onto how local religious tastes and political opinions were nationalized in a federal institution during an era of radical decentralization. West Point also serves as a reminder that the antebellum period witnessed a great deal of religious experimentation, differentiation, and innovation in both the structure and practice of American religious groups. The effects of these changes extended beyond religious groups and institutions, however. Their consequences spilled out across American life, influencing ideas about the state and state institutions such as West Point. Amanda Porterfield's insightful critique that certain "religious institutions grew as much to manage mistrustful doubt as to relieve it...feeding the uncertainty and instability they worked to resolve" could also be applied to the Academy ([3], p. 2). To be sure, as John Fea and others have shown, Christian nationalism meant different things across the North and South in the leadup to the Civil War ([4], pp. 12–21). Even so, the Academy's interaction with Christian nationalism—while initially haphazard—would grow more focused and deliberate as the war drew closer.

2. A Church in the Service of the State

West Point's mission was to mold the U.S. Army's officer corps through devotion to transcendent ideals of Christian nationalism. Chief among these ideals was the sovereignty of the Republic. Sovereignty, as understood at the Point, was the legitimate use of power and military force. The Academy's unique religious atmosphere came of age in the late 1820s alongside hugely divisive issues such as the Tariffs of 1824 and 1828 (the latter being the so-called "Tariff of Abominations") and the subsequent Nullification Crises. In this context, the great achievement of the Academy was not simply to imbue the state with theological significance, but to instill in cadets a sense of personal connection *to* the state as a theological object. Not surprisingly, as the political atmosphere grew more heated and the prospect of civil war became a reality, the Army increasingly relied on West Point's ability to manufacture a distinctly federal product. Religious ideas were used to build the connection between cadet and state, and this process took place seemingly everywhere across the Academy. The classroom, the chapel, the laboratory, and the drill field were all part of this experience.

A key function of West Point was to stamp out sectional or regional loyalties ([5], p. 10). The rhetoric of the non-sectarian and neutral cadet was taken seriously at the Academy, and cadets were drilled on its importance. Cadet George Strong remembered how his instructors inquired about his politics. Strong responded with what he thought was the safest answer: "I'm an administration man, Sir." Disappointed, his instructor sighed and replied, "Just as I expected...It is evident you have mistaken your calling. You should have known, ere this, that an officer of the Army has nothing to do with politics" ([6], p. 195). Cadets were taught that to be a proper Army officer was to engage in a delicate balancing act: they must be neutral between administrations (but loyal to the commander in chief) and nonsectarian (yet Episcopal in disposition).

Denominational differences were flattened as well. Rather than deal with a fractious religious atmosphere on post, the Academy's administration simply made it a requirement that all services were Episcopal. All cadets, including non-Christians, were required to attend the Episcopal chapel service on Sunday ([7], p. 21). Simon Magruder Levy, a Maryland Jew, was an inaugural West Point cadet at a time of pervasive anti-Semitism. Levy graduated second in his class of two, allowing cadets at the West Point Jewish Chapel (built in 1984) to claim that the first West Point graduating class was "50% Jewish" ([8]; [9], p. 415). Additionally, the Episcopal Church's avoidance of a major pre-war schism made it appear even more attractive to an explicitly federal and tenuously apolitical institution such as the Army ([6], p. 31). Whereas questions over slavery had worked to sunder the Presbyterians in 1837, Methodists in 1844, and Baptists in 1845, the Episcopal Church kept its theological divisions internal. Even so, membership in the Episcopalian Church did not exempt one from involvement in long running sectional controversies. Episcopalians participated in the debates and, of course, in the eventual war itself. Instead, the Army and the Academy understood Episcopalianism as a proper religion for "gentlemen" ([6], p. 31). They understood it as a religious identity well-suited to emphasize the qualities that they prized in cadets. Chief among those qualities was discipline, and chief among what cadets were to be disciplined in was loyalty to their senior officers and to their country.

The most important aspect of religious life at the antebellum Academy was the working relationship between the Academy's administration and the Episcopal Church. Begun under the auspices of West Point Superintendent Sylvanus Thayer and Episcopal Chaplain Charles P. McIlvaine in the 1820s, the pseudo-establishment of the Episcopal Church on post served the needs of both the church and state. The church gained a foothold in both the federal government and U.S. Army officer corps, while the Academy could leverage the moral authority of the church in order to teach "proper" notions of American citizenship while maintaining the appearance of a religiously non-sectarian government institution. This relationship culminated in the revival of 1826, cementing the place of a nationalist Christianity as the focal point of West Point's character education in the early republic.

3. The Revival of 1826

The foundations of West Point's antebellum religious culture, and its advocacy of Christian nationalism, lay in the revival of 1826. This revival looked different from those led by Charles Finney or Lorenzo Dow, however. It renewed cadets' devotion to American federal government as much as to any doctrinal claims. Nathan Hatch's *Democratization of American Christianity* (1989) argued that the Second Great Awakening was a liberating, democratic experience for its American participants [10]. Hatch writes that during this period "common people" worked to spread a sentiment of political and religious freedom rather than reinforce authority or attempt to control the masses ([10], p. 9).

The Revival of 1826 suggests that something entirely different was also occurring during the Awakening. The revival was a story of two figures: Chaplain Charles P. McIlvaine, the religious authority behind the revival, and Academy Superintendent Sylvanus Thayer, who permitted and tacitly encouraged the outbreak of religious enthusiasm on post. West Point witnessed a revival in which the religious authorities were carefully selected, hired, and paid by the federal government of the United States for expressly religious purposes, and its intended audience—the Corps of Cadets—was mandated to listen and sworn to obey the military hierarchy.

When Superintendent Sylvanus Thayer assumed command of the Academy, he inherited a military school lacking basic discipline and respect for authority. Over a period of several years, Superintendent Thayer slowly instituted radical changes in curriculum, decorum, dress, and even eating habits. These changes were promulgated in an attempt to enforce a radical sense of uniformity among cadets. Treated with ambivalence under previous superintendents, religion was also brought to heel. Though attendance at chapel was mandatory, religious instruction was largely ignored by cadets ([11], p. 89). The incumbent chaplain, Thomas Picton, was not popular. The cadets dismissed Chaplain Picton's lessons as simply "truisms they learned as children" ([12], p. 96).

Rather than reduce cadets' religious obligations—or, worse, allow a variety of Christian denominations on post and risk religious disunion—Superintendent Thayer chose to enforce the chapel attendance policy and simply replace the chaplain. The new chaplain, the Episcopalian minister Charles P. McIlvaine, arrived shortly thereafter. In his memoirs, Chaplain McIlvaine remembered how the job of chaplain was broached to him by his friend John C. Calhoun, then serving as Secretary of War. While taking tea at Calhoun's home one evening, the Secretary asked McIlvaine if he might be interested in the position of Professor of Ethics, and thus chaplain, at West Point ([13], p. 286). McIlvaine was interested but worried his young age might be a problem. Calhoun dismissed McIlvaine's worries in a manner perhaps indicative of Superintendent Thayer's priorities: "[Calhoun] answered that he preferred a young man who would grow to the place, rather than one whose habits of mind were so fixed by age that they could not be molded," McIlvaine later recalled ([14], p. 20). Like other revivalists working in 1825, McIlvaine was young. Yet he boasted an unusual resume for a revivalist. He had just finished serving as the Chaplain of the U.S. Senate, making McIlvaine one of the few explicitly religious professionals with work experience at the federal level.

McIlvaine landed at West Point in the spring of 1825 and quickly learned that he had his work cut out for him. Upon his arrival, he remarked that except for "three or four ladies...there was a most chilling want of any manifestation of sympathy with the Gospel" ([14], pp. 24–25). McIlvaine was warned that religious services were not taken very seriously by either cadets or professors. Friends familiar with the culture of West Point had confided that there was widespread atheism and agnosticism at the school ([15], p. 198). Cadets reported that reading coursework and sleeping during sermons was common ([11], p. 89).

McIlvaine wasted little time. He distributed religious tracts around post and sought out students for conversation. On Sundays, cadets remarked that his sermons became "hotter and hotter" ([14], p. 26). Yet the chaplain had to walk a fine line. West Point was suspicious of emotional appeals. The cadets thought of themselves as Enlightenment thinkers, pursuing education at West Point largely because of the school's expertise in engineering. Emotionalism was out of place. Chaplain McIlvaine policed himself, writing that he knew "Had I gone on with a sermon which I was preaching to them, I verily believe I should not have been able to moderate or control their feelings. I had to stop, I did stop" ([14], p. 177).

Even so, McIlvaine's message got through. The first cadet to respond was Leonidas Polk of North Carolina. McIlvaine would later write of Polk's first meeting that, "I was amazed at the depth and power of his convictions and anxieties, and his readiness for whatever might be required of him as a servant of Christ." Cadet Polk's conversion offers a striking contrast to traditional narratives of Second Great Awakening revivalism. Polk would explain his decision as the result of the tracts and McIlvaine's masterful series of sermons on the evidences of Christianity, which helped Polk ease his "skepticism" [16]. After joining the chaplain in prayer, Polk "became tranquil" and asked for McIlvaine's help in his conversion ([11], p. 92).

Chaplain McIlvaine instructed Polk to come forward in the next mandatory chapel service. When the call for confession went out, Polk quietly left his seat, walked toward the front of the chapel, and silently knelt. McIlvaine described the scene from the pulpit: "When the confession in the service came, I could hear his movement to get space to kneel, and then his deep tone of response as if he was trembling with new emotion, and then it seemed as if an impression of solemnity pervaded all the congregation" [16]. McIlvaine later wrote that, "It was a new sight, that single kneeling cadet. Such a thing had not been supposed to be possible" ([11], p. 92). Polk would write to his brother, confiding that "This first step was my most trying one, to bring myself to renounce all of my former habits and associations, to step forth singly from the whole corps acknowledging my convictions of truth" ([17], p. 175). Being the first cadet in the history of the Academy to openly convert on post, Polk understood the challenges ahead of him. McIlvaine instructed Polk that the cadet would now be "watched in chapel" and Polk felt the need for the "greatest circumspection" ([11], p. 92).

Despite Chaplain McIlvaine's measured tone, the conversion of Polk brought about a whirlwind of enthusiasm on post. Cadets began taking an interest in Polk's new-found religious beliefs and requested meetings with McIlvaine [16]. So many came to McIlvaine that he began holding group meetings at his home. Before long, however, the meetings grew too large for the chaplain's quarters. Polk requested, and received, permission from Superintendent Thayer to move the nightly revival meetings into the prison, which was then the single largest room available on post. Cadets and faculty began noticing changes in the campus atmosphere. General Wright observed that:

> At length the whole corps was roused as by a thunder-clap at the announcement that Leonidas Polk and others had been 'converted,' and that Polk was to lead a 'praying squad' in the prison, which was the only unoccupied and quiet room in the barracks. I and many others stood on the stoop to see them go by and find out who they were. Polk, calm and

fearless, with earnest anxiety in his look, headed the squad of 'converted' men. From day to day the number increased, and finally it became so large that they were obliged, for want of room, to adjourn to the chapel. There was a veritable revolution in the barracks and the corps of cadets ([11], p. 89).

McIlvaine would write that Polk's "conviction was complete, and in the spirit of the missionary he laboured among his fellows with a zeal which showed the earnestness of his character" ([14], p. 176). Yet this was an unusual revival: a series of sermons on the rational, logical nature of Christianity at an institution which celebrated scientific empiricism brought forth a curious cadet who helped instigate a "solemn" revival, who in turn led a series of "calm" and "fearless" nightly revival meetings in a prison.

McIlvaine's concerns about emotion are understandable in light of how the revival was seen by those living outside of West Point. Neither the Episcopal Church nor the US Army wanted the public to associate wild, unchecked emotionalism or religious fervor with the military. As the revival progressed, McIlvaine sought advice from Episcopal Bishop James Milnor. During a lengthy exchange of letters, Milnor confided in McIlvaine that he heard grumblings about the revival at West Point. Milnor stressed the importance of maintaining the Episcopal Church's mutually beneficial relationship with West Point and the nation's military. Milnor's letters suggest broader military worries about the religious occurrences at West Point. Milnor related a conversation with a Major in the New York militia who felt:

deep regret at your fanatical proceedings. You were, he said, turning a military academy into a theological seminary, and aiming to make young men soldiers in the Church militant, (he meant ministers,) whom the government intended to train for its army; he understood you met them for prayer every morning at daylight, and encouraged them to neglect other studies for that of religion; that the most serious apprehensions were entertained of the consequent degradation, if not ruin of the institution ([18], p. 264).

For Bishop Milnor, this was a dangerous turn of events. Milnor reiterated that McIlvaine must keep religious excess under control and suggested that converted cadets make clear how their newfound religious belief made them better soldiers: "What can even unbelievers object to the operation of inward religion on the minds of these young men, when its practical effects are seen, not in the deterioration, but in the improvements of their character as members of your very excellent and useful institution?" ([19], p. 267). The Episcopal church enjoyed its preeminent position at West Point and was uninterested in risking a scandal which could jeopardize it. "The peculiar circumstances in which you are placed require a course of conduct very different from that followed in ordinary revivals," Milnor wrote, and "if your removal should take place...the effect would be disastrous as it respects West Point, and injurious in a vast variety of ways, which will as readily suggest themselves to your mind as they have to my own" ([20], p. 270). Milnor was well aware of how word of revival at West Point under an Episcopal chaplain could create unwanted public relations problems for the Episcopal Church or the Army as a whole.

For his part, Superintendent Thayer helped the revivals continue. He was interested in the revival because it promoted Christian nationalism and helped keep away hints of larger, national divisions on the horizon. Through his support of Chaplain McIlvaine's revival, Superintendent Thayer made clear that he did not understand religious excitement to promote disunion. On the contrary, Thayer recognized that the religious life of cadets would also have to be uniform if the Academy was to produce soldiers who were ideologically committed to the defense of the Republic. Yet Chaplain McIlvaine was no willing dupe of the Superintendent. He understood the importance of cementing campus unity and obedience to the federal government, and he recognized that his evangelicalism complemented these pursuits.

The taxpayer-funded educational system at West Point negotiated disestablishment by collapsing distinctions between the church and state. West Point accomplished this by quietly maintaining, and even strengthening, its own church and carefully molding this new, quasi-established order to reflect West Point values and support its military mission. West Point's Episcopal Church became an ad hoc establishment of religious nationalism. It was also an increasingly vocal mouthpiece for religious arguments, echoing most of the Army's officer corps that it served. West Point's Episcopal church preached a religion of union, of *Federal* Union, that prized conformity and obedience to the will of Washington, D.C. while effectively diminishing the authority of individual state governments. The pulpit at West Point's Episcopal Chapel rough drafted many of the theological arguments which would echo throughout the pulpits north of the Mason-Dixon during the Civil War. The starting point for this was the religious revival that McIlvaine helped to spark in 1826. Chaplain McIlvaine wanted souls; Superintendent Thayer wanted obedience to the federal government. Both had a vested interest in making this instance of pseudo-establishment succeed. West Point is one example of how US military leaders sought to harness the political support of religious groups and transform it into a supporting plank of national security policy.

The faculty at West Point were expected to model proper citizenship, and thus proper religious observance, for the cadets. When several faculty members protested that mandatory chapel attendance breached their constitutional rights, for example, Superintendent Thayer quietly forwarded their protest to his friend, Secretary of War John C. Calhoun. Calhoun replied that "[the Secretary] was farthest from any desire to interfere in the least with their conscientious scruples, and would, therefore, send them where attendance upon Divine service would not be deemed necessary," and reassigned the objecting faculty members to frontier forts, the same locations that the lowest ranking members of each West Point graduating class fought to avoid ([12], p. 152). The message was received and there were no further constitutional objections raised. Informally establishing the Episcopal Church on post had consequences for the Army for decades. Faculty correspondence makes clear that within two decades of Chaplain McIlvaine's struggles to install Episcopal religious services at the Academy, there was an outcry among military officers because the Chaplain provided by Congress for the school was *not* an Episcopalian. Furthermore, school records show that by mid-century, between 80% to 90% of West Point faculty members and their families were registered Episcopalians [21].

Thayer also used McIlvaine to build a space on campus which would transform potentially destabilizing ideas—such as religious emotionalism—into aids for cementing unity and obedience. Thayer may not have anticipated the revival, but he did manage to use it for his own ends. The newly religious environment of West Point was designed to subvert outbursts of emotionalism by channeling the efforts of cadets to buck the system into the very process which sought to mold them into radical equals. Reckless emotionalism suggested that individualism could corrode the culture of West Point if it was not carefully controlled. This was due, at least in part, to the emotionally disciplined culture at West Point. The Academy was known almost exclusively as a school for engineering. As a bastion of Enlightenment thinking, West Point prized scientific thought; emotion was untrustworthy, a poor guide for officers who were taught to be dispassionate in all considerations. This may be in part why, in his own memorialization of the revival, McIlvaine goes to great lengths to portray the revival as powerful yet "solemn" and reasonable ([14], p. 29).

Furthermore, West Point was made up of men who were previously ambivalent about attendance at religious service. Christine Leigh Heyrman's *Southern Cross* (1997) suggests that a Southern culture of manly honor conflicted with religious participation in the first few decades of the 19th century. Heyrman suggests that this was overcome in part because religious leaders began equating religious struggle with military conflict ([22], p. 244). Southern gentleman saw that religion could aid in the burgeoning sectional crisis by "spiritualizing [all] assertions of southern manliness, militancy, and masterly prerogative" ([22], p. 249). Particularly for the first two converts, Polk (of North Carolina) and William B. Magruder (of Virginia), Heyrman's hypothesis helps explain the marriage of the revival with martial imagery and military concerns.

Emotion played a peculiar role in the religious changes at the Point. Judging by the surviving accounts, the most enduring image of the Revival of 1826 is the scene of Polk kneeling at the front of the chapel and responding with a forceful "amen" in response to McIlvaine's call. "Do you remember the scene of the baptism of Cadet Polk in the chapel," McIlvaine wrote to Thayer later in life, "...and how, in response to some charge to be faithful, he broke out with a deep 'Amen', as if it came from *de profundis?*" ([14], p. 209). This was the dramatic crescendo—such as it was—of the revival: Polk quietly kneeling in front of the chapel. McIlvaine would likely have disagreed that this was a revival "of the head and not the heart," yet overt emotionalism was warily kept in check by McIlvaine. As the awakening spread from "room to room" and "heart to heart", McIlvaine wrote that, "Had I gone on with a sermon which I was preaching to them, I verily believe I should not have been able to moderate or control their feelings. I had to stop, I did stop" ([14], p. 177). Similarly, McIlvaine was clear that cadets were involved in the revival as the result of a rational choice on their part. When writing about the baptism of Polk, McIlvaine explained that, "[Polk's] baptism now was not hurried; due time was given him to try and examine himself, and know it was no mere sudden impulse of excitement that had taken possession of him" [16]. For McIlvaine, it was important that the cadets under his command be understood as acting for themselves and not under the chaplain's emotional influence.

Yet the tale of a quiet, contemplative revival was not the story that leaked out of West Point in 1826. Bishop Milnor, for one, apparently had heard conflicting tales about "Polk's 'Amen'" and found himself troubled. Milnor was unsure if Polk's exclamation should be read as a hysterical scream or a quiet word, and asked McIlvaine for clarification. After exchanging a flurry of letters with McIlvaine, the Bishop appears to have been calmed. "I thank you for the explanation of that ominous 'amen' and hope that every Christian cadet, whatever prudence may direct in regard to the utterance of the *lips*, will always be ready, with the feelings of his *inmost soul*, to make this response to such a desire as that which you expressed at the conclusion of your sermon" [19].

The Academy's effort to manage religious emotionalism paid dividends almost immediately. Chaplain McIlvaine reported that, before his conversion, Cadet Polk—the revival's first convert—had been far from a model cadet. Polk was more likely to be found drinking, smoking, or gambling (or, better yet, doing all three simultaneously) than studying. The chaplain was perhaps putting it diplomatically when he said that Cadet Polk was, "not unwilling to join in certain not perfectly temperate frolics with his companions" [16]. After Polk's conversion, the change in his behavior was abrupt and, from the perspective of both Superintendent and Chaplain, much for the better. Superintendent Thayer made his pleasure known by rewarding those who converted with leadership positions within the Corps of Cadets. Chaplain McIlvaine later recalled asking Thayer why the converts had been chosen for the task at hand.

> 'The truth is,' answered [Thayer], 'we had to take them...I thought these young men could be relied on to do their duty at all hazards.' [Thayer] was right. They did it. They were memorialized and threatened, and the alternative was put to them either to resign or allow the traditional right practice to go on. They quietly answered that neither would be right, and after a while they had no difficulty [16].

In other words, the revival continued to receive Thayer's support because it served Thayer's ends. A renewed devotion to God enabled a renewed devotion to Nation.

The Academy's religious practices during the period of disestablishment is one instance of the tension between the categories "religion" and "secular" in the early Republic. The example of West Point suggests that such easy divisions used to identify and assess American religious impulses—*this* religious, *this* not—is complicated by attention to how historical actors understood the role of religion in society. In West Point's informal establishment, the righteousness of the American military and the justness of American foreign policy were rendered self-evident. This is not to suggest that the process of disestablishment simply swapped long-held established religion for a kind of militarized religious nationalism wholesale. The reality was far more gradual and ambiguous as government-backed Christian nationalism became an increasingly important part of the national security strategies taught at West Point.

4. Assessing the Revival

One way to assess the revival of 1826, and the legacy of Christian nationalism it helped install at West Point, is to consider how well it focused cadet loyalty away from individual states and toward the federal government. Given the politics of the antebellum United States, the Academy was concerned about loyalty to individual states trumping loyalty to the Union. Yet the Academy was reasonably assured that even if cadets first considered themselves a "Virginian" or "Texan", they each also had an American identity. As John Barnard, a graduate of the class of 1833, described West Point, "The first duty [the U.S.M.A.] requires is obedience. [The U.S.M.A.] is the teacher of the purest patriotism, of the most fervent love of country" ([7], p. 22).

Yet religion presented a more complex problem. Unlike statehood, religious affiliation was a more difficult "loyalty" to track and one that was difficult for the Academy to reliably correlate with political affiliation. West Point was presented with the vexing problem of how to respond to an "invisible" loyalty such as religion. Informally establishing the Episcopal Church on post helped address this problem. The establishment of a religious common ground was, for the Army, the express goal of the Episcopal involvement at West Point. It was intended to mirror the homogenized nationalism inculcated into cadets. Yet for all the Academy's careful planning, West Point's pseudo-establishment of the Episcopal Church was not free of division. Much like the Academy's attempt to enforce egalitarianism, this religious "common ground" was recognized by cadets as one particular political orthodoxy among others. Ulysses S. Grant (class of 1843), for example, wrote that it was doubly "not republican" to be marched to religious service, and an Episcopal one at that ([12], p. 151). Considering the antebellum divisions in American political and religious life, it is remarkable that West Point's efforts to cultivate unity among its cadets succeeded as well as it did. Ensuring obedience to the federal government in a time of trial was at the heart of West Point's antebellum mission, and developing a potent mixture of Christian nationalism helped the Academy fulfill that mission.

5. Conclusions: The *Practical Ethics* of Christian Nationalism

The changes wrought by McIlvaine and Thayer shaped the spiritual life of West Point for decades. The position of chaplain, and the role of religion on post, would never again be neglected as they had been before McIlvaine's arrival. Future chaplains and religious leaders on post included Martin Parks (himself a former cadet and member of the converted during the Revival of 1826) who followed McIlvaine as chaplain in the 1840s as well as Cadet O. O Howard (class of 1854), a devout Episcopalian and the officer responsible for a resurgence of religious piety at West Point in the 1850s. Howard would later be described by fellow cadet Morris Schaff as "probably known more widely among the church-going people of our country than any officer of his time" ([23], p. 70). In the mold of McIlvaine, Parks, and Howard was John W. French.

As the chaplain who served West Point during the Civil War, French was a fitting culmination to this legacy of religious leadership. Serving as Chaplain and Professor of Ethics from 1856 to 1871, French presided over the religious life of West Pointers during a particularly trying time. Following in McIlvaine's footsteps, French inherited a chapel that was quite unlike any other church in the nation. Hanging over the pulpit was "Peace and Freedom," a giant mural depicting an eagle protecting the American flag. The eagle was flanked by the Roman Goddess of Peace and the God of War. The bottom of the painting was inscribed with Proverbs 14:34: "Righteousness exalteth a nation; But sin is a reproach to any people."

Last in the pre-war line of Episcopal chaplains, French worked hard to maintain cadet loyalty to the federal government. French worked with Professor O.O. Howard to encourage a resurgence in Bible study groups and prayer sessions, in the hope that it would help defray some of the rising sectional tensions among cadets. Howard and French were successful to a degree—another revival broke out on post—but it was not enough to deter the growing tension ([17], p. 313). French corresponded regularly with Jefferson Davis, a close friend and former West Point cadet, pleading with him to do what he could to avoid conflict. It was French's "truly prophetic" soul, according to Howard, that led him to obsess over the threat of war. Howard recalled how in the winter of 1859–1860 "[French] worked day and night...in correspondence with [Davis] with ever-decreasing hope" ([24], pp. 99–100).

Chaplain French's work offers an insight into how West Point's Christian nationalist identity was maintained over time. While teaching at West Point, French developed his own textbook, *Practical Ethics*, which he assigned to his students and which remained in regular use at the Academy until 1877 ([25]; [26], p. 152). Chaplain French, much like his predecessor Chaplain McIlvaine, discovered the most effective pedagogical techniques to be the ones that engaged cadets' scientific and mathematical schooling. *Ethics* itself is filled with theological equations, breaking down solemn duties and ethical values into rational formulations and logical proofs. Cadet Schaff, who served as French's teaching assistant, explained that French "seemed to think that, in view of our perpetual use of mathematical symbols, the only way cadets could appreciate anything was by being shown that something was equal to something else. Therefore, in teaching practical ethics he would go to the blackboard and write, 'Virtue = Morality' etc." ([23], p. 106).

For French, *Practical Ethics* represented the fullest realization of what each West Point cadet should be taught. The book is broken down into several categories revolving around "duty": "Duties Above Us", "Duties Within Us", and "Duties Around Us". One of the most important themes in French's *Practical Ethics* is the role of authority. Authority is a legitimating force, enabling and justifying actions which a cadet's duty might require.

French approached the question of authority through a series of orderly flowcharts ([25], pp. 10–12). French placed both the nation *and* God as the highest point of authority: "The Virtues which are first in order are those which regard the Deity and objects, such as Government and Law, which are greater than self" ([25], p. 13). Closely linking the "Deity" and the "Government" in the same chain of command, French was able to outline a very powerful role for the Constitution: "The nation has an organic law, called the Constitution. Being the supreme law, it demands special reverence and obedience from all the members of a nation. The correspondent virtue thus required is called LOYALTY" ([25], p. 14). The ends to which French applied loyalty are illuminating. French wrote:

> The nation...exists through centuries, for the welfare of its members, through successive generations. As one of the family of nations, it exists for the welfare of the world. The good which the nation thus promotes is called the public good...The correspondent obligation resting on every member of a nation is, to love that public good more than any private good for himself or others. The virtue which observes this obligation is called PATRIOTISM, or THE LOVE OF THE COUNTRY. It requires that every member of a nation shall be ready to sacrifice his life, property, liberty and inclination, when required for the public defence and welfare ([25], p. 14).

This was the theology of West Point: a divine mandate to uphold the sovereignty of the nation.

Once the authority and legitimacy of the Constitution is established, French begins to craft one of the book's core themes: a hatred of disunion and the justification of force to prevent it. For example, cadets read that "for a nation to fulfill its great office, harmony and tranquility, amongst its great constituent parts are indispensable" ([25], p. 15). In case there was any doubt, French employed a liberal approach towards capitalization in order to argue that "The faults opposed to these are TREASON, DISLOYALTY, REBELLION, CONSPIRACY, SEDITION, DISRESPECT TO SUPERIORS, SELFISHNESS OR INDIFFERENCE TO THE PUBLIC WELFARE, REFUSAL TO ACT OR SUFFER FOR THE PUBLIC GOOD, AGITATION BY THE DEMAGOGUE" ([25], p. 15). Cadets would also have to be vigilant in guarding against these faults for the duration of their lives: French instructed his students that "Any violation of these reciprocal obligations by one party does not absolve the other party from his obligations. The duties *to* the nation from every member of it, and duties *from* it, remain. They are formed not by a temporary bargain, but by *relations* which the Creator has established" ([25], p. 16). This was totalizing enough to make any tent-pole revivalist proud. The relation between cadets and the nation, cadets learned, was "ineffaceable...except by death" ([25], p. 30).

This sentiment can be seen in the cadets who worked with *Practical Ethics*, particularly as the prospect of civil war became reality. While responses from the cadets who worked with *Practical Ethics* in their curriculum are hard to come by, one surviving letter which mentions the textbook is from cadet Tully McCrea of Ohio. On 12 December 1858, McCrea wrote to his cousin that:

> I have just returned from church where I heard a sermon from the text, "Thou shalt not kill", and I thought that it was a singular one for [Professor French] to select to preach to officers and cadets, but he twisted it around to suit all cases...[French] is no more qualified to fill the place than the man in the moon. He is a very good preacher and a very smart man and would make a very good professor in some theological college, but he is out of his sphere at the military academy. He is always introducing something into the course that is of no practical use. Last year he introduced a work of his own, "Practical Ethics" which is merely a collection of verses from the Bible...It is needless to say that the Professor is very unpopular with the cadets ([27], p. 29).

After a few more years with Chaplain French, however, Cadet McCrea's opinions underwent a transformation. A mere three years later as the war raged in 1861, McCrea wrote another letter testifying to his changing opinions:

> I have just returned from church where I heard a sermon from Professor French to the graduating class. It was very eloquent and affecting and a great many realized the truths it contained. The graduates looked very serious and it is very easy to see that they are awake to the painful circumstances which are the cause of their graduating before the proper time ([27], p. 92).

Throughout the antebellum period, the twin sins of individuality and state-loyalty threatened loyalty to the federal government as well as West Point's unique religious landscape. The Academy's culture of Christian nationalism worked to defang these threats by training cadets as radical equals, in politics as in religion.

While reminiscing about his experiences as a West Point student under Chaplain French, former Cadet Morris Schaff paused to consider what he would ask his former professor if he had the opportunity to speak with French again after the passage of decades: "If I could see the old professor now I should like to talk to him...he might make plain the mysterious relations and affinities that a man's ideals have with his surroundings. What, for instance, have the scenery, the historic associations, the ceremonials at West Point to do, not with the mere matter of its concrete education, but with those high and abstract conceptions connected with it that we call honor and duty and truth?" ([23], p. 105).

Schaff's question is an important one. From Mark Noll's "evangelical synthesis" to Harry Stout's chronicling of how Americans sacralized the Civil War, historians of American religion have investigated how changing ideas about Christianity—as well as about the United States itself—influenced American religious culture in this period [7,28]. The curious religious establishment at antebellum West Point was one important example in this longer history of the development of Christian nationalism during the 19th century.

The example of West Point's religious revival provides one specific point at which historians can examine the relationship between religion, nationalism, and early ideas about national security. With the case of West Point, Nathan Hatch's argument that the Second Great Awakening represented "the influence of popular religion in a culture shifting from classic republican values to those of a vulgar democracy and entrepreneurial individualism" becomes forcefully inverted: revivalistic religion was used to keep out "vulgar democracy" and create a space in which "classic republican values" could be nurtured and protected within the state's own classrooms and chapels ([10], p. 222).

Indeed, these very same "republican values" became weaponized at the Point, and their deadly product was subsequently brought to bear on the same individual manifestations of religious freedom which Hatch holds up for admiration. It was Robert E. Lee (class of 1829) who captured and hanged

John Brown, enraging his abolitionist sympathizers in and out of the black church. Albert Sydney Johnston (class of 1826) led the Federal Army west to punish the Mormons in the Utah War. Both Lee and Johnston were cadets under Chaplain McIlvaine, but there are examples from other periods of West Point's antebellum history too. It was James Forsyth (class of 1854) who, during the Ghost Dance Revival, oversaw the massacre of at least 150 Lakota at Wounded Knee. As these examples illustrate, West Point's sense of Christian nationalism was not uniform. It was not directed consistently at a single target, or understood by its practitioners in precisely the same way. It was, like the country of which it was a part, an idea still under construction. Instead, the religious legacy of antebellum West Point should remind us that revivalistic religion—and Christian nationalism—offered as many opportunities to enforce authority as to challenge it.

Conflicts of Interest: The author declares no conflicts of interest.

References

1. Alexander William Doniphan. *Address by A. W. Doniphan, of Missouri, to the West Point Graduating Class of 1848*. New York: W. L. Burroughs, Printer, 1848.
2. Jeffrey L. Pasley. *"The Tyranny of Printers": Newspaper Politics in the Early American Republic*. Charlottesville: University of Virginia Press, 2001.
3. Amanda Porterfield. *Conceived in Doubt: Religion and Politics in the New American Nation*. Chicago: University of Chicago Press, 2012.
4. John Fea. *Was America Founded as a Christian Nation? A Historical Introduction*. Louisville: Westminster John Knox Press, 2011.
5. John C. Waugh. *The Class of 1846: From West Point to Appomattox: Stonewall Jackson, George McClellan, and Their Brothers*. New York: Warner, 1994.
6. Glenn Robins. *The Bishop of the Old South: The Ministry and Civil War Legacy of Leonidas Polk*. Macon: Mercer UP, 2006.
7. Harry S. Stout. *Upon the Altar of the Nation: A Moral History of the American Civil War*. New York: Viking, 2006.
8. "West Point's Centennial." *New York Times*, 11 May 1902.
9. James S. Robbins. *Last in Their Class: Custer, Pickett, and the Goats of West Point*. New York: Encounter, 2006.
10. Nathan O. Hatch. *The Democratization of American Christianity*. New Haven: Yale University Press, 1989.
11. Leonidas Polk. *Leonidas Polk: Bishop and General*. Edited by William M. Polk. New York: Green and Longmans, 1915, vol. 1.
12. Stephen E. Ambrose. *Duty, Honor, Country: A History of West Point*. Baltimore: Johns Hopkins, 1966.
13. Theodore J. Crackel. *West Point: A Bicentennial History*. Lawrence: University of Kansas, 2002.
14. Charles P. McIlvaine. *Memorials of the Right Reverend Charles Pettit McIlvaine*. New York: Thomas Whittaker, 1882.
15. James W. Kershner. "Sylvanus Thayer: A Biography." Ph.D. Dissertation, West Virginia University, Morgantown, WV, USA, 1977.
16. Charles P. McIlvaine. "Leonidas Polk, the Bishop-General Who Died for the South. Interesting Reminiscence of Life at West Point of the Gallant Churchman and Soldier." *Richmond Times*, 2 August 1890.
17. George S. Pappas. *To the Point: The United States Military Academy, 1802–1902*. Westport: Praeger, 1993.
18. "Letter of 8 June 1826." quoted in James Milnor; In *A Memoir of the Life of James Milnor, D.D.: Late Rector of St. George's Church, New York*. Edited by John S. Stone. New York: American Tract Society, 1848.
19. "Letter of 17 June 1826." quoted in James Milnor; In *A Memoir of the Life of James Milnor, D.D.: Late Rector of St. George's Church, New York*. Edited by John S. Stone. New York: American Tract Society, 1848.
20. "Letter of 28 June 1826." quoted in James Milnor; In *A Memoir of the Life of James Milnor, D.D.: Late Rector of St. George's Church, New York*. Edited by John S. Stone. New York: American Tract Society, 1848.
21. Suzanne Geissler. "Professor Dennis Mahan Speaks out on West Point Chapel Issues." *The Journal of Military History* 69 (2005): 505–19. [CrossRef]
22. Christine L. Heyrman. *Southern Cross: The Beginnings of the Bible Belt*. New York: Knopf, 1997.
23. Morris Schaff. *The Spirit of Old West Point: 1856–1862*. Boston: Houghton Mifflin, 1909.
24. Oliver O. Howard. *Autobiography of Oliver Otis Howard, Major General, United States Army*. New York: Baker & Taylor, 1907.

25. John W. French. *Practical Ethics*. New York: D. Van Nostrand, 1860.
26. Sidney Forman. *West Point: A History of the United States Military Academy*. New York: Columbia UP, 1950.
27. Tully McCrea. *Dear Belle: Letters from a Cadet & Officer to His Sweetheart, 1858–1865*. Edited by Catherine S. Crary. Middletown: Wesleyan UP, 1965.
28. Mark Noll. *America's God: From Jonathan Edwards to Abraham Lincoln*. Oxford: Oxford University Press, 2005.

religions

MDPI

Article

"Our Country Is Destined to be the Great Nation of Futurity": John L. O'Sullivan's Manifest Destiny and Christian Nationalism, 1837–1846

John D. Wilsey

Southwestern Baptist Theological Seminary, 2001 W. Seminary Drive, Fort Worth, TX 76115, USA; jwilsey@swbts.edu

Academic Editor: Mark Edwards
Received: 12 December 2016; Accepted: 14 April 2017; Published: 17 April 2017

Abstract: As founding editor of the *United States Magazine and Democratic Review*, John L. O'Sullivan (1813–1895) preached a particular form of Christian nationalism that centered on expansionist fever occurring during the 1830s and 1840s. O'Sullivan's Christian nationalism was known as "Manifest Destiny". He famously coined the term in 1845 while defending the right of the United States to annex the Republic of Texas. The central argument of this essay is that Manifest Destiny, as O'Sullivan articulated it in the pages of the *Democratic Review*, follows the contours of the innovative and heterodox political religion developed by Elie Kedourie and expounded upon by Anthony D. Smith. O'Sullivan's Manifest Destiny was a conglomerated nationalistic paradigm consisting of elements from Protestant theology, Lyman Beecher's vision for civilizing the West, and German idealism via George Bancroft's use of historicism in his *History of the United States of America, from the Discovery of the American Continent*. As a form of Christian nationalism located in the context of antebellum America, Manifest Destiny is helpful to historians as they trace both continuity and change over time in how Americans have self-identified in religious terms since their origin as a collection of colonial, and later independent, polities.

Keywords: Manifest Destiny; nationalism; national identity; antebellum America

1. Introduction

As founding editor of the *United States Magazine and Democratic Review*, John L. O'Sullivan (1813–1895) preached a particular form of Christian nationalism that centered on expansionist fever occurring during the 1830s and 1840s. O'Sullivan's Christian nationalism was known as "Manifest Destiny". He famously coined the term in 1845 while defending the right of the United States to annex the Republic of Texas. The central argument of this essay is that Manifest Destiny, as O'Sullivan articulated it in the pages of the *Democratic Review*, follows the contours of the innovative and heterodox political religion developed by Elie Kedourie and expounded upon by Anthony D. Smith [1,2]. O'Sullivan's Manifest Destiny was a conglomerated nationalistic paradigm consisting of elements from Protestant theology, Lyman Beecher's vision for civilizing the West, and German idealism via George Bancroft's use of historicism in his *History of the United States of America, from the Discovery of the American Continent*. As a form of Christian nationalism located in the context of antebellum America, Manifest Destiny is helpful to historians as they trace both continuity and change over time in how Americans have self-identified in religious terms since their origin as a collection of colonial, and later independent, polities.

2. The *Democratic Review,* John L. O'Sullivan, and Manifest Destiny

O'Sullivan founded the *Democratic Review* with his brother in law, Samuel Daly Langtree, in 1837. He was the proprietor, editor, and regular contributor of the journal until 1846, when he sold it to Henry Wikoff for between five and six thousand dollars ([3], p. 84). Landon Fuller wrote that O'Sullivan had two major goals for the magazine from the outset. First, the *Democratic Review* was to be an outlet advancing "the fundamental principles of American democracy" ([3], p. 2). In doing so, O'Sullivan hoped to cast American democracy as the most ideal society on earth. Further, O'Sullivan consistently argued, from the beginning of his tenure as editor until the end, that America was destined to go from strength to strength in future years, and by its pure example, fulfill its God-given mission to overspread the entire North American continent. In an 1838 analysis of Alexis de Tocqueville's recently published first volume of *Democracy in America*, O'Sullivan predicted, "We see no reason, other than the merely material inconvenience of assembling representatives from so great a distance, why the Union may not cross the Rocky Mountains with as much facility as it has done the Alleghanies [*sic*], and spread itself from the Arctic Sea to the Gulf of Mexico with as much safety as it did of old from Maine to Georgia" ([4], p. 354). Just before he sold the *Democratic Review* in 1846, he wrote, "Is there one who does not hope for—nay, does not foresee—...that the future is to extend to all the people of the American continent, if true to their trust, institutions based upon the light of reason and truth, upon the benefits and inherent and equal rights of all men, and upon that fraternal bond of union which alone can give promise of universal peace?" ([5], p. 64).

Second, Fuller wrote that the *Democratic Review* was "to promote the development of American literature on a national and democratic basis" ([3], p. 2). O'Sullivan believed that, despite America's greatness as a pure experiment in democracy, the nation did not have a literary tradition or identity to match its political exceptionalism. A great nation ought to have an equally great body of literature. He wrote in 1842, "The spirit of literature and the spirit of Democracy are one" ([6], p. 196). Americans ought to have literature and arts that emerge out of the shadow of Europe to surpass their former masters. In 1839, O'Sullivan lamented, "And our literature!—Oh, when will it breathe the spirit of our republican institutions? When will it be imbued with the God-like aspiration of intellectual freedom—the elevating principle of equality? When will it assert *its* national independence, and speak the soul—the heart of the American people? Why cannot our literati comprehend the matchless sublimity of our position amonst the nations of the world—our high destiny—and cease bending the knee to foreign idolatry, false tastes, false doctrines, false principles?" ([7], p. 428).

O'Sullivan's stress on both politics and literature was one of the unique features of the *Democratic Review*. It was broader in scope than most of its contemporary outlets. Fuller compared the *Democratic Review* to the *American Quarterly Review* (which he described as "notoriously dull" ([3], p. 10)), the *Knickerbocker Magazine*, and the *Southern Literary Messenger*. He said that while these outlets were interested in literary developments, they were not so interested in politics. Others offered political commentary, but little in the way of literary content. Fuller cited a letter from George Bancroft to Jared Sparks to describe what, in his view, the *Democratic Review* accomplished under the editorship of O'Sullivan: "A vein of public feeling, of democratic independence, of popular liberty, ought to be infused into our literature. Let Mammon rule in the marts; but not on the holy mountain of letters. The rich ought not to be flattered; let truth, let humanity speak through the public journals and through American literature" [8]. And while the *Democratic Review* was an advocate of Democratic party principles, the literary figures who contributed were mostly non-partisan. Auspicious writers such as Nathaniel Hawthorne, Edgar Allan Poe, Ralph Waldo Emerson, Henry David Thoreau, Walter Whitman (as he was then called), James Kirke Paulding, William Gilmore Sims, Alexander H. Everett, Parke Godwin, Evert A. Duyckinck, and Henry T. Tuckerman were among the frequent men of letters who contributed to the poetry, fiction, and essay sections of the magazine. Political figures (and Democratic partisans) who contributed were equally famous: Benjamin F. Butler, Lewis Cass, Caleb Cushing, Samuel J. Tilden, Henry Gilpin, and Orestes A. Brownson joined their voices with O'Sullivan's [3].

Other journals that advanced Manifest Destiny were the *New York Herald* under the editorship of James Gordon Bennett and the New York *Sun*, edited by Moses Y. Beach. New York City was the source of most of the journals advocating for Manifest Destiny, and these two in particular boasted the largest circulation of the New York journals. Bancroft edited the *Bay State Democrat* in Boston, and he and O'Sullivan were in frequent correspondence during this period ([9], p. 35). The *Democratic Review* did not have the largest circulation of the Democratic outlets, but it had a national audience and was credible enough to attract some of the most influential figures as contributors under O'Sullivan's editorship. Anders Stephanson wrote that under O'Sullivan, the *Democratic Review* "became such a thorn in the side of conservatives that the *American Whig Review* was revamped in 1845 into a political counterpart" ([10], p. 39).

Unfortunately, comparatively little is known about O'Sullivan. Edward L. Widmer marveled that "[H]e was unusually intimate with eminent writers and politicians, yet there exists almost no likenesses of him, nor any substantial manuscript collections" ([11], p. 29). His father, John O'Sullivan, who drowned after attempting to rescue sailors after their ship ran aground off the coast of South America, was a source of romantic inspiration to him. He matriculated into Columbia College at the age of fourteen and finished his freshman year at the top of his class. He was allowed to skip his sophomore year, and the trustees of the college even permitted him to complete his studies without attending classes. Decades later, the president of the college mused of O'Sullivan, "it presents an example of native ability combined with resolute industry, and crowned with distinguished success, to which I do not know a parallel" ([12], pp. 4–5). He graduated with an A.B. degree in 1831 at the age of eighteen and spent two more years at Columbia serving as a tutor and instructor. In 1835, he was admitted to the New York bar.

After his education was complete, O'Sullivan's mother moved the family down to Washington, D.C. where she hoped to settle claims against the US government. Just prior to his death in 1825, the elder John O'Sullivan had purchased a merchant ship, the *Dick*, which was subsequently seized as a pirate ship by the American government in Buenos Aires. With the help of Martin Van Buren and Democratic Congressman Churchill C. Cambreleng of New York City, Mrs. O'Sullivan was awarded $20,210 from the US Treasury as compensation for the unfounded seizure of the *Dick*. This influx of money served as the basis for the founding of the *Democratic Review*. O'Sullivan sold the *Democratic Review* in 1846, and actively filibustered for Cuba against Spain for ultimate annexation to the United States. He was tried for violating the Neutrality Act and acquitted in 1852. He became minister to Portugal from 1853 to 1857 during the Pierce administration, and advocated on behalf of secession and state rights leading up to the Civil War. During the war, O'Sullivan took to England with his reputation tarnished, not returning to the United States until the late 1870s. By this time, he had been nearly forgotten in the United States and he died in 1895 impoverished and obscure. Adam Gomez wrote, "[h]aving once been the voice of the radical Democrats, O'Sullivan at his death was less than an embarrassment; he was barely a memory" ([13], p. 255).

O'Sullivan is probably most famous for having coined the term "Manifest Destiny" in 1845. Widmer observed, "[a]lmost every history of the Jacksonian period contains a one-sentence summation of O'Sullivan as the author of the phrase" but O'Sullivan himself seems to have been oblivious to the significance of this fact. Widmer wrote, "he never claimed his territorial rights to it, despite his self-aggrandizing personality" ([11], p. 31). The context for the origin of the term was the issue of Texas annexation. In April 1844, O'Sullivan wrote "[t]hat Texas is to be, sooner or later, included in the Union, we have long—nay, ever since the battle of San Jacinto [21 April 1836]—regarded as an event already indelibly inscribed in the book of future fate and necessity" ([14], p. 423). Just over a year later in July 1845, O'Sullivan advocated in favor of annexation and criticized the intrigues of European powers, namely Great Britain and France, as they sought to undermine the relationship between Texas and the United States. He accused Europe of "thwarting our policy and hampering our power, limiting our greatness and checking the fulfillment of our manifest destiny to overspread the continent allotted by Providence for the free development of our yearly multiplying millions" ([15], p. 5). Texan annexation was completed by the end of 1845, and was one of the background causes for the Mexican American War, which broke out in the spring of 1846.

Interestingly enough, while O'Sullivan clearly thought the United States had a rightful claim to Texas, he was strongly opposed to any conquest of Texas or any other lands, for that matter. When advocating for annexation in 1844, O'Sullivan insisted, "[n]or ought the Annexation be made without the consent of Mexico, or her recognition of the independence of her successfully revolted province. We must avoid even the appearance of evil" ([14], p. 430). O'Sullivan maintained his anti-war of conquest stance consistently because since it was America's God-given destiny to possess North America in time, and since it would betray the principles of American democracy, it was futile and hypocritical for the United States to take by force any territories [16]. Still, expansionism in the 1840s would not wait.

While expansionism and Manifest Destiny were powerful nationalistic expressions during this period, these were not without their opposing positions. Expansionism was mainly found in the Democratic party, and especially among Democrats in the states of the Old Northwest. These wanted to see the United States annex Texas, northern Mexico, and the Oregon Country up to 54° 40'. Their opponents in the Whig party, centered primarily in the Northeast, did not want the United States to acquire any new territories. Whigs believed that America had a divine mission just as Democrats like O'Sullivan did, but according to Daniel Walker Howe, "[t]hey saw America's moral mission as one of democratic example rather than one of conquest" ([17], p. 706). President James K. Polk settled on the 49th parallel as the northernmost American claim to Oregon, but was determined to have northern Mexico—placing him in the position of a centrist ([18], p. 357).

There were two powerful dynamics behind Manifest Destiny, one practical and one religious. Practically speaking, many believed that the annexation of territories south and west would alleviate the slavery problem. David M. Potter observed that "expansionism meant expansionism southward, and expansion southward meant the extension of slavery" ([19], p. 197). By the 1850s, expansion of slavery into the territories was a sectional issue, but prior to the Mexican American War this was not yet the case. O'Sullivan agreed with Mississippi Senator Robert J. Walker, who according to Sean Wilentz, "argued that annexation would lead to a dispersal of the slave population through the West and into Latin America, hasten slavery's demise, and leave behind an all-white United States—a rehashing of the old Jeffersonian 'diffusion' idea" ([20], p. 63). O'Sullivan sided with Free Soil, but his views on slavery were not strongly abolitionist. Tocqueville believed that African Americans would eventually emigrate to Latin America and the islands of the Caribbean, a position which O'Sulllivan found to be "extremely probable." Furthermore, O'Sullivan did not think that African Americans were the moral or intellectual equals of whites. He wrote, "[t]he attempt to raise [African Americans] to a political equality with the white race, has not succeeded in practice in the States where it has been carried into effect in theory" ([4], p. 352).

Related to this position was the notion that Anglo Americans were the only people able to civilize the land and make it productive. In his 1845 article "Annexation", O'Sullivan stated that Mexicans lacked the ability to govern California. The result was that Mexico had no rightful claim to the territory, and it was thus *de facto* independent and open for the taking by the United States. "Imbecile and distracted, Mexico never can exert any real governmental authority over such a country" ([15], p. 9). Later in 1845, when considering how to treat the people of Mexico in the event that the United States annexed that country, he stated what he really thought of the Mexican people's ability to live and possess a stake in a republic. "Beyond a question the entire Mexican vote would be substantially below our national average both in purity and intelligence. The Mexican people are unaccustomed to the duties of self-government, and for years to come must travel up through numberless processes of political emancipation before they can dispense with restraints which the Saxon family threw off more than three hundred years ago" ([21], p. 245).

O'Sullivan's view was not uncommon. It is related to a commonly held racist position on the dominion mandate in the nineteenth century. The dominion mandate was the commandment of God given to humans shortly after Creation to "be fruitful and multiply and fill the earth and subdue it and have dominion over the fish of the sea and over the birds of the heavens and over every living thing that moves on the earth" (Gen 1:28, ESV). The racist view of the dominion mandate lurked behind Andrew Jackson's 1830 justification for the removal of Native American from their homes in the South. In his Second Annual Message to Congress of December 6, 1830, Jackson said that removal would "place a dense and civilized population in large tracts of country now occupied by a few savage hunters...It will...cause them gradually, under the protection of the Government and through the influence of good counsels, to cast off their savage habits and become an interesting, civilized, and Christian community" ([22], III.1083). Sam Haselby wrote that Jackson's message represented "the first explicitly racist statement on the political community from a sitting US president, and it was also the first time a US president turned to a theological justification for an imperial act" ([23], p. 312).

Mexicans, according to many Americans of the 1840s, were unable or unwilling to fulfill the dominion mandate. Thus, by not fulfilling the dominion mandate, a nation forfeits its title to any tract of land. For example, in arguing for conquest of northern Mexico, Congressman Timothy Pillsbury of Texas said, "[a] country kept vacant by the policy of a nation which claims the right of ownership over it is common property, and reverts to the situation in which all land was before it became property, and is open to be occupied, subdued, and cultivated by man—by those who will do so—as the Creator designed it should be" ([24], p. 194). Ex-president and Massachusetts Congressman John Quincy Adams expressed similar views on the floor of Congress, arguing for the annexation of all of Oregon Country. Richard Kluger wrote that Adams, a committed abolitionist, wanted all of Oregon "to offset the Texas annexation". Adams said, "We claim that country...to make the wilderness bloom as the rose, to establish laws, to increase, multiply, and subdue the earth, which we are commanded to do by the first behest of God Almighty". He went on to excoriate the British, who were doing nothing in his view to develop the land, but simply sought "to keep it open for navigation, for hunters to hunt the wild beasts...for the buffaloes, braves, and savages of the desert" ([25], pp. 428–29).

In addition to these factors, technological advancements like the steam engine and the telegraph had the effect of practically shortening vast distances between spaces in the republic and creating demand for access to new lands. Also, the Panic of 1837, America's worst economic crisis to that date, contributed further to this demand. Thus, Frederick Merk called Manifest Destiny a "reform" of the 1840s advanced by emerging politicians and thinkers known as "Young America." Some figures associated with Young America were O'Sullivan, Stephen O. Douglas, William Allen, Andrew Kennedy, Thomas Ritchie, and James K. Polk who became president in 1845. Polk, at 49, was the youngest person to date to be elected president. Merk wrote, "[y]outh was responsible, doubtless, for such characteristics of Manifest Destiny as its grandeur and scope, and for the moral exaltation with which it was set forth" ([9], pp. 54–55). But Manifest Destiny ultimately paved the way for the Civil War by exacerbating the slavery issue, transforming it into the most divisive economic, social, political, and moral problem of the 1850s. James M. McPherson said "[t]he triumph of Manifest Destiny may have reminded some Americans of Ralph Waldo Emerson's prophecy that 'the United States will conquer Mexico, but it will be as the man swallows the arsenic, which brings him down in turn. Mexico will poison us.' He was right. The poison was slavery" ([26], p. 50).

3. Manifest Destiny and Christian Nationalism

How do we assess Manifest Destiny as Christian nationalism? Anthony D. Smith's engagement with Elie Kedourie's landmark work on nationalism is particularly helpful as we consider the meaning of nationalism as an idea and the relationship that Christianity might have with nationalism. Smith divided Kedourie's modernist understanding of nationalism into three positions: (1) "secular replacement" whereby traditional religion is replaced by a "secular, revolutionary nationalism" (as in revolutionary France or Soviet Russia), (2) "neo-traditional", in which religion serves as an "ally" of nationalism (as in, say, the nineteenth century Church of England), and (3) "a secular version of millennial 'political religion'" which "depicts nationalism as a new *ersatz* and heterodox religion opposed to conventional, traditional religions, yet inheriting many of their features" ([2], p. 13). It is this third position which seems to comport best with Manifest Destiny as we assess it as a form of Christian nationalism. His aim was not to advance or advocate for a Protestant theology *per se*, but to strive for, in Smith's words, "the attainment and maintenance of autonomy, unity, and identity on behalf of a population some of whose members deem it to constitute an actual or potential 'nation'" ([2], p. 24). In so doing, O'Sullivan appropriated certain Protestant theological themes in order to advocate for America's Manifest Destiny, which we will discuss later.

Kedourie's third sense of nationalism illustrates how nationalists appropriate religions to advance their purposes, thereby putting forth a political religion with the nation at its center. A religion's themes and figures are put to use in the service of a particular nation in order to advance the nation's interests. So, Kedourie wrote, "[m]en who thought they were acting in order to accomplish the will of God...are suddenly seen to have been really acting in order that the genius of a particular nationality should be manifested and fostered" ([1], p. 69). He provided the historical examples of Abraham, Moses, Muhammad, and Luther as figures prominent in Judaism, Islam, and Christianity which are reinvented in the present by nationalists to serve the political purpose of galvanizing the concept of the Jewish, Arab, or German nation respectively. Thus, Kedourie wrote, "[n]ationalists make use of the past in order to subvert the present" ([1], p. 70). In other words, nationalists distort the histories of particular religions in order to develop a political religion that casts a nation in metaphysical terms in the present. As they do this, the nationalist ideology and the religion it appropriates are often at odds with one another. Commenting on Kedourie's paradigm of nationalism as political religion, Smith wrote "while modern nationalisms often incorporate motifs from earlier, traditional religions, they also reject many of their ideas and practices, particularly those that hold out the prospect of seeking salvation from a cosmic, other-worldly source" ([2], p. 17).

This is exactly what we see in how O'Sullivan framed Manifest Destiny—his American Christian nationalism. Throughout his writings in the *Democratic Review*, he took the figure of Christ and Christ's messages and marshaled them in the service of American ideals. Christ was no longer the suffering servant, despised and rejected of men, and giving his life as a ransom for many, as the Tanak book of Isaiah and the gospel of Mark portrayed him. He was not the savior of the world through his death, burial, and resurrection as the four gospels described him. O'Sullivan replaced Christ with democracy as the savior of the human race. For example, in 1839, he wrote that "democratic liberty" had its source in the American founding documents, and that it was the "source of true civilization". Neither Christ nor the gospel, but democratic liberty ushered in a world order "destined to cease only when every man in the world should be finally and triumphantly redeemed" ([27], p. 213). O'Sullivan also used Christ as the embodiment of the expressions of equality and natural rights in the Declaration of Independence. He further saw Christ as exemplar of human progress, the champion of liberty, and the enemy of tyranny. In 1840, he wrote, "Christianity struck its first blow at the vitals of unjust power. The annunciations of its lofty Teacher embodied truths after which the nations in their dim twilight had long struggled in vain" ([28], p. 228).

O'Sullivan hosted editorialists who also transformed the biblical Christ into a political savior. An editorialist known as simply "D.D.F." commented on an address given by Mark Hopkins, the president of Williams College, on the fiftieth anniversary (1844) of the school's founding. Hopkins' address was entitled, "The Law and Progress of the Race." In that address, Hopkins recast Christianity from a theological system centered on the atonement of Christ to a political theology advancing the upward progression of the human race in history via the inherent freedom of the individual. Furthermore, the religion founded by Christ was the only system that, in Hopkins' words, "could have amalgamated materials so discordant as the northern barbarian and the effeminate Roman" and without Christianity, there could be no way that "Europe could have been freed from the curse of domestic slavery and of feudal institutions". The editorialist D.D.F. took Hopkins to mean that American civilization was the perfection of a Christian society—not in terms of literature, heroism, the arts, or "the production of noble men", necessarily. But more importantly for D.D.F., American civilization champions the

"rights of man as man". Finally he wrote, "In our days man is invested with a certain sanctity....
He has rights too sacred for man to touch, born with him, and inalienable." And what is the source
of America, this pinnacle of civilization? Simply put, Christianity. The editorialist took the Christian
religion and recast its essence from the gospel of Christ and transformed it into an ideology setting
America above other nations, including Germany and England, upon highest pedestal of human
society. D.D.F. asked in conclusion to his essay, "who shall presume to set limits to [Christianity's]
work of regeneration?" ([29], p. 202). D.D.F. even changed the term "regeneration" from its New
Testament meaning in Tit. 3.5 to a political meaning with America as the medium through which
Christianity's liberal regeneration of humanity would take place in future time. Conrad Cherry
observed this departure from Protestant theology—"According to the exponents of Manifest Destiny,
God's New Israel was elected for clear or *manifest* reasons—because of its superior form of government,
its geographical location, and its beneficence" ([30], p. 117).

Clearly then, Manifest Destiny entailed more for America than simply existing as "a Christian
nation". It was an exceptional Christian nation, because it was the divine choice of God for the
political salvation of the world. Mark Noll's analysis of Christian nationalism is particularly helpful
here. He distinguished between two types of Christian nationalism: "strong" and "weak Christian
America" ([31], pp. 7–13). Advocates of strong Christian America posit the nation as "an extension
of the history of salvation" and are convinced that "God must have providentially intervened in that
conflict on the side of 'his people,' the Americans". America is an "anointed land, set apart by a divine
plan for an extraordinary existence as a nation and an extraordinary mission to the world" ([31], pp. 7–8).
By contrast, advocates of a weak Christian America would hesitate from providential certainty and
assess the American experience by thinking historically and along the pattern of traditional orthodoxy
in order to critically understand America's past. Noll wrote of weak Christian America, "[b]y reasoning
from theological principle and historical actuality—rather than from intuitions about God's secret
providence—it should be possible to say that some aspects of a nation's history comport better than
generally Christian principles than do other aspects of that history" ([31], p. 10). O'Sullivan posited a
"strong Christian America" in the pages of the *Democratic Review*.

So, we have located Manifest Destiny on Kedourie's map of nationalism as, what Smith described,
"a secular version of millennial 'political religion'" ([2], p. 13). We have also identified Manifest Destiny
as consistent with Noll's model of "strong Christian America." As such, O'Sullivan incorporated
elements from disparate sources to construct Manifest Destiny, his particular brand of Christian
nationalism, which served as a political religion of the antebellum period in American history.
These sources include Protestant theology, a vision of westward expansion advocated by Lyman
Beecher, and George Bancroft's writing of history, which was informed by German historicism.

First, what Protestant theological themes can be found in Manifest Destiny? As we begin to think
about this question, it is helpful to broadly consider the Christian America thesis, that is, the notion
that America is, and always has been, a Christian nation. As John Fea has noted, most generations
of Americans have believed they were living in a Christian nation. And more particularly, America
was probably more of a Christian nation during the antebellum period than at any other time in its
history. Fea wrote, "[i]f the United States was ever a 'Christian nation', it was so during the period
between the ratification of the Constitution (1789) and the start of the Civil War (1861)" ([32], p. 4).
An obvious example of the Protestant religiosity of the American people is in the evolution of Federalist
engagement with American religion, politics, and society in the early republican period. Jonathan Den
Hartog traced this evolution, identifying three successive stages occurring among Federalists between
the Revolution and the 1820s in their attitudes concerning how best to maintain the virtue of the
United States as a Protestant Christian nation. Den Hartog's categories are (1) "a Republican attitude"
that prevailed from the Revolution through the end of Washington's administration; (2) "a Combative
perspective" from the 1790s to the War of 1812; and (3) "a Voluntarist strategy" which occurred after
1815 and the subsequent fracturing of the Federalist Party. Den Hartog noted that the Federalists
sought to adapt themselves to the developing democratic impulse in the new nation in the first decades

of its existence, while simultaneously working to maintain the nation's identity in decidedly Protestant terms. What they failed to do by political means, they sought to carry on their mission through voluntary religious societies. Den Hartog wrote, "[Federalists] were pushed out of politics in the face of Democratic electoral success, but they were also pulled in the direction by the successes they saw resulting from early voluntarist endeavors" ([33], p. 7).

As a nineteenth century nationalist articulation of strong Christian America, O'Sullivan's Manifest Destiny appropriated the Protestant metaphysical and ethical themes of providence, innocence, mission, and millennialism. First, let us consider O'Sullivan's use of Protestant themes in his expression of Manifest Destiny as nationalism. The most prominent Protestant theme appearing in O'Sullivan's nationalistic writings is providence. Providence is the unifying concept in Manifest Destiny, and scarcely does O'Sullivan describe America without somehow appealing to providence. Providence permeates O'Sullivan's nationalism, and O'Sullivan clearly believed that he could have certainty with regard to God's purposes. For him, it was God's will to bring history to an ideal state, and American democracy was the medium by which God would accomplish his purposes. In 1839, he wrote, "[i]n its magnificent domain of space and time, the nation of many nations [that is, America] is destined to manifest to mankind the excellence of divine principles; to establish on earth the noblest temple ever dedicated to the worship of the Most High—the Sacred and the True." Earlier in the same essay, he asserted, "[w]e are the nation of human progress, and who will, what can, set limits to our onward march? Providence is with us, and no earthly power can. We point to the everlasting truth on the first page of our national declaration, and we proclaim to the millions of other lands, that 'the gates of hell'—the powers of aristocracy and monarchy—'shall not prevail against it'" ([7], p. 427). In these lines, O'Sullivan accomplished several nationalistic objects simultaneously: he spoke with certainty about God's will with regard to America, he claimed America to be the chosen people of God, he explained the millennial purpose God had bestowed upon America, and he conflated the Christian gospel with the ideals expressed in the American Declaration of Independence.

Innocence is a second key ethical Protestant theme O'Sullivan adopted for his nationalism. Gomez observed that because of the workings of providence through the chosen people, America is thus a morally regenerate nation. America's sinlessness comes by virtue of its being the agent of God's providence and in the sense that America is the paragon of what O'Sullivan called "the democratic principle" ([13], p. 240). In O'Sullivan's 1837 inaugural editorial for the *Democratic Review*, he said, "[w]e feel safe under the banner of the democratic principle, which is borne onward by an unseen hand of Providence, to lead our race toward the high destinies of which every human soul contains the God-implanted germ..." ([34], p. 9). For O'Sullivan, the past is irrelevant and the only history that matters is future history. America is the nation of the future, and thus it is America that will define future history under the hand of providence. Furthermore, all morality must be defined according to the democratic principle. The upshot of this is that America, being the ideal democratic nation, is morally pure. "All history has to be re-written; political science and the whole scope of all moral truth have to be considered and illustrated in the light of the democratic principle" ([34], p. 14).

Mission is another Protestant theme found O'Sullivan's Manifest Destiny. Gomez wrote that for O'Sullivan, "America does not *have* a mission, it *is* a mission, and the spread of American government is always the spread of human liberty..." ([13], p. 252). Spreading democracy across the North American continent, and ultimately, to the whole of humanity was at the center of O'Sullivan's understanding of mission. God has chosen America, not in a passive way but in an active way. America has been chosen not to *be* something, but to *do* something. O'Sullivan defined the mission as being "the entire development of the principle of our organization—freedom of conscience, freedom of person, freedom of trade and business pursuits, universality of freedom and equality....For this blessed mission to the nations of the world, which are shut out from the life-giving light of truth, has America been chosen; and her high example shall smite unto death the tyranny of kings, hierarchs, and oligarchs, and carry the glad tidings of peace and good will where myriads now endure an existence scarcely more enviable than that of the beasts of the field" ([7], p. 430). Thus, O'Sullivan transformed the Christian gospel—the "glad tidings" of Isa 52:7, Matt 24:14, Luke 2:10, and Rom 10:15—into another gospel of salvation in American democracy in his nationalism.

Finally, O'Sullivan annexed millennialism to Manifest Destiny. Recall that Kedourie observed that a key feature of nationalism as political religion occurs when a central religious figure is recast from his traditional, orthodox role to a new role that serves the interests of the nation. O'Sullivan took the figure of Christ and recast him, from the orthodox pattern of Suffering Servant, Son of God, Savior of world, and eschatological Judge of all humankind to the preacher of American democracy who will ultimately bring about the Kingdom of God on earth. In 1843, he said, "those principles and those precepts of Him who spoke as never man spake, which it is henceforth the joint and blessed mission of both to apply in practice to the regeneration of human society, to realize that inconceivably glorious result, of the coming of the Kingdom of God upon the earth, of which He himself promised the attainment, as well as taught the way" ([35], p. 567). So American democracy was the gospel of Christ who brought forth the United States into the world sinless to serve as the example to all humankind and the usher in the kingdom that would be defined by personal liberty and equality.

O'Sullivan imported these and other important Christian themes from Protestant theology to Manifest Destiny. He was not the first to do this. The history of the use of Protestant themes to situate the identity and significance of the nation goes back to the early seventeenth century Puritans who established the New England colonies. It continues into the eighteenth century as American colonists adapted the way they self-identified to the colonial wars and the Revolution. And Americans continued to use theological themes after their independence in the late eighteenth century and into the nineteenth. O'Sullivan's Manifest Destiny is the antebellum iteration of a long tradition of religious exceptionalist ideas that emerged in the American colonies and later, the nation [36][1].

No genealogical accounting of Manifest Destiny is complete without a consideration of how westward expansion inspired its adherents, particularly O'Sullivan. In particular, the rapid westward expansion of the United States, beginning with the Louisiana Purchase of 1803, seemed evidence to many that the nation was chosen by God to fulfill a special destiny on the continent that would extend to the world. Westward expansion gave a new significance to the Protestant theological vocabulary that had been in use since the seventeenth century. And while Manifest Destiny did signal the beginning of sectionalism in the nation, nevertheless, the rhetoric its advocates used to promote it was nationalistic in its scope.

Lyman Beecher (1775–1863) expressed his vision for expansion into the west in his 1835 book, *A Plea for the West*. Beecher's vision provides the means by which we may place the Christian nationalism of Manifest Destiny in its antebellum context. John C. Pinheiro argued in his religious history of the Mexican-American War that Americans took the concepts of Anglo-Saxonism, Protestantism, and anti-Catholicism to arrive at what he termed the "Beecherite Synthesis" [37][2], a new providentialist and destinarian language of exceptionalism befitting the growth of the American population, the expansion of its territory, and the democratization of its Christianity. The Beecherite Synthesis evolved from the 1830s through the Texas annexation debates of 1844–45 and culminating in the Mexican-American War from 1846–48. By the time open hostilities had broken out between the United States and Mexico in April 1846, Pinheiro argued O'Sullivan's Manifest Destiny and the Beecherite Synthesis had become nearly synonymous.

In *A Plea for the West*, Beecher admitted he was initially skeptical about the idea of a divinely-ordained destiny reserved for the United States. But upon reflection on the history of

---

[1]   See John D. Wilsey. *American Exceptionalism and Civil Religion: Reassessing the History of an Idea* for a historical and theological consideration of American exceptionalism from the colonial period to the present.

[2]   Pinheiro carefully examines how the concept of race went far beyond distinctions of color, e.g., black/white. He demonstrates that in nineteenth century discourse on race could be broadly understood to refer to color, religion, ethnicity, nation, and other factors. Other excellent treatments on race and nationalism can be found in Reginald Horsman, *Race and Manifest Destiny: The Origins of American Racial Anglo-Saxonism* (Cambridge: Harvard University Press, 1982) [38] and Nicholas Guyatt, *Providence and the Invention of the United States, 1607–1876* (Cambridge, UK: Cambridge University Press, 2007) [39].

western expansion to his own time, he confessed he had come to see the light. Whereas he once found the idea of divine destiny for America "chimerical", he came to believe, "there is not a nation upon earth which, in fifty years, can be all possible reformation place itself in circumstances so favorable as our own for the free, unembarrassed applications of physical effort and pecuniary power to evangelize the world" ([40], p. 123). And how would America make good on fulfilling its divine destiny? It would do so by securing civil and religious liberty through a concerted effort of education in Protestant theology and morals. Beecher asserted, "the conflict which is to decide the destiny of the West, will be a conflict of institutions for the education of her sons, for purposes of superstitions, or evangelical light; of despotism, or liberty" ([40], pp. 123–24).

Central to Beecher's work was the notion that Catholicism and liberty were mutually exclusive, and one must win out completely over the other when they come into conflict. At the national founding, there was not much concern among Americans about a Catholic threat—in 1800, Catholics represented only about 1.7% of the total population ([37], p. 41). But because of the Second Great Awakening and the influx of immigrants during the early decades of the nineteenth century, that percentage jumped to 3.5% by 1840 ([37], p. 41). According to Pinheiro, by 1830 "there were over a dozen Catholic seminaries and colleges and the number of monasteries and convents were approaching forty" ([37], p. 42). For Beecher, the rising tide of Catholicism in the United States threatened to undermine its destiny to civilize the west. If Americans did not awaken themselves to the Catholic threat and establish Protestant institutions in the west, then the fabric of republicanism in the nation could be torn asunder. But, Beecher urged, "if this work be done, and well done, our country is safe, and the world's hope is secure. The government of force will cease, and that of intelligence and virtue will take its place" ([40], p. 130).

When *A Plea for the West* appeared in 1835, Beecher's anti-Catholicism was aimed primarily at Catholic immigrants coming into the United States. But by the mid 1840s, the Beecherite Synthesis shifted its focus from American Catholics to Roman Catholic Mexico. Pinheiro traced this evolution from the writings of Charles Joseph Latrobe, George Wilkins Kendall, William H. Prescott, Brantz Mayer, and William Stapp. These authors characterized Mexican society as dilapidated, indolent, bigoted against Protestants, and the Mexican people as racially inferior. Anglo-Saxons were, in contrast, freer, more enlightened, more industrious, and most obviously favored by God over all other racial groups in the world. Pinheiro wrote, "by 1846, America's identity seemed most intelligible only when defined in contradistinction to Mexico: Protestant, not Catholic; Anglo-Saxon not Indian/Mestizo/Spanish (i.e., white not non-white or black); republican not tyrannical; industrious not slothful" ([37], p. 65). But it was O'Sullivan that culminated this shift in his "Annexation" essay published just less than a year out from Polk's war address of May 11, 1846. According to Pinheiro, O'Sullivan transformed the Beecherite Synthesis "by spelling out the shape of the Catholic menace, relocating it for the time being in Mexico, and reinforcing the divinely ordained American role in the advancement of civil and religious liberty" ([37], p. 65). O'Sullivan's writings lack the strenuous anti-Catholic and covenantal elements found in Beecher's book—he was after all, the son of Irish immigrants and was raised Catholic. Still, O'Sullivan's exultations over the superiority of Anglo-Saxonism in the pages of the *Democratic Review* neatly situate his Manifest Destiny within the Beecherite Synthesis.

As Christian nationalism then, O'Sullivan's brand of Manifest Destiny bears the marks of a political religion that contrasts with Christianity while simultaneously appropriating themes from Protestant theology; and it fits within the antebellum context via the Beecherite Synthesis. Lastly, Manifest Destiny is a Christian nationalism informed by the Enlightenment, and perhaps most significantly, from nineteenth century German idealism. It accurately represents the Enlightenment's emphasis on human progress, and it bears resemblance with certain characteristics of G. W. F. Hegel's philosophy of history. While it is unclear whether or not O'Sullivan was familiar with Hegel's writings, it is clear that he was personally acquainted with historian and diplomat George Bancroft (1800–1891), and had knowledge of his work in American history. Bancroft serves as the connection between O'Sullivan's Manifest Destiny and German idealism, via the historicism he had adopted while studying at universities in Berlin, Heidelberg, and Göttingen, where he earned his doctorate in 1820.

The influence of the German Enlightenment is clear in O'Sullivan's writings. For example, with regard to the doctrine of providence, O'Sullivan followed the leading philosophers and historians of his day in assuming that providence was the way in which the past itself and knowledge of the past were reconciled [41][3]. Jonathan Boyd, in his dissertation on Bancroft, wrote that providentialists "argued consistently that there is *no dichotomy*—no divide between natural law and providence, between justice and caprice, between mechanism and agent, or between reason and history" ([42], p. 36). O'Sullivan clearly espoused that view of providence in his writings. Also, like Bancroft, O'Sullivan believed that nations possess a life span of their own, much like a human being. They have a birth, maturity, and old age. And as Boyd wrote, "nations are the individuals, the moral agents with which the historical narrative must deal" ([42], p. 187). By God's hand of providence, nations fulfill the purpose for which God calls them into being, and that purpose transcends their own interest and identity. Boyd, writing of Bancroft's concept of the American nation, said that America is providentially subsumed under "the international shape of world history, wherein all nations derive their identity, their calling, and their destiny from the larger pattern of history in its forward march of liberty" ([42], p. 200). A similar concept of nation is found in O'Sullivan's writings on the American nation.

Before we explore how, let us first consider some key tenets of the Enlightenment. "Enlightenment" is often used ambiguously—people use it assuming there is a universally understood and simple definition that everyone intuitively comprehends. Of course, the Enlightenment is enormously varied and complex. Still, there are a some elements of Enlightenment that we can identify that are common from the seventeenth century to the twentieth century as it appeared in all its forms on the European continent, the British Isles, and America. Henry F. May summarized Enlightenment thought by saying, "[l]et us say that the Enlightenment consists of all those who believe two propositions: first, that the present age is more enlightened than the past; and second, that we understand nature in man best through the use of our natural faculties" ([43], p. xiv)[4]. Entailed in May's first tenet is the idea of inevitable progress. Inevitable progress is the insistence that human civilization, knowledge, morality, etc. were perpetually on the advance. Charles Van Doren wrote that the "eighteenth century not only believed in progress, it even began to believe in *necessary* progress; things *had* to get better, because that was the nature of things" ([44], p. 217).

O'Sullivan's writings are fraught with the concept of inevitable progress. "Our national birth," O'Sullivan wrote, "was the beginning of a new history, the formation and progress of an untried political system, which separates us from the past and connects us with the future only;...we may confidently assume that our country is destined to be *the great nation* of futurity. It is so destined, because the principle upon which a nation is organized fixes its destiny, and that of equality is perfect, is universal" ([7], p. 426). He went on to assert that American laws, education, literature, and culture "are carried onward by the increasing tide of progress; and though they cast many a longing look behind, they cannot stay the glorious movement of the masses, nor induce them to venerate the rubbish, the prejudices, the superstitions of other times and other lands, the theocracy of priests, the divine right of kings, the aristocracy of blood, the metaphysics of colleges, the irrational stuff of law libraries" ([7], p. 429). But this advancement was not for America alone. Recall that America's mission, for O'Sullivan, was to bring the light of the democratic principle to the whole world. "The movement of man, then, must be upward. The virtue of earth and the holiness of Heaven, are pledged to his support. May God hasten the day of his complete final success!" ([28], p. 229). Thus was America's mission a world movement of liberation and of the establishment of the kingdom of God.

---

3   See G. E. Lessing. *Lessing's Theological Writings* for Lessing's famous "ditch." Lessing posited, "accidental truths of history can never become the proof of necessary truths of reason." Lessing meant that events and truths were of two separate categories, and must not be conflated. His view of history was purely secular, in that he asserted that one could not attain knowledge of God from historical events. Claims about God fall into the realm of faith, not knowledge.

4   May categorized four periods of Enlightenment thought in the eighteenth and nineteenth centuries.

What marks of Hegel does O'Sullivan's Manifest Destiny bear? First, let us explore Hegel's philosophy. Hegel's thought is notoriously opaque. Bertrand Russell drily noted that Hegel "is, I should say, the hardest to understand of all the great philosophers" ([45], p. 730). But Hegel is not impossible to understand, and his philosophy of history in particular is recognizable in O'Sullivan's nationalism.

Hegel was a monist, in other words, he saw reality as a singular whole unified by logic, which to him was identical to metaphysics. The One, the Absolute Idea, for Hegel was God, or *Geist*, meaning "Spirit". *Geist*, wrote Russell, "is the only reality, and that its thought is reflected into itself by self-consciousness." Furthermore, "[t]he Absolute Idea [again, *Geist*] is pure thought thinking about pure thought. This is all God does throughout the ages—truly a Professor's God" ([45], pp. 734–35). History is the act of God in the process of becoming through the stages of the dialectic: thesis, antithesis, and synthesis. The process of time, for Hegel, is a movement from the less perfect to the more perfect, to finally culminate in an ideal logical end. Russell described it this way: "logical perfection consists in being a closely-knit whole, without ragged edges, without independent parts, but united, like a human body,...into an organism whose parts are interdependent and all work together towards a single end; and this also constitutes ethical perfection" ([45], pp. 735–36).

As *Geist* moves through a process of becoming, Hegel identified three phases: the Oriental, the Graeco-Roman, and the German. Each phase is recognized by a certain level of freedom. Hegel said, "[t]he East knew and to the present day knows only that *one* is free; the Greek and Roman world, that *some* are free; the German world knows that *all* are free. The first political form therefore which we observe in history, is *despotism*, the second *democracy* and *aristocracy*, the third *monarchy*" ([46], p. 203). Hegel also cast the nations representing historical development in organic terms. The Oriental stage "is the childhood of history". The Greek stage "would be the boyhood of history". The Roman stage, "the *manhood* of history"; and Hegel described the final, German stage as "the periods of life human life to its *old age*." In contrast to the physical, the "*spirit* is its perfect maturity and *strength*, in which it returns to unity with itself, but in its fully developed character as *spirit*" ([46], pp. 204–5). Once the Absolute Idea, or *Geist*—or God—has completed the process of becoming (and we must understand "God" as everything that is), then, wrote Hegel, "[f]reedom has found the means of realizing its ideal—its true existence" ([46], p. 206). Of course, time is a mirage, and the dialectical process of history—God working through a process of becoming—proceeds through eternity. But for Hegel, the German state represents the *telos* of history, the logical and ethical end of process in which perfect freedom exists [47].

Hegel located the fulfillment of historical *telos* in Germany, while O'Sullivan clearly located it in America. Hegel's ethical *telos* was perfect freedom—as was O'Sullivan's, although Hegel's notion of freedom was not the liberal brand of the eighteenth century British or American Enlightenment. Russell said that for Hegel, freedom "means little more than the right to obey the law" ([45], p. 737). Still, Hegel shows up in O'Sullivan's writings through his conceptions of progress, *telos*, and freedom.

For example, in his "On the Intelligence of the People", O'Sullivan embraced the notion of *vox populi, vox Dei*. God's providence is such that it works through even the destructive tendencies of humans. God is the "Governor of the universe" and "is literally...the life and soul...directing [man] in every thought and action that he may attain to the true ends of his being..." ([48], p. 361). Most strikingly, in his essay "The Course of Civilization", O'Sullivan posits an order of progression of human civilization that resembles that articulated by Hegel. The first stage of history, O'Sullivan called the "theocratic" stage and "was born among the oldest people in the East, in Judea, Persia, India....Little social elevation, and less of personal freedom, could be found under such a dominion." O'Sullivan's second stage was the Graeco-Roman stage, and was marked by "the indisputable supremacy of the State." The third stage, or the "aristocratic order of civilization" was defined by power, which when wielded by the elites was done for the purpose of "mutual envy and ambition." Finally, the last stage was the "democratic" which "received its first permanent existence in this country." The Declaration of Independence "established the direct existence of democracy as a social element, and began a reform destined to cease only when every man in the world should be finally and triumphantly redeemed" ([27], pp. 209–13). For O'Sullivan, human civilization and human freedom are synonymous with salvation, and these are culminated in American democracy. "Nothing short of the broadest reception of the principles of democracy can regenerate man" ([27], p. 216). The working out of human salvation—equated by O'Sullivan with American democracy—is the work of divine providence, and not an accident of history. "The spirit is that of the Christian gospel—working sometimes most powerfully through many of those who are the most unconscious of the source from which their inspiration and stimulus have been derived" ([35], p. 563). Gomez described O'Sullivan's views of the *telos* driven course of civilization in this way: "O'Sullivan believes that the *telos* of politics, and thus of history, is human liberation. Liberty is for him a primary political good, being both the will of God and the universal human interest" ([13], p. 246). While O'Sullivan had no developed philosophy of history on the plane of Hegel, these elements of Hegelian idealism can be recognized in O'Sullivan's Manifest Destiny. O'Sullivan's ontology is understood, not as a German *telos*, to be sure, but certainly as an American one.

The most direct connection O'Sullivan had with German idealism in general is through Bancroft's historicism. Boyd described the historicism of German idealists like Johann Gottfried Eichhorn, F. D. E. Schleiermacher, Johann Gottfried Herder, and Hegel as "a developing historical consciousness...which centers on historical change, on history itself as the ultimate locus of reality" ([42], p. 59). For German historicists such as these and others like Bancroft's mentor Arnold H. L. Heeren and Leopold von Ranke, providence was integral to the interpretation of history. Also for them, providence was the activity of a God who was strictly immanent and impersonal. For American providentialists like Bancroft, God was at all times personal, immanent, and transcendent.

Boyd noted three prominent themes in historicism: the idea of flux (emphasizing the importance of causation and history's coherence), contingency (i.e., "that historical events are shaped by and contingent upon their immediate historical surroundings" ([42], p. 74)), and anachronism (in that all historical events and periods are distinct from one another, thus the past is foreign to the present). In addition to these themes, Boyd stressed the nature of history as an active participant in the flow of events, rather than an abstract hermeneutical category. He wrote that historicism recognizes that "history has such great power over the objects caught up in its currents that historical understanding becomes a—if not *the*—central avenue for the knowledge of reality" ([42], p. 76).

The historicism utilized by German idealists was *Historismus* and Bancroft spent years immersed in it while he studied in Europe. A central presupposition in *Historismus* was that history can be known, understood, and communicated. Through the use of primary sources, text criticism, and narrative historiography, historians in this classical historicist school approached history as, in Boyd's words, being "metaphysically integrated" ([42], p. 84). Thus, ideas in history grew from infancy to maturity, just as all living things do including nations. History, then, provides access to ultimate reality and the mind of God. Boyd stated it this way: "[m]etaphysical historicists—among them the classical German historicists (and, to jump ahead, Bancroft in America)—believed in a reality that transcended the material world and included the real existence of the ideal" ([42], p. 85). Because the metaphysical historicists invested history with such power, providentialism was necessary to the study of history. As Boyd wrote describing Bancroft's use of providence in history-writing—"[his] providentialism asserts the reality of that divine intelligence which gives foundation to his romantic idealism, that intelligence who things the great thoughts which come to life in history" ([42], p. 107). And it is a similar approach to providentialism that is a necessary element in O'Sullivan's Manifest Destiny.

To be sure there are differences between Bancroft and O'Sullivan in the ways they understood America as a providential nation. Bancroft's historicism led to a cyclical view of history (e.g., Hegel's dialectical process of becoming), with an emphasis on coherence amid change over time (e.g., flux). O'Sullivan was not a trained historian in the German idealistic tradition, and his rhetoric about the United States representing something utterly new reflects that whatever influence he felt from historicism was limited in its scope. He still carried significant characteristics of pre-historicist, linear history when thinking of inevitable progress and America representing "futurity". Furthermore, both Bancroft and O'Sullivan had to deal with the problem of the lifespan of the American nation as an organic being with a birth, maturity, and old age. Would America ultimately die, as other nations had? Would it usher in the millennium? Or would it live on in another form, carrying its providential purpose into another age? Bancroft's developed historicism offers more coherent solutions, whereas O'Sullivan's prehistoricism limits his solutions to only one: that America would itself be the millennial kingdom of Protestant theology. These differences are helpful in preventing us from overstating the weight of German idealism upon O'Sullivan's nationalism.

Still, that influence is there and it is evident in O'Sullivan's association with Bancroft. They were connected through both diplomatic and literary circles. They corresponded with one another frequently on the issues of their day. In 1841, O'Sullivan wrote to Bancroft on his opposition to the death penalty ([11], p. 45). In the months preceding the American annexation of Texas on the issue of possible war with Mexico, O'Sullivan expressed concern to Bancroft about the bellicose attitude America was taking toward Mexico ([11], p. 31). O'Sullivan also commended Bancroft as an example of a true historian of the American mold. In 1842, he wrote, "[w]e are happy to see the latest of the great historians, Bancroft (a name to be placed close to Hume and Tacitus) tracing the growth of the democratic principle in our colonial history with nicety and profound research" ([6], p. 199). Two years later, O'Sullivan referred to Bancroft as "the most democratic historian of modern times" in a piece for the *New York Morning News* ([11], p. 41). In addition to providing his own endorsement of Bancroft's writing, he featured an opinion of Bancroft from the literary critic W. A. Jones in an essay entitled "Unitarian Portraits". Jones described Bancroft as a historian who "possesses the most philosophical spirit of any writer of history in England or in this country since Hume". Jones noted that Bancroft's work was marked by "great ingenuity and boldness" and, in pure O'Sullivan style, he said that Bancroft "is the historian for the people....He traces, with a masterly hand, the progress of the democratic principle,—the ultimately sovereign power in the State" ([49], p. 391). Widmer asserted that the unique nature of the *Democratic Review* under O'Sullivan's editorship—as a political-literary outlet—united the spread-eagle rhetoric of Manifest Destiny with "Bancroft's delineation of the democratic principle in his history" ([11], p. 63). The combination of nationalistic flair with literary sophistication were not found only in the *Review*, but according to Widmer, "never in so dramatic a fashion, with so public a manifesto, such ardent energy, and such a clear intention of presenting literature and politics as part and parcel of the same idea" ([11], p. 63). While O'Sullivan was not directly influenced by Hegel in particular, or nineteenth century German philosophy in general, through his personal and professional association with Bancroft, his reading of Bancroft's history, and his affinity with Bancroft's historical method, it seems clear that his Manifest Destiny was informed in part by German idealism.

4. Conclusions

Manifest Destiny, as it appeared during O'Sullivan's tenure at the *Democratic Review* from 1837 to 1846, conformed to patterns around the specific historical context of the day. By the 1850s, Manifest Destiny had played out—at the end of the Polk administration, the United States had acquired more territory in four years than in any equivalent period before or since. The Civil War shattered the political framework of the early republican period, but Manifest Destiny would achieve a revival in the late 1890s with the American victory over the Spanish and the resulting acquisition of overseas colonies in the Pacific and Caribbean. This second emergence of Manifest Destiny was different than the first because it arose in different historical circumstances. At every period of American history, Christian nationalism has taken a particular form: the Christian republicanism of the 1770s and 80s; Manifest Destiny of the 1840s and 1890s; Christian civilization of 1917–1919; the Manichean division between the free and Communist worlds of the 1950s–1980s; and the Christian America thesis of the 1970s–present to name a few manifestations that Americans have embraced over time [36][5]. While much has changed

---

[5]   See John D. Wilsey. *One Nation Under God? An Evangelical Critique of Christian America* for a philosophical, historical, and theological assessment of the Christian America thesis as it has been articulated from 1977 to the present [50].

in terms of how Americans have self-identified using religious terms, much has stayed the same. Smith defined national identity as "the maintenance and continual reinterpretation of the pattern of values, symbols, memories, myths, and traditions that form the distinctive heritage of the nation, and the identification of individuals with that heritage and its pattern" ([2], pp. 24–25). Smith noted both *maintenance* and *continual reinterpretation* in his definition. Americans have always believed their nation was exceptional, and have always believed that it enjoyed a special relationship with God which entailed particular duties in the world. How that exceptionalism should be defined, and what America's privileged status has meant to its people has changed significantly depending on both internal and external circumstances. It has been thus since the origins of the nation, and will likely be thus for the foreseeable future. For these, and other reasons, Christian nationalism is a theme worthy of continual historical and religious study.

Conflicts of Interest: The author declares no conflict of interest.

References

1. Elie Kedourie. *Nationalism*, 4th ed. Oxford: Blackwell, 2000.
2. Anthony D. Smith. *Chosen Peoples: Sacred Sources of National Identity*. Oxford: Oxford University Press, 2003.
3. Landon Edward Fuller. "The United States Magazine and Democratic Review, 1837–1859: A Study of its History, Contents, and Significance." Ph.D. dissertation, University of North Carolina, Chapel Hill, NC, USA, 1948.
4. John L. O'Sullivan. "European Views of American Democracy—No. II." *The United States Magazine and Democratic Review* 2 (1838): 337–57. Available online: http://ebooks.library.cornell.edu/cgi/t/text/text-idx?c=usde;cc=usde;view=toc;subview=short;idno=usde0002-4 (accessed on 7 November 2016).
5. John L. O'Sullivan. "America in 1846: The Past—The Future." *The United States Magazine and Democratic Review* 18 (1846): 57–65. Available online: http://ebooks.library.cornell.edu/cgi/t/text/text-idx?c=usde;cc=usde;view=toc;subview=short;idno=usde0018-1 (accessed on 7 November 2016).
6. John L. O'Sullivan. "Democracy and Literature." *The United States Magazine and Democratic Review* 11 (1842): 196–200. Available online: http://ebooks.library.cornell.edu/cgi/t/text/text-idx?c=usde;cc=usde;view=toc;subview=short;idno=usde0011-2 (accessed on 7 November 2016).
7. John L. O'Sullivan. "The Great Nation of Futurity." *The United States Magazine and Democratic Review* 6 (1839): 426–30. Available online: http://ebooks.library.cornell.edu/cgi/t/text/text-idx?c=usde;cc=usde;view=toc;subview=short;idno=usde0006-4 (accessed on 7 November 2016).
8. George Bancroft to Jared Sparks, 22 August 1834, quoted in Fuller, *United States Magazine and Democratic Review*, p. 11.
9. Frederick Merk. *Manifest Destiny and Mission in American History: A Reinterpretation*, 2nd ed. Cambridge: Harvard University Press, 1995.
10. Anders Stephanson. *Manifest Destiny: American Expansion and the Empire of Right*. New York: Hill and Wang, 1995.
11. Edward L. Widmer. *Young America: The Flowering of Democracy in New York City*. Oxford: Oxford University Press, 1999.
12. Robert D. Sampson. *John L. O'Sullivan and His Times*. Kent: Kent State University Press, 2003.
13. Adam Gomez. "*Deus Vult*: John L. O'Sullivan, Manifest Destiny, and American Democratic Messianism." *American Political Thought* 1 (2012): 236–62. [CrossRef]
14. John L. O'Sullivan. "The Texas Question." *The United States Magazine and Democratic Review* 14 (1844): 423–30. Available online: http://ebooks.library.cornell.edu/cgi/t/text/text-idx?c=usde;cc=usde;view=toc;subview=short;idno=usde0014-4 (accessed on 7 November 2016). Ironically, O'Sullivan's anti-war position was more consistent with the Whigs' position on expansion, who were exemplarist rather than imperialist in their attitudes toward Texas, Mexico, and Oregon.
15. John L. O'Sullivan. "Annexation." *The United States Magazine and Democratic Review* 17 (1845): 5–10. Available online: http://ebooks.library.cornell.edu/cgi/t/text/text-idx?c=usde;cc=usde;view=toc;subview=short;idno=usde0017-1 (accessed on 7 November 2016).

16. John L. O'Sullivan. "Hurrah for a War with England! " *The United States Magazine and Democratic Review* 9 (1841): 411–17. Available online: http://ebooks.library.cornell.edu/cgi/t/text/text-idx?c=usde;cc=usde; view=toc;subview=short;idno=usde0009-5 (accessed on 7 November 2016).

17. Daniel Walker Howe. *What Hath God Wrought: The Transformation of America, 1815–1848.* Oxford History of the United States. Edited by David M. Kennedy. New York: Oxford University Press, 2007.

18. David S. Reynolds. *Waking Giant: America in the Age of Jackson.* New York: HarperCollins, 2008.

19. David M. Potter. *The Impending Crisis: America before the Civil War, 1848–1861.* Completed and edited by Don E. Fehrenbacher; New York: Harper Perennial, 2011, First published 1976.

20. Sean Wilentz. *The Rise of American Democracy: Jefferson to Lincoln.* New York: Norton, 2005.

21. John L. O'Sullivan. "Territorial Aggrandizement." *The United States Magazine and Democratic Review* 17 (1845): 243–48. Available online: http://ebooks.library.cornell.edu/cgi/t/text/text-idx?c=usde;cc=usde;view=toc; subview=short;idno=usde0017-3 (accessed on 8 November 2016).

22. Andrew Jackson. "Second Annual Message, December 6, 1830." In *A Compilation of the Messages and Papers of the Presidents.* New York: Bureau of National Literature, 1897, vol. III, pp. 1063–92.

23. Sam Haselby. *The Origins of American Religious Nationalism.* Oxford: Oxford University Press, 2015.

24. Thomas R. Hietala. *Manifest Design: American Exceptionalism and Empire,* Revised ed. Ithaca: Cornell University Press, 1985.

25. Richard Kluger. *Seizing Destiny: How Americans Grew from Sea to Shining Sea.* New York: Knopf, 2007.

26. James M. McPherson. *Battle Cry of Freedom: The Civil War Era.* Oxford: Oxford University Press, 1988.

27. John L. O'Sullivan. "The Course of Civilization." *The United States Magazine and Democratic Review* 6 (1839): 208–17. Available online: http://ebooks.library.cornell.edu/u/usde/usde.1839.html (accessed on 8 November 2016).

28. John L. O'Sullivan. "Democracy." *The United States Magazine and Democratic Review* 7 (1840): 215–29. Available online: http://ebooks.library.cornell.edu/cgi/t/text/text-idx?c=usde;cc=usde;view=toc;subview=short; idno=usde0007-2 (accessed on 8 November 2016).

29. D. D. F. "The Law of Progress of the Race." *The United States Magazine and Democratic Review* 15 (1844): 195–203. Available online: http://ebooks.library.cornell.edu/u/usde/usde.1844.html (accessed on 28 March 2017).

30. Conrad Cherry, ed. *God's New Israel: Religious Interpretations of American Destiny,* Revised ed. Chapel Hill: University of North Carolina Press, 1998, First published 1971.

31. Mark A. Noll. *One Nation under God? Christian Faith and Political Action in America.* San Francisco: Harper and Row, 1988.

32. John Fea. *Was America Founded as a Christian Nation: An Historical Introduction.* Louisville: Westminster John Knox, 2011.

33. Jonathan Den Hartog. *Patriotism and Piety: Federalist Politics and Religious Struggle in the New American Nation.* Charlottesville: University of Virginia Press, 2015.

34. John L. O'Sullivan. "Introduction." *The United States Magazine and Democratic Review* 1 (1837): 1–15. Available online: http://ebooks.library.cornell.edu/cgi/t/text/text-idx?c=usde;cc=usde;view=toc;subview= short;idno=usde0001-1 (accessed on 7 November 2016).

35. John L. O'Sullivan. "The Christian Union." *The United States Magazine and Democratic Review* 12 (1843): 563–67. Available online: http://ebooks.library.cornell.edu/cgi/t/text/text-idx?c=usde;cc=usde;view=toc; subview=short;idno=usde0012-5 (accessed on 7 November 2016).

36. John D. Wilsey. *American Exceptionalism and Civil Religion: Reassessing the History of an Idea.* Downers Grove: IVP Academic, 2015.

37. John C. Pinheiro. *Missionaries of Republicanism: A Religious History of the Mexican-American War.* Oxford: Oxford University Press, 2015.

38. Reginald Horsman. *Race and Manifest Destiny: The Origins of American Racial Anglo-Saxonism.* Cambridge: Harvard University Press, 1981.

39. Nicholas Guyatt. *Providence and the Invention of the United States, 1607–1876.* Cambridge: Cambridge University Press, 2007.

40. Lyman Beecher. "A Plea for the West." In *God's New Israel: Religious Interpretations of American Destiny,* Revised ed. Edited by Conrad Cherry. Chapel Hill: University of North Carolina Press, 1998. First published 1971.

41. G. E. Lessing. *Lessing's Theological Writings.* Library of Religious Thought; Stanford: Stanford University Press, 1957, p. 53.

42. Jonathan Boyd. "This Holy Hieroglyph: Providence and Historical Consciousness in George Bancroft's Historiography." Ph.D. dissertation, Johns Hopkins University, Baltimore, MD, USA, 2001.
43. Henry F. May. *The Enlightenment in America*. New York: Oxford University Press, 1976.
44. Charles Van Doren. *A History of Knowledge, Past, Present, and Future: The Pivotal Events, People, and Achievements of World History*. New York: Ballantine, 1991.
45. Bertrand Russell. *The History of Western Philosophy*, 2nd ed. New York: Touchstone, 1972.
46. Georg Wilhelm Friedrich Hegel. *The Philosophy of History*. The Great Books of the Western World, no. 46. Edited by Robert Maynard Hutchins. Chicago: Encyclopedia Britannica, 1952, pp. 151–369.
47. I must acknowledge that this description is a massive simplification of Hegel's philosophy of history. I also want to clearly state that my reading of O'Sullivan does not entail a direct influence from Hegel's philosophy. I am only asserting that Hegel's philosophy can be recognized in O'Sullivan's nationalism, albeit in an unrefined and Americanized form.
48. John L. O'Sullivan. "On the Intelligence of the People." *The United States Magazine and Democratic Review* 8 (1840): 360–66. Available online: http://ebooks.library.cornell.edu/u/usde/usde.1840.html (accessed on 8 November 2016).
49. W. A. Jones. "Unitarian Portraits." *The United States Magazine and Democratic Review* 15 (1844): 389–97. Available online: http://ebooks.library.cornell.edu/u/usde/usde.1844.html (accessed on 28 March 2017).
50. John D. Wilsey. *One Nation Under God? An Evangelical Critique of Christian America*. Eugene: Pickwick, 2011.

religions

MDPI

Article

Beyond Christian Nationalism: How the American Committee on Religious Rights and Minorities Made Religious Pluralism a Global Cause in the Interwar Era

David Mislin

Intellectual Heritage Program, Temple University, 1114 Polett Walk, Philadelphia, PA 19122-6090, USA; dmislin@temple.edu

Academic Editor: Mark T. Edwards
Received: 4 October 2016; Accepted: 8 December 2016; Published: 16 December 2016

Abstract: During the 1920s and 1930s, the American Committee on Religious Rights and Minorities offered a potent challenge to the view of the United States as a Christian nation. The Protestant, Catholic, and Jewish members of the committee drew on a wealth of interfaith commitments to develop a critique of religious persecution around the world, especially the increasing anti-Semitism across Europe. In an era marked by isolationism, nationalism, and Christian triumphalism, the committee offered a competing vision of pluralist internationalism.

Keywords: pluralism; internationalism; religious minorities; interwar Europe

---

In January of 1927, the queen of Romania arrived for an official visit to the United States. She promptly found herself greeted by a charitable yet unquestionably forceful rebuke. The protest came from an interfaith committee that objected to the treatment of the minority religious communities of her nation by its majority Orthodox community. Signed by the committee's distinguished membership, the petition implored the queen to devote "personal consideration to those religious minorities in Roumania suffering under the practice of discrimination," a reference in particular to a new wave of anti-Semitic violence that had begun the previous year and had already sparked an outcry from prominent Americans. Despite the fact that this committee was affiliated with the Federal Council of Churches, an ecumenical organization representing the mainline Protestant denominations in the U.S., its members included Roman Catholics and Jews, and their petition expressed concern not only for Romania's Baptists, Lutherans, and Presbyterians, but for its Roman Catholic, Jewish, and Unitarian residents as well. "It is our conviction that if your royal influence could be further exerted on their behalf their present condition would be vastly improved," committee members declared, signaling their conviction that Americans had both the right and the responsibility to directly lobby foreign leaders in matters of interreligious relations [1,2].

Issuing petitions such as this one represented the principal work of the American Committee on Religious Rights and Minorities (ACRRM), which had been established as an informal working group in 1920 with the initial goal of examining the "status of religious minorities" in the newly independent nations of Eastern Europe. In its initial statement of purpose, the group declared its mission to be investigating the plight of "Protestants, Roman Catholics, Jews and Greeks where any or all of these religious bodies are being restricted in the exercise of their right." Throughout the twenties and thirties, the committee formalized its structure and expanded its efforts more broadly across the globe, though its work increasingly came to be dominated by efforts to combat the growing anti-Semitism in Europe [3].

The ACRRM represented a who's who of the U.S. religious and political establishment of the interwar period. At various points during the twenties and thirties, its members included political luminaries such as Herbert Hoover, William Jennings Bryan, Charles Evans Hughes, and William Howard Taft. The many notable religious leaders affiliated with it included a number of leading Protestants: the committee's chairman, Arthur J. Brown, a noted Presbyterian minister and missionary; Charles S. Macfarland, who served as general secretary of the Federal Council of Churches; Charles H. Brent, an Episcopalian bishop who had served as chief of the military chaplaincy during World War I; and Ralph Sockman, a New York Methodist who earned national fame with his weekly radio broadcasts. The influential theologian Reinhold Niebuhr, though he did not officially join the committee, nevertheless attended its meetings during the early thirties. Equally prominent Catholics and Jews joined the group. Cardinal James Gibbons, who was widely revered as the de facto leader of the U.S. Catholic Church, and James J. Walsh, a Catholic physician and dean of the school of medicine at Fordham University, were among the representatives of Catholicism (though Gibbons served only a short time before his death). The rabbi Stephen Wise and Oscar Straus, who years earlier had become the first Jewish cabinet member in the U.S., represented Judaism [3,4].

The existence of a committee made up of powerful religious and political leaders who were committed to advancing the interests of minority faith communities abroad challenges many conventional understandings of American religion during the interwar period. On the surface, any group that advocated the greater involvement of the United States on the world stage seems aberrant in a decade best remembered for the isolationist "return to normalcy." Yet the ACRRM seems anomalous even in the context of those Americans who did support continued engagement abroad.

As many recent scholars have noted, the allied victory in World War I reignited a spirit of Christian triumphalism in the U.S. Believing that the armies of good had slain the forces of evil, leading Christians—in reality, leading Protestants—sought to sustain the American presence on the world stage through a variety of movements intended to foster global peace. Especially during the twenties, Christian pacifists forged international connections in various arenas in an attempt to prevent future calamitous wars. Underlying all of these efforts, however, was the fundamental assumption that the U.S. was a Christian nation with the responsibility of exporting Christian values to a world in desperate need of them [5–9].

However, the very existence of the ACRRM challenges this simple characterization of Americans' self-understanding in the interwar period. Committee members were clearly committed to exporting American values to the rest of the globe, but those values were neither exclusively Protestant nor Christian. Rather, they sought to transmit a more recently articulated value: that religious pluralism represented a positive benefit to society. Those on the ACCRM championed this view, which had begun to circulate among elites during the final decades of the nineteenth century and had gained widespread currency among progressive political and religious leaders during World War I. Two facets of this view bear noting. First, for most observers in the interwar years, religious diversity meant the presence of Roman Catholics and Jews. Efforts to expand inclusiveness to members of other faith traditions, which had occurred fleetingly at the close of the nineteenth century, largely diminished in the early twentieth. Second, despite the spread of these views in elite circles, it would take World War II and the Cold War for such values to pervade the general population. Nevertheless, when it came to Catholics and Jews, the view of prominent leaders in the political and religious realm was that rather merely being tolerated, members of these communities should be welcomed as partners and contributors in national life [10,11].

The ACRRM took this view a step further, however. Drawing on an increasingly widespread commitment to minority religious rights, its members advocated a pluralist internationalism that sought to instill such views in other countries, particularly newly independent ones. To be sure, this concern was not new. Governments in Western Europe—and, at times, even U.S. presidential administrations—had sporadically expressed concern for the protection of the rights of Jewish minorities in Eastern Europe since the late nineteenth century. However, what was novel was the level of sustained commitment to minority rights that developed in the U.S. during the post-World War I years, and the way in which that commitment merged with a changed understanding of the nation's own pluralism [2,9].

In this essay, I argue that the ACRRM offers a lens through which to consider a conception that held that the United States was a religiously pluralistic society whose citizens could advance respect for religious diversity in the international realm. By tracing the evolution of the committee's work, it will become clear that what began as an informal group with a limited internationalist vision rapidly grew in confidence and expanded the scope of its work. I will further demonstrate that the committee did not exist in a vacuum. Its members were religious and political leaders who had embraced ideals of pluralism within American society, and who matched their defense of religious minorities abroad with a commitment to an inclusive view of minority faith traditions at home.

Ultimately, I will suggest that despite its failure to meaningfully prevent religious persecution, the ACRRM nevertheless proved extraordinarily significant. Over the course of two decades, its members combined two commitments that had emerged independently: an increasing enthusiasm for religious pluralism and the belief that American ideals represented a beacon for the rest of the world. Furthermore, in these commitments, the ACRRM exemplified a broader phenomenon of the 1920s: the emergence of combined efforts by Protestants, Catholics, and Jews to advance a progressive internationalism, over and against continued conservative, evangelical arguments for Christian nationalism.

1. The Founding and Influence of the ACRRM

What became the American Committee on Religious Rights of Minorities began as a special committee within the Federal Council of Churches, an ecumenical body which, having reaped the benefits of a close relationship with the federal government during World War I, greatly expanded the scope of its work during the interwar period. Yet, despite its connection to a Protestant interdenominational organization, the ACRRM included Roman Catholics and Jews from the outset. This reflected the increasingly common perception that the religious culture of the United States encompassed those three traditions. During the early 1920s, the committee appears to have met sporadically (the records of meetings from the early years are incomplete). In its early years, the ACRRM seemed to lack confidence about acting on its own. Instead, it sought greater involvement of the U.S. in the League of Nations. Committee members argued that success in shaping global affairs—especially those related to minority religious groups—would be best accomplished by linking Americans' endeavors with the work of the newly formed international body. Such a position was unsurprising. The majority of the ACRRM's members were staunch internationalists who lamented the isolationist turn in Washington that had kept the U.S. from joining the League. The Federal Council of Churches was itself a staunch advocate of American membership in the international body, endorsing the organization as "an earnest endeavor to establish the principles of the Kingdom of God among nations" [2,9,12].

Thus, it was unsurprising that, in 1923, committee member and former Harvard University president Charles Eliot urged the group to push for "the immediate entrance of the United States into the League of Nations," which he believed to be "the best way to secure the rights of religious minorities." In the same spirit, the ACRRM requested that the federal government appoint a delegate to represent the U.S. in the League's Commission on Minorities. "We believe that the unnecessary suffering of minorities in the various countries," the committee declared, "will be greatly relieved in the interest of the United States in their welfare is made evident." That the U.S. had become an influential global power was beyond dispute among committee members [13,14].

As the twenties progressed, however, isolationist sentiments took deeper root in the American psyche. It became clear that repeated petitions and demands had not moved the U.S. any closer to membership in the League of Nations. Nor was the League itself proving particularly successful in achieving large-scale improvements for religious minorities. The ACRRM therefore formalized its work and increasingly began to act as a force for direct change rather than as an agent lobbying the federal government. Committee members believed that "the treatment of religious minorities" constituted "one of the chief problems which have followed the World War" and decided to act on the belief that "entire freedom is the right of every religious body the world over" [2,3,15].

And act they did. Dissatisfied with the response to the petition it issued to the queen of Romania on her visit to the U.S. in 1927, the committee dispatched an investigative group to her country the following year. Upon its return, the group reported continued hostility to various Protestant sects and to Roman Catholics, but it expressed its greatest concern for "Anti-Jewish propaganda," which it denounced as a "widespread and ugly manifestation of racial and religious hatred." The full committee issued a 143-page report detailing the treatment of members of Romania's various faith communities, which was publicized widely by the Federal Council of Churches [16,17].

The crises of the 1930s pushed the ACRRM to maintain its focus to the "countries of Eastern and Southeastern Europe," while expanding to new areas of concern, including Mexico, Egypt, Palestine, and, in particular, Soviet Russia. In increasingly forceful rhetoric, members demanded that U.S. leaders "use their great influence to secure the universal recognition of the principle that religious freedom or the right to worship God freely according to the dictates of conscience is a primary human right." In one of its most widely reported actions, the committee circulated a public statement denouncing the persecution against Jews, Protestants, and Catholics in the Soviet Union—persecution, it noted, that was "on a scale unprecedented in modern times." The *New York Times* cheered the "clearness and disinterestedness" of the committee's discussion of the "human issues involved in violation of religious liberty in Russia," and urged that the report "have the widest possible circulation" [18–20].

That Americans at large would endorse such a project is unsurprising; religious liberty had, after all, long been a core tenet of the political culture of the United States. What is extremely noteworthy here, however, is that the acceptance—indeed, the embrace of—religious minorities had now become a value that leading Americans sought to export abroad. Even more telling of the cultural shift was the way in which the *New York Times* viewed the committee's membership. For the newspaper's editors, it was to be expected that an interreligious body would speak for the views of leading Americans. The differences separating Protestants, Catholics, and Jews had become akin to divergences of political affiliation. They were minor distinctions that in no way rendered someone less deserving of the right to speak for the nation.

Indeed, as the 1930s progressed, the concerns of non-Protestant minorities occupied an ever-growing focus of the ACRRM. Its members expressed concern for Roman Catholics following a "great ... demonstration" against them in Northern Ireland. The group also raised anxieties about Orthodox minorities in Poland, which marked a notable shift, given that Orthodox churches had often been the source of persecution of minorities elsewhere in Eastern Europe [21,22].

However, by far the greatest occupier of the committee's time during the 1930s was the explosion of hostility toward Jews throughout Europe. Within a year of Hitler's rise to power, the group issued a statement—again, circulated in the press—that denounced as "deplorable" the increasing "persecution of Jewish citizens" in Germany. As they had done for over a decade, committee members grounded their critique in assertions of a fundamental right to free religious practice. "We are concerned solely with the question of justice and humanity, the common, inalienable rights of men everywhere, irrespective of race or religion." As the decade progressed, "anti-Semitism was growing by leaps and bounds in Germany, Italy, Poland, Hungary, and Roumania," and combatting it demanded larger and larger effort. Moreover, it increasingly seemed that values of pluralism at home had come under attack. In one public statement, the ACRRM blasted the "cold pogrom" against German Jews, but, even more worryingly, the desire of the Nazis to spread anti-Semitism to the rest of the world, including the United States [21,23,24].

The specter of the various crises of the 1930s also inspired the ACRRM to adopt a more public presence. At a 1935 event at the Carnegie Hall Free Synagogue, committee members sought to expand public awareness of persecution against minority faiths—especially Jews—in Russia, Mexico, and Germany. The three speakers chosen reflected the interfaith membership of the group: ACRRM chairman Arthur Brown spoke for Protestant communities, while diplomat William Sands represented

Catholicism and former New York attorney general Carl Sherman represented Judaism. In its report on the event, the *New York Times* noted the "closely integrated fight" by members of all three faiths. Such language reinforced the degree to which Protestants, Catholics, and Jews were viewed as equal partners in these efforts. However, the story noted another development as well: with the Great Depression continuing, economic anxieties had trumped religious ones. Concern for the preservation of religious values was increasingly seen as less important than policy reforms to ease hardship. This reality would hinder the ACRRM all the more as the decade progressed [25].

Yet the significance of the ACRRM was not limited to its success or to the scope of its work. It was noteworthy for its approach to religious pluralism in four important ways. First, it was not merely a group of Christian—or Protestant—Americans demanding religious toleration abroad. On the contrary, the committee always maintained an inclusive membership. If a Catholic or Jewish representative needed to resign, another member of the same faith was quickly appointed. The committee's publicity likewise emphasized the makeup of the group. Media reports noted that membership consisted of "men of differing political and religious convictions—Jews, Protestants, and Catholics" and saw this as an asset as it made its case both domestically and abroad. Most notably, despite the committee's formation under the umbrella of the Protestant Federal Council of Churches, the Catholic and Jewish representatives were not relegated to second-class status in the group. They were fully integrated into the group's work, so much that the prayer of invocation at meetings rotated among representatives of the three faiths [4].

Second, and closely related, their documentation of the plight of religious minorities abroad pushed ACRRM members to think critically about religious and racial minorities in the United States. At a 1939 meeting, George Haynes, the founder of the Urban League and a professor at the City College of New York, urged committee members to recognize that from the perspective of "Negroes, Indians, Mexicans and Orientals in the United States," it seemed that "organized religion is failing them in their struggles for justice and goodwill." During the interwar period, the committee never matched its enthusiasm for activism on behalf of religious minorities with support for racial and ethnic minorities in the United States, though some of the committee's members were active in other programs of the Federal Council of Churches that did seek to improve race relations in the U.S. Regardless, the committee's invitation to Haynes emphasized the extent to which its members envisioned a broadly pluralistic society rather than one dominated by a specific ethnic and religious identity [13,26].

Third, the diversity of the ACRRM and the breadth of its activities assured its focus was on all minority faiths, which set it in stark contrast to its counterparts in Europe. Throughout the 1920s, the committee maintained close contact with politicians and groups that shared its commitment. Yet, these Europeans were often far narrower in their definition of religious minorities than were members of the American committee. In its own report on the condition of "religious minorities" in Romania, one organization noted that "Roman Catholics and Protestants" had leveled complaints against the majority Orthodox community. While the ACRRM made the plight of Jewish Romanians a constant focus of its work, such concerns went largely unaddressed by European Christian groups [27].

Finally, the broadness of the committee's inclusiveness grew even more expansive as time progressed. By the late twenties, the ACRRM began to press even beyond the threefold Protestant-Catholic-Jewish representation of religious diversity in the United States. In 1930, its members passed a resolution calling for religious communities in the United States to "use every proper resource consistent with their faith and practice to keep alive and develop a stronger moral consciousness of the inestimable value of the principles of religious freedom for the welfare of religion and of humanity." The resolution was directed not only to churches and synagogues but also to "the representatives of other religions" [18].

Thus, the ACRRM represented a body fully committed to the ideal of pluralism. Whether in details as small as the prayers at meetings or as large as its definition of minority faiths in other nations, it was broadly inclusive of Catholics and Jews. Moreover, despite its limited view of American diversity as consisting of Protestantism, Catholicism, and Judaism, the committee's constant attention to the plight of minority communities pushed its members to think about diversity in new ways. Thus, the ACRRM embodied an expanding understanding of pluralism as it exported its vision to the world at large.

2. The ACRRM and American Opinions on Pluralism

Despite its tireless efforts, the ACRRM was, on the face of it, a failure. In the two decades between the World Wars, the committee, like other similar endeavors, failed to meaningfully alter the status of religious minorities in most of the countries targeted by its efforts. However, as much attention as its members called to the growing persecution of Jews in Germany and Nazi-controlled territories, as well as hostility to minority faiths elsewhere, there existed little political will in the United States to act in the international realm. By the outbreak of World War II, the committee found itself impotent as it continued its denunciations of Nazi Germany.

Despite its inability to end the rampant persecution of minority religious communities during the interwar period, however, the ACRRM had enormous significance. It marked the first sustained attempt by leading Americans to articulate a new view of religious pluralism on the global stage. While much of the group's rhetoric was couched in language of tolerance of minorities, the fundamental premise of their work was that religiously diverse societies should be embraced as the norm. Committee members took as their starting-point the conviction that Protestants, Catholics, and Jews—and, by 1930, adherents of other traditions as well—were all important contributors to the civic life of the United States.

It was no coincidence that many of the members of the ACRRM had long records as champions of an inclusive, pluralistic religious culture in the United States. Foremost in this realm was Charles Henry Brent, an Episcopalian who served as a bishop in upstate New York and who had been the chief of chaplains of the American Expeditionary Force in Europe during World War I. Brent had used the chaplaincy corps as a vehicle for enacting an inclusive vision of national life. During the war, he had emphasized his commitment to fostering "a sense of brotherhood among the chaplains," and to ensuring that, regardless of whether they were Protestant, Catholic, or Jewish, all chaplains would have "a spirit of respect for one another's convictions." Brent himself had emphasized that all religions shared a common interest. At the headquarters of the military chaplaincy, he had staff members from all three faiths, and "each of us had to care for the interests of the others as he would care for his own." Such an approach helped to alleviate the sense that Catholics and Jews were religious minorities in a Protestant army. Brent further contributed to such a spirit by participating in a Rosh Hashanah celebration by Jewish soldiers during the war [28–30].

During the 1920s, Brent became active in efforts to foster this spirit of religious pluralism back in the United States. He joined the American Association on Religion in Universities, an interfaith effort of Protestants, Catholics, and Jews to encourage inclusiveness on college campuses. The group—which was active for much of the twenties and which achieved its greatest success in the establishment of a school of religion at the University of Iowa—sought to challenge the perception of students who witnessed "divisions and competitions" or "strife" among faith traditions, rather than "the undergirding unity" that existed among Protestantism, Catholicism, Judaism, and, ultimately, other religions as well [31].

While Charles Brent enjoyed enormous stature from his prominence during World War I, many other noted Protestants joined or contributed to the efforts of the ACRRM. Many of these men had demonstrated an equally longstanding commitment to the endorsement of pluralism in the United States. Charles Macfarland, another founding member of the committee and a key figure in the Federal Council of Churches, served on the Federal Council's Committee on Goodwill between Jews and Christians. That body, formed in the early 1920s, sought to "promote understanding" between the two traditions through pulpit exchanges, community discussions, and a curriculum for schools that would promote "studies of the contribution of the Jew, the Catholic, and the Protestant" to national life. The work of the Committee on Goodwill was built on the foundational belief that members of all three faiths represented stakeholders in American society [32,33].

Other Protestants in the orbit of the ACRRM were equally involved in the interfaith movement of the twenties and thirties. The noted Union Seminary theologian Reinhold Niebuhr, who did not join the committee but attended several of its meetings, stressed in correspondence his affinity for Judaism and his sense of having "more in common" with many liberal Jews than with conservative Christians. Another contributor to the ACRRM was Everett Clinchy, who became director of the National Conference of Christians and Jews (NCCJ), which was established in the late twenties. Under Clinchy's leadership, the NCCJ exemplified the ideals of a pluralistic nation. Responding to the "spiritual, moral and social issues" that resulted from the Great Depression, the new interfaith organization proclaimed that "as Catholics, Jews, and Protestants we regard society as a cooperative human brotherhood." Echoing the same critique that the ACRRM directed abroad, NCCJ members lamented that American society failed "to reflect the principles of justice and brotherhood which our religious teachings share in common." Thus, even as they expressed their pluralist vision internationally, religious leaders such as Clinchy did not lose sight of imperfections at home. Two other ACRRM members, Charles Brent and Charles Macfarland, also joined the NCCJ, which became the lasting institutional embodiment of the interfaith movement of the twenties [34–36].

Roman Catholic members of the ACRRM likewise demonstrated a longstanding commitment to a broader idealization of religious pluralism. In large part, this was due to the reality of life as a minority faith community, and it reflected a pragmatic solution to the realities of American society more than a shift in outlook. Nevertheless, regardless of their motivation, Catholics' rhetoric invoked a newfound embrace of diversity. The aging Cardinal James Gibbons, who was a member of the committee in its earliest days, had long denounced any claim of conflict between Roman Catholicism and citizenship. He insisted that there was "no barrier" that separated Catholics from other Americans. Gibbons also acknowledged that an "overwhelming majority" of non-Catholic Americans "understand and appreciate" their Catholic neighbors. Indeed, on occasion Gibbons drew direct parallels between the experience of Catholics and that of Jews in the United States, highlighting the status of both as minority faiths whose presence was valued in a pluralistic society. Another Catholic member of the ACRRM, New York physician James J. Walsh, devoted his career to demonstrating the compatibility between Catholic faith and the commitment to education and progress that defined American culture in the early twentieth century. This was precisely the ideology that the committee would itself embody and export abroad: that differences of religion were minor and in no way affected a person's ability to be a good citizen [37,38].

As an even smaller minority, and, unlike Roman Catholics, existing outside the boundaries of Christianity, Jews likewise felt an obligation to prove their commitment to American ideals. Like Gibbons and Walsh, the Jewish members of the ACRRM articulated a positive vision of pluralistic societies and actively participated in efforts to build acceptance of religious diversity within the United States. Oscar Straus had long championed inclusion, and as early as the 1890s had publicly denounced the "bigoted fanatics" who falsely claimed "that this is a Christian country in the sense that Protestant Christianity is the basis of our government, and that the rights of Catholics, Jews and Free-thinkers need not be considered." During the 1920s, he became involved with various interfaith organizations as he used the Protestant periodical *Outlook* to emphasize his personal history of support for religious minorities abroad. Likewise, Stephen Wise worked with Charles Macfarland and other members of the Committee on Goodwill between Jews and Christians. The rabbi served as a speaker for one of the public addresses to businessmen's clubs that became a core aspect of the committee's efforts to expand the popularity of its ideals among respectable professionals. Like their Protestant counterparts on the ACRRM, both Wise and Straus became involved with the National Conference of Christians and Jews [39–42].

As the religious leaders affiliated with the ACRRM offered a voice for pluralism, their message was echoed by the various political luminaries aligned with the committee. Charles Evan Hughes, one of the initial members of the group and the eventual Chief Justice of the Supreme Court, served as a public face for one of the most prominent interfaith events of the 1920s: the Goodwill Dinner held in New York City in 1926. The evening, organized by the Committee on Goodwill between Christians and Jews, drew a crowd in the hundreds and included representatives of major Protestant denominations and the three principal branches of Judaism. Hughes guided the festivities, and in his keynote address emphasized that the U.S. represented "a nation which was founded in neither race nor creed," and thus it was essential to foster a spirit of "mutual understanding, friendly accord, and earnest cooperation for the common good" among Christians and Jews alike. This was precisely the view of a healthy society that the ACRRM worked to transmit abroad in the same years [43].

Herbert Hoover, who served alongside Hughes on the ACRRM in its earliest days (both men withdrew as they rose to higher office in the twenties), likewise had a longstanding commitment to the advancement of pluralism. Despite the anti-Catholic rhetoric that would tarnish his 1928 campaign against Al Smith, Hoover had been instrumental in fostering the inclusion of Catholics in national life during World War I. Early in the war, he identified the benefits of embracing Catholics as full partners in the war effort, and, in correspondence with Charles Brent, came to emphasize an inclusive vision. During the 1920s, Hoover sustained personal ties with Protestant and Jewish leaders of the interfaith movement, including several members of the Committee on Goodwill Between Jews and Christians [44,45].

3. Conclusions: Legacies of the ACRRM

In the decades between the two World Wars, the American Committee on Religious Rights and Minorities brought together influential figures from the political realm and from the three major faith traditions in the United States in support of a common cause: a pluralistic international vision. The Protestant, Catholic, and Jewish members of the committee all shared a longstanding commitment to advancing the belief that religious pluralism represented a social strength, not a weakness that should cause concern. These luminaries worked to foster an embrace of diversity within the United States, and in the early 1920s formed the committee to spread this value to the world. Despite powerful countervailing forces at home and abroad, ACRRM members publicized, combatted, and tried in vain to build support against the rampant persecution of minority faiths in Eastern Europe, Latin America, the Middle East, and, most tragically for the course of history, in Nazi Germany.

The ACRRM offers a critical challenge to assumptions about Christian nationalism in the United States amid the rampant isolationism of the 1920s and 1930s. First and foremost, the committee was internationalist, not nationalist. Its members recognized the value of international organizations such as the League of Nations, and they believed that the United States had an obligation to actively participate in global affairs. However, unlike many other internationalist movements in the U.S. during the same period, the ACRRM was intentionally inclusive rather than exclusively Christian. It modeled interfaith interaction in the minute details of its work, and in its public actions it gave equal prominence to its Catholic and Jewish members. In both its words and its deed, the committee offered a new ideal of pluralist internationalism, which proved to be its lasting legacy. Though its message did not become dominant during the interwar period, the ideals it cultivated became core values that permeated American society during the second half of the twentieth century [46–48].

Conflicts of Interest: The author declares no conflict of interest.

References

1. Minutes of the Meeting of the American Committee on the Rights of Religious Minorities (ACRRM), 27 January 1927, folder 18, box 18, Records of the Federal Council of the Churches of Christ in America, Presbyterian Historical Society, Philadelphia. 1927.
2. Carole Fink. *Defending the Rights of Others: The Great Powers, the Jews, and International Minority Protection, 1878–1938.* Cambridge: Cambridge University Press, 2004, vol. 3, pp. 5–7, 151–60, 274–83, 317.

3. Minutes of the Special Committee for the Protection of the Rights of Religious Minorities in Other Countries, 7 April 1920. Federal Council Records, Presbyterian Historical Society, Philadelphia.
4. Minutes of the ACRRM, June 7, 1929, folder 18, box 18, Federal Council Records, Presbyterian Historical Society, Philadelphia.
5. Michael G. Thompson. *For God and Globe: Christian Internationalism in the United States between the Great War and the Cold War*. Ithaca: Cornell University Press, 2015, chap. 1, 2.
6. Andrew Preston. *Sword of the Spirit: Religion in American War and Diplomacy*. New York: Alfred A. Knopf, 2012, pp. 297–303.
7. Richard M. Gamble. *The War for Righteousness: Progressive Christianity, the Great War, and the Rise of the Messianic Nation*. Wilmington: ISI Books, 2003, pp. 224–31, 239–49.
8. Matthew Avery Sutton. *American Apocalypse: A History of Modern Evangelicalism*. Cambridge: The Belknap Press of Harvard University Press, 2014, pp. 207–25.
9. Cara Lea Burnidge. *A Peaceful Conquest: Woodrow Wilson, Religion, and the New World Order*. Chicago: The University of Chicago Press, 2016, chap. 4.
10. Kevin M. Schultz. *Tri-Faith America: How Catholics and Jews Held Postwar America to its Protestant Promise*. New York: Oxford University Press, 2011.
11. Matthew S. Hedstrom. *The Rise of Liberal Religion: Book Culture and American Spirituality in the Twentieth Century*. New York: Oxford University Press, 2013.
12. David Mislin. *Saving Faith: Making Religious Pluralism an American Value at the Dawn of the Secular Age*. Ithaca: Cornell University Press, 2015, chap. 4, 6.
13. "Faith in League of Nations Re-Affirmed." *Federal Council Bulletin* 3 (1920): 9.
14. Minutes of the ACRRM, 18 January 1923, folder 18, box 18, Federal Council Records, Presbyterian Historical Society, Philadelphia.
15. Mark Mazower. "The Strange Triumph of Human Rights, 1933–1950." *The Historical Journal* 47 (2004): 379–98. [CrossRef]
16. "Treatment of Religious Minorities." *Federal Council Bulletin* 11 (1928): 29.
17. "Safeguarding Religious Minorities." *Federal Council Bulletin* 11 (1928): 10.
18. Minutes of the ACCR, 29 January 1930, folder 18, box 18, Federal Council Records, Presbyterian Historical Society, Philadelphia.
19. "Religious Persecution in Russia." *New York Times*, 24 March 1930, p. 16.
20. "Mexico Atheistic, Lay Report Finds." *New York Times*, 14 October 1935, p. 6.
21. Minutes of the ACRRM, 17 October 1938, folder 18, box 18, Federal Council Records, Presbyterian Historical Society, Philadelphia.
22. Minutes of the ACRRM, 16 May 1939, folder 18, box 18, Federal Council Records, Presbyterian Historical Society, Philadelphia.
23. "Leaders Protest Nazi 'Persecution'." *New York Times*, 29 January 1934, p. 4.
24. "Nazi 'Pogrom' Protested." *New York Times*, 13 May 1935, p. 10.
25. "Religious Liberty Urged By 3 Faiths." *New York Times*, 11 November 1935, p. 7.
26. Minutes of the ACRRM, 22 March 1939, folder 18, box 18, Federal Council Records, Presbyterian Historical Society, Philadelphia.
27. European Central Bureau. "Report of the Present Conditions of Religious Minorities." 1926, folder 18, box 18, Federal Council Records, Presbyterian Historical Society, Philadelphia.
28. Charles H. Brent to Cameron J. Davis, 10 August 1918, folder 6, box 15, Charles H. Brent Papers, Library of Congress, Washington, DC.
29. Charles H. Brent to J.S. Williamson, 18 February 1929, folder 9, box 16, Brent Papers.
30. Charles H. Brent diary entry for 6 September 1918, May 1918 to August 1919 Diary, Box 3, Brent Papers.
31. "Suggestions on the American Association on Religion in Colleges and Universities." Attachment to O.D. Foster to David Philipson, December 3, 1926, folder 5, box 1, series A, David Philipson Papers, Jacob Rader Marcus Center of the American Jewish Archives, Cincinnati, Ohio.
32. Agenda for the Meeting of the Committee on Goodwill between Jews and Christians, 7 January 1926, folder 18, box 18, Federal Council Records, Presbyterian Historical Society, Philadelphia.
33. Minutes of the Committee on Goodwill between Christians and Jews, November 20, 1929, folder 13, box 2, series B, Philipson Papers.

34. Reinhold Niebuhr to Isidore Singer, September 20, 1929, folder 5, box 1, Isidore Singer Papers Jacob Rader Marcus Center of the American Jewish Archives, Cincinnati, Ohio.
35. Attachment to Everett R. Clinchy to David Philipson, March 8, 1933, folder 2, box 1, Philipson Papers.
36. Benny Kraut. "A Wary Collaboration: Jews, Catholics, and the Protestant Goodwill Movement." In *Between the Times: The Travails of the Protestant Establishment in America, 1900–1960*. Edited by William R. Hutchison. New York: Cambridge University Press, 1989, pp. 193–230.
37. James Gibbons. "The Church and the Republic." In *A Retrospect of Fifty Year*. New York: Arno Press, 1972, pp. 211–12, 232.
38. David Mislin. "Roman Catholics." In *The Idea that Wouldn't Die: The Warfare between Science and Religion: Historical and Sociological Perspectives*. Edited by Jeff Hardin and Ronald L. Numbers. Baltimore: Johns Hopkins University Press, forthcoming.
39. Oscar Straus. *Religious Liberty in the United States*. New York: Philip Cowen, 1896, pp. 24–25.
40. Oscar Straus. "Under Four Presidents: The World War." *Outlook*, 22 November 1922, p. 514.
41. "Tentative Program, Federal Council's Committee on Goodwill between Jews and Christians." 1926, folder 13, box 2, Philipson Papers.
42. Everett R. Clinchy to Boris D. Bogen, 6 January 1929, folder 13, box 2, Philipson Papers.
43. "Keynote of Dinner is Religious Amity." *New York Times*, 24 February 1926, p. 19.
44. Charles H. Brent to Herbert Hoover, 13 June 1917, folder 2, box 14, Brent Papers.
45. Herbert Hoover to Charles H. Brent, 15 June 1917, folder 2, box 14, Brent Papers.
46. William R. Hutchison. *Religious Pluralism in America: The Contentious History of a Founding Ideal*. New Haven: Yale University Press, 2003, pp. 196–218.
47. Wendy L. Wall. *"Inventing the American Way": The Politics of Consensus from the New Deal to the Civil Rights Movement*. New York: Oxford University Press, 2008, pp. 132–62.
48. David A. Hollinger. *After Cloven Tongues of Fire: Protestant Liberalism in Modern American History*. Princeton: Princeton University Press, 2013, pp. 20–49.

religions

MDPI

Article

The Protestant Search for 'the Universal Christian Community' between Decolonization and Communism[†]

Gene Zubovich

John C. Danforth Center on Religion and Politics, Washington University in St. Louis, 1 Brookings Dr,
St. Louis, MO 63130, USA; gzubovich@wustl.edu; Tel.: +1-314-935-8328

† The author would like to thank the John C. Danforth Center on Religion and Politics at Washington University
  in St. Louis and its director, Dr. R. Marie Griffith, for providing the support that made writing this
  article possible.

Academic Editor: Mark T. Edwards
Received: 2 December 2016; Accepted: 19 January 2017; Published: 24 January 2017

Abstract: This article investigates the history of American Protestant thought about peoples living
beyond the North Atlantic West, in Asia in particular, from 1900 to the 1960s. It argues that Protestant
thought about the Global South was marked by a tension between universalism and particularism.
Protestants believed that their religion was universal because its core insights about the world were
meant for everyone. At the same time, Protestant intellectuals were attentive to the demands of
their coreligionists abroad, who argued that decolonization should herald a greater appreciation for
national differences. The article traces three distinct stages of Protestant attempts to resolve these
tensions; support for imperialism in the early twentieth century, then for human rights at mid-century,
and finally for pluralism in the 1960s. In doing so, it shows that the specter of the Soviet Union
intensified the Protestant appreciation of national differences and ultimately led to the disavowal of
Protestant universalism.

Keywords: Protestantism; human rights; communism; Soviet Union; Cold War; World Council of
Churches; William Ernest Hocking; Wilfred Cantwell Smith; pluralism

1. Introduction

In 1900, evangelist John R. Mott called for missionaries to 'give all men an adequate opportunity
to know Jesus Christ as their Savior and to become His real disciples' ([1], p. 3). Mott's clarion call
expressed the optimism of his fellow Protestants that they could reach every corner of the world with
their message 'in this generation'. This massive undertaking would be one step in the ultimate goal
of Christianity, which Mott described as 'a means to the mighty and inspiring object of enthroning
Christ in individual life, in family life, in social life, in national life, in international relations, in every
relationship of mankind' ([1], p. 16).

At the beginning of the twentieth century, Protestant leaders insisted that Protestant values could
become part of a universal system of international relations. In articulating these global ambitions,
they had to present their system in such a way that, by their standards, it could make do with the range
of racial, religious, and cultural diversity of the world. By claiming that their religion was universal,
Protestant intellectuals were forced to reinvent Christianity as a worldview that would find common
ground among all the peoples of the world. This article argues that, ultimately, Mott's project was
disavowed by American Protestants because they were unable to meaningfully explain to themselves
why everyone should embrace Protestant values as decolonization and demands for the recognition
of national differences were gaining momentum in the mid-twentieth century. Although they fell

well short of making Protestantism acceptable to the whole world, that process nonetheless pushed Protestant intellectuals to become less tribal, to embrace human rights and decolonization, and to ultimately espouse a more pluralistic understanding of international relations.[1]

Protestant intellectuals developed a Protestant internationalism not only in competition with other religious traditions but also in opposition to political systems they viewed as 'secular'.[2] The clash between Protestant universalism and the particular demands of Protestants in the Global South took place in what Protestant intellectuals saw as a competition with socialism, whose banner would be taken up by the Union of Soviet Socialist Republics (USSR) following World War I (WWI). Rather than simply being anti-communist, Protestant intellectuals were deeply enmeshed with this secular state and its ideology, which they condemned and praised, fought and mimicked. This article argues that Protestant intellectuals worked out their conflicting ideological instincts about their religion and its relationship to ethno-nationalism through their relationship with the Soviet Union and other communist nations [7].

This article focuses on the ecumenical 'Protestant establishment', those non-fundamentalist elites in the 'mainline' denominations who, like Mott, held a great deal of sway in American religious and political life for the first half of the twentieth century.[3] In doing so, it offers a corrective to the literature on Cold War Christian nationalism in the United States, which shows that the United States was portrayed as a religious nation in order to emphasize the country's superiority over its irreligious enemy [11–13]. If the bipolar Christian nationalism of Billy Graham and John Foster Dulles was premised on their belief in irreconcilable differences between a Judeo-Christian America and an atheistic Soviet Union, Protestant internationalists held a multipolar view of international affairs and saw the Cold War as a conflict between people of the same faith, not between religion and irreligion. Their experiences were shaped by global institutions that put them in contact with fellow Christians behind the 'iron' and 'bamboo' curtains, who saw no conflict between communism and Christianity. From the vantage point of Protestant internationalists, who viewed the diversity of their religion rather than the threat of atheism as their great challenge, one can see that Protestant attempts to reckon with the Soviet Union began almost as soon as the Soviet Union did—far earlier than most works on Cold War nationalism acknowledge. Stepping back from Cold War era religious mobilization into a longer chronological frame also helps explain why the hold of the Cold War and Christian nationalism over the American imagination came to such a sudden end in the 'Sixties'.

The article begins by surveying the development of an international Protestant politics in the early twentieth century, as leaders from the North Atlantic West created international institutions that included more and more leaders from the Global South. It then looks at how the existence of a socialist alternative to Protestant internationalism pushed some religious leaders to act more forcefully against imperialism and racism, two of the key concerns of Asian leaders. The article

---

[1] This was not the first time that Protestants imagined their religion as a political system. During the European reformation, Protestantism became a state religion in a number of German principalities. See [2]. In British North America, European exiles created a Puritan commonwealth on the principles of a particular dissenting branch of Protestantism. See [3]. While these nation-building projects had come and gone over the centuries, what stood out about the twentieth century was the Protestant attempt to transcend national boundaries and, instead, to formulate an international Protestant politics.

[2] Recent works on 'secularism' have emphasized criticism of the concept's historical construction. In particular, some scholars have emphasized secularism's Protestant roots. This 'Protestant secularism', they argue, has an embedded bias against religions that emphasize practice and ritual, like Catholicism and Islam. Whether or not Protestant assumptions were embedded in notions of the secular in the United States, Protestant intellectuals continued to self-consciously define themselves in relation to a domestic and international 'secularism'. For an overview of the 'Protestant secularism' literature, see [4]. On the origins of an oppositional relationship between Protestant internationalism and secularism, see [5,6].

[3] This article focuses on those intellectuals and leaders in positions of power in ecumenical Protestant organizations centered on the Federal (after 1950, National) Council of Churches and the World Council of Churches. William R. Hutchison refers to this group as 'the Protestant Establishment', whose membership mostly came from the 'mainline; denominations, including the Northern Methodists, Northern Presbyterians, Congregationalists, Episcopalians, Disciples of Christ, American Baptists, and Evangelical Lutherans. See [8]. Although Mott's emphasis on evangelization would be taken up self-consciously by the neo-fundamentalists of the 1940s, the institutions he helped create were firmly in the hands of the Protestant establishment. On the neo-fundamentalists, see ([9], pp. 15–35). On the invention of the Protestant 'mainline', see [10].

concludes by showing how the questions of race and colonialism so drastically transformed Protestant internationalism by the 1960s that it bore little resemblance to Mott's original enthusiasm for evangelization. Despite the abandonment of Mott's project of converting the world, the search for a yet more universal Protestantism moved the Protestant establishment toward ideas and practices that would remake America's relationship to the world.

2. Universal or Indigenous? The Ambiguity of Protestant Internationalism

In 1900, the same year that Mott called for the "evangelization of the world in this generation," hundreds of thousands of people gathered together in New York City to celebrate a century of missionary work. Called the 'Ecumenical Conference on Foreign Missions', it was attended by past, present, and future presidents, including William McKinley, Benjamin Harrison, and Teddy Roosevelt, along with dignitaries from the North Atlantic West [14]. Missionaries from around the world were in attendance. At Carnegie Hall, the white missionaries were seated together: 'To the left of the main isle were placed delegates from Japan, Korea, Oceanica, the West Indies, China, Central America, Mexico, and South America. To the right were Siam, India, Ceylon, Burma, Assam, Syria, Egypt, Turkey, North and South America, Persia, Arabia, and Africa.' [15]. For several weeks in New York, Protestant clergy and laity boasted about the worldwide reach their missionaries had created over the previous century, often with the help of imperialism. 'When the American flag shook out its starry folds at Santiago and Manila, the question of sovereignty, and also of responsibility, was settled', one speaker declared to thunderous applause. 'For better or for worse, we are in for it. The white man's burden is on us. The Lord give us straightness of shoulder and stiffness of backbone to bear it' [16].

A decade later Mott brought together many of the same missionaries in Edinburgh, Scotland, to continue the negotiations that took place in New York. Comity agreements, which divided up the world between Protestant denominations, were formalized at Edinburgh and a permanent International Missionary Council was created soon after the 1910 meeting to ensure continued cooperation between Protestants worldwide. Again, this was an overwhelmingly Euro-American affair with only a few exceptions [17].

In other ways, Edinburgh was a turning point. Although the meeting was dominated by North American and European representatives,[4] it was the first major international missionary gathering to articulate the idea that the non-Western religions, including Hinduism, Islam, and Buddhism, were not enemies of Christianity and that non-Western Christians would be partners in a global Christian movement ([17], pp. 205–47).

With the gradual inclusion of non-western Christians, some Protestants began to rethink their earlier endorsement of imperialism. When the Boxer Rebellion in China in 1900 and the Amritsar protests in India in 1919 were put down by European armies, missionaries largely sympathized with the colonial powers. But the rebellions did make them increasingly attentive to the twentieth century reality that colonial peoples would not stomach imperialism for much longer.

With the post-WWI trouble in Europe, and especially with the rise of communism and fascism in the interwar era, ecumenical Protestants began reconceiving their religion as a supranational political force that provided a necessary antidote to the petty nationalisms and materialism they believed were rising across the world [5,6,18–20]. They called for unity among Protestants, at home and abroad, at this crucial hour. As Theodore Trost argues, 'for many leaders...the impulse toward church union was anchored not so much in ecclesiology or church doctrine as in the sense of responsibility for a world torn asunder by war during the first half of the twentieth century' ([21], p. 2). Bringing Protestants from across the world together would be a political act in opposition to the forces tearing it apart.

---

4   Since the conference was a gathering of missionaries and representation was based on the money they devoted to missionary work, the 1215 delegates were comprised of 509 British missionaries, 491 North Americans, 169 continental Europeans, and 27 South African and Australians. Only 19 were not of European descent.

By the time the International Missionary Council met in Jerusalem in 1928, the self-conscious attempt to create a universal Protestant body out of a diversity of races and cultures was well underway. The meeting site itself stood as a symbol of the new emphasis on diversity, conceived by the conveners as a meeting point between East and West. At Edinburgh in 1910, only 10 of the 1356 delegates came from outside the North Atlantic West. At Jerusalem in 1928, conveners made sure that half of the total delegates came from non-Western nations. As Michael G. Thompson argues, 'the [International Missionary Council] implemented a kind of early affirmative action quota system', which resulted in 'the first truly representative global assembly of Christians in the long history of the Church' ([19], p. 109).

Four years later, philosopher William Ernest Hocking took stock of the missionary situation in East Asia. The investigation in 1932 was prompted by the Great Depression, which forced missionary groups to tighten their belts. He reported on the ineffectiveness of missionaries, who needed more and better education. The calls for greater efficiency in Hocking's report, however, were obscured by the withering critiques of the old ideology of missions. No longer can imperialism be supported, Hocking insisted, in Asian nations where mass movements protested against Western rule. He reassured his readers that the 1900 Boxer rebellion had been 'the last serious act of... resistance' against 'the flood of international idea and practice'. Now, 'newer nationalism is inclusive' and takes the best of Western ideas 'as its own' ([22], p. 22). Partly because of the widespread anti-Western sentiment and partly because the new nationalism was not as threatening to the West, Christian institutions should be handed over to locals as quickly as possible, he advised. Social development—building schools, hospitals, orphanages—should be emphasized over conversion. And common ground must be found between Christianity and other world religions.

The problem, as Hocking saw it, ran deeper than the tarnishing of Christianity because of its close association with colonialism. Spreading Christianity could itself be a form of cultural imperialism because the religion is so embedded in a distinctly Euro-American history and culture. Therefore, he came to believe that Christianity, in its current state, could not be exported to Asia. As read by many admirers and critics, Hocking indicted the whole missionary project as hopelessly parochial and a barrier to the search for the unity of mankind [23]. But what to do about the problem of a religion rooted in 'Western' culture that claimed it was for everybody was less than clear. According to Hocking, the Protestant church had done more than any other group to create 'the universal Christian community', which is now functioning 'as preparation for world unity in civilization'. The philosopher argued that:

> The world must eventually become a moral unity: to this end, it was necessary that the apparent localism of Christianity should be broken down. It must not be thought of as solely the religion of the West. It was because Christianity is *not* western, but universally human, that it must be brought back to the Orient and made at home there. ([22], p. 8)

Hocking's criticism moved in two contradictory directions. First, he wanted push forward the political project of Protestant universalism to find a stripped-down Christian core and use it to bind together all nations in a way that no other faith could do. Second, he wanted missionaries to respect cultural differences and to indigenize the Christian faith, which implied pluralism and a weakening of the ties that bind nations together [24–32].

These two parallel commitments of universalism and national particularity went unreconciled in Hocking's thought. Indeed, they were irreconcilable. Should Protestant Christianity be made indigenous, making it more Chinese and Japanese, or should it be made more universal by stripping away its Western particularities to get at a core universal message? Was 'the apparent localism of Christianity' to 'be broken down' or was Christianity to be 'made at home' in the Orient? This was the central, unresolved ambiguity in the Protestant international project.

Hocking did not recognize the tension between the universal and the indigenous in his thought. He emphasized instead that both positions meant that Protestants should renounce cultural imperialism. As a practical matter, missionaries should talk less and listen more, they should respect and cooperate with independence movements, and they should forfeit some of their institutional power so that non-Western Christians could have more of it. The 1932 Hocking report was, to date, the most important attempt to sever the missions project from its historical role of justifying and supporting Western imperialism. Would the emergence of the post-colonial nation-state in East Asia help or hinder 'world unity in civilization'? Hocking did not tell us.

3. Protestant Internationalism as an Alternative to Socialism

The great competitor of Protestant internationalism for much of the twentieth century was socialist internationalism. As Samuel Moyn argues, by the 1930s Protestant internationalists positioned themselves in relation to 'a Soviet enemy that claimed for itself the mantle of secularism'. ([18], p. 24). The Soviet Union was promoting the cause of national independence throughout the world in a more vociferous and sustained way than Protestant internationalists were doing, so too did Soviet intellectuals posit a universal system of values that purported to solve the political crises of the era. Through the Third International, activists in China, colonial Southeast Asia and Africa, Latin America, and India came to envision the universal system of socialism as the best means for attaining national independence and developing their young nations [33]. At a time when the United States championed white supremacy and the European powers swapped colonies between themselves, socialist internationalism found many sympathetic ears in the Global South. American missionaries in Asia noted this development and sent reports back home about the popularity of socialism abroad.

While the ur-theorist of socialism, Karl Marx, wrote about imperialism as a force that would thrust the backwards peoples of Asia into the modern world, Lenin instrumentalized anti-imperialism in his revolutionary struggle in Russia. During WWI and the civil war that followed, he renounced territorial concessions, called for national independence for colonized nations, and granted cultural autonomy to many nationalities in the former Russian Empire. According to Francine Hirsch, Soviet experts pursued a policy of 'double assimilation' within the USSR, which encouraged people to become Soviet by becoming members of an ethno-nationality ([34], p. 14). Lenin created new republics, like the Belarussian and Uzbek Soviet Socialist Republics, which would have some linguistic and cultural autonomy, while remaining part of the Soviet Union's political community. This was a compromise reached after a debate between rival factions in the Bolshevik party. Some members of the party had maintained, according to Terry Martin, that 'once the proletariat had seized power... national self-determination became irrelevant' ([35], p. 2). The simultaneous promotion of nationality and Soviet unity was a compromise between the universalist ambitions of Soviet socialism and a recognition of the vigor of nationalism among certain ethnic communities during World War I. 'In an effort to reconcile their anti-imperialist position with their strong desire to hold on to all of the lands of the former Russian Empire,' Hirsch writes, 'the Bolsheviks integrated the national idea into the administrative-territorial structure of the new Soviet Union' ([34], p. 5).

The challenge for Protestant intellectuals was not simply that there was a competing universalist ideology that promised to solve the same problems of colonialism and international disorder. Ecumenical Protestant leaders were forced to deal with attacks from the right that used the USSR as a reference point. Similarly, many Protestant intellectuals were influenced by the social gospel and their program for reform was described as 'communistic' by American conservatives [36–42]. Socialism also claimed to be secular and scientific, opposed to what Soviet leaders saw as the superstition of religious leaders. Many of the ecumenical Protestant intellectuals likewise saw themselves as invested in science against their anti-Darwinian fundamentalist opponents [43,44]. Americans involved in international Protestant ventures defined themselves in relation to this socialist other, but, while fundamentalists and many Catholics positioned their faith as communism's polar opposite, ecumenical Protestants had a more ambivalent relationship with the Soviet Union, which was full of fear, jealousy, mimicry, and compromise. In the complicated relationship with the USSR, communism acted as a mirror to the parochialism of American Protestantism, moving them further in their aspiration to discard their cultural baggage and emerge as a yet more universal force on behalf of social justice in the world.

The Protestant intellectuals most closely engaged with the Soviet Union were not just church leaders; they were experts in foreign affairs before the professionalization of foreign policy analysts took place during WWII and the Cold War. For example, the future Methodist Bishop G. Bromley Oxnam travelled to the USSR in 1926 on a fact-finding mission that met with Stalin and other high-ranking officials, and he gave a series of public talks on everything from the Soviet New Economic Policy to the condition of the peasantry [45].

During his trip, Oxnam met with Soviet Foreign Minister Georgy Chicherin, who he described as 'one of the ablest diplomats in Europe.' At the meeting, Oxnam 'was struck immediately by the number of pictures of Oriental leaders' on Chicherin's wall ([45], p. 67). The Soviet Union was leading a great anti-imperialist drive across the world, Oxnam concluded, that was already succeeding in places like Persia and China. If Americans cling to imperialism, he instructed his fellow Protestants, they will find that 'there are lined up in the East one billion out of a total world population of one billion seven hundred or eight hundred million' led by the USSR ([45], p. 75). For Oxnam, accepting the inevitability of decolonization was a dramatic turnabout. In 1919, just seven years earlier, he had personally witnessed a riot in India and he recoiled at the burning of several Christian churches by Hindu nationalists. His diaries record him praising the actions of the British troops at the Amritsar massacre, which left 379 unarmed protesters dead. 'The Indians little realize the power of modern weapons, but I understand they were taught something of a lesson at Amritsar,' he wrote. 'One feels terrible over the whole situation. It means that mission work will be slowed up for years' ([46], pp. 93–97). It took a trip to the USSR for Oxnam to disavow imperialism.

Oxnam called for the recognition of the Soviet Union soon after he returned from his trip, a move that found support among ecumenical Protestants but one that was largely opposed by fundamentalist Protestants and the Catholic clergy who, in very different ways, feared the spread of atheistic communism. In the 1930s, as Oxnam became involved in popular front groups that aided republican fighters in Spain, he found himself clashing once more with Catholic supporters of Francisco Franco. For Oxnam, genuine concern about the Vatican's policies and the American Catholic hierarchy's resistance to a variety of liberal values merged with historic Protestant antipathy toward Catholics. His resistance to joining Catholics in the 'Judeo-Christian' Cold War alliance against the Soviet Union would bring him before the House Un-American Activities Committee in 1953 ([12], pp. 105–56; [20], pp. 128–51; [46]).

During World War II, Oxnam lead his fellow Methodists in transforming the values of the Jerusalem Conference of 1928 and the Hocking report of 1932 into a political program for the reconstruction of international affairs after the war. Oxnam orchestrated the Methodist Crusade for World Order, which was among the most impressive mobilizations on behalf of the United Nations and human rights in the 1940s ([47], pp. 161–62). At this moment, they turned to human rights as a political framework that best expressed Hocking's ideas. It occurred at a historical moment when the wartime alliance with the Soviet Union muted criticism of the communist nation and when the spirit of wartime unity meant that universalist ideals were ascendant and pluralism was looked upon with suspicion.

In 1943, Methodists gathered at Ohio Wesleyan University to discuss the postwar peace. At this meeting, Methodist Bishop Francis J. McConnell explained to the audience at the university that human rights stood at the heart of Christian civilization. For McConnell, Christian civilization was not an immanent development but a long-term project. He told listeners that it took millions of years of the earth's physical development to allow life to be created and it took thousands of years of Judaism to make people receptive to Christianity. In the same way, it will take a long era of human rights to create the groundwork for Christian civilization, McConnell argued. In the midst of global war against nations that rejected the basic premises of liberalism, it was the grounds on which Christianity rested that had to be defended, which included 'freedom to think, to question established beliefs and institutions, and to publish results, to work with some degree of security as to livelihood'. For Christianity to thrive, 'a basis must be kept under Christianity,' McConnell argued ([48], p. 32).

McConnell's assertion that Christianity must stand on liberal values clashed with the analysis of Reinhold Niebuhr, whose 1944 book *Children of Light and Children of Darkness* was a critique of liberalism. Niebuhr was insistent that only the insights of Christianity on the nature of man could serve as a grounding for liberal democracies. Those insights included a belief in a power beyond mankind, awe at the vastness of the universe, and a chastened sense of the power of individuals and nations. Christianity should come to the aid of liberalism, Niebuhr argued, not the other way around [5,49,50].

Niebuhr developed a distinctly religious international politics, but he narrowed the meaning of Protestant internationalism in two ways. First, he argued that Protestant Christianity did not have a monopoly on ultimate values and that Jews and Catholics, too, could come to liberalism's defense through their particular values. Secondly, Niebuhr's conception of what counted as religious resources was remarkably thin. As David Hollinger argues, 'Niebuhr presented a series of quite general virtues as products of Christianity, without explicitly denying the possibility that these virtues might be cultivated and propagated without Christianity' ([51], p. 218).

Together, McConnell and Niebuhr represented diverging ways of dealing with the problem of translating Protestant principles into universal political ideas that could make do with the ethnic, racial, and cultural diversity of the world. How could Protestant values be sold to Buddhists and Hindus, let alone to the Soviet Union? Niebuhr doubled-down on the important role of Christianity and called on his coreligionists to oppose the USSR [11–13]. McConnell, on the other hand, saw no easy path to reconciling Protestant values with a diverse world, and he retreated to what he believed was the more neutral language of secular liberalism. He was not unusual in this regard. O. Fredrick Nolde, the Protestant liaison to the State Department and United Nations on human rights, likewise believed that Protestant principles must be translated into a language that was more universal than Protestantism, if human rights were to make any headway in a world organization that included the officially-atheistic USSR ([52], pp. 98–100). 'We must reckon with government in its international form,' he told his colleagues in 1946. The 'problem is: here the Churches [represent only] a minority of the earth's population' ([53], p. 86).

Most Protestant intellectuals continued to have it both ways in the 1940s. They continued to preach both universalism and pluralism, as Hocking himself had done in the prior decade. The Methodist missionary and best-selling author E. Stanley Jones wrote in 1944 that 'each nation must dare to be itself, must dare believe that it has a call and a commission to offer humbly to the rest its own interpretation of the Universal Fact. Just as each individual must allow the Spirit of God to pull out the stops and play all over the keyboard of his life, so each nation must present itself to God to be played over so that its notes, definitive and distinctive, may be a part of the universal harmony' ([54], p. 8). Jones' line of reasoning left unanswered why Christianity must be the score that the world plays and why the new nations of the Global South would remain in the orchestra.

The vibrant discussions among Protestant intellectuals in the 1940s inspired the Methodist Board of Missions to carefully consider the issue of racism. The final product of dozens of ensuing study groups and conferences was Edmund Soper's *Racism: A World Issue*, published in 1948 [55]. The book's chapters covered the major regions of the world and offered an appraisal of the history and current state of race relations in each country. It was among the most careful and nuanced studies of racism available in the 1940s. The book was meant to explain to its readers the problem of racism across the world and to encourage them to take action against it.

The exploration of racial practices in the Soviet Union, in particular, was designed to provincialize American racism. For Soper, the Soviet Union provided a model for how to deal with a plurality of racial minorities in one nation. He looked to a country that, according to Yuri Slezkine, 'was the world's first state to institutionalize ethnoterritorial federalism, classify all citizens according to their biological nationalities and formally prescribe preferential treatment of certain ethnically defined populations' ([56], p. 415). Soper concluded that the differences between the USSR and US resulted from the different legal systems. In the United States, immigrants are expected to 'merge, lose their former distinctive features, and become completely amalgamated,' whereas the USSR had a policy of 'local and racial autonomy' and the stated purpose was 'to retain [the nationality's] own distinctiveness, language, traditions, and customs' ([55], p. 80). Soper believed that human rights could function along the lines of the 1936 Soviet Constitution, which protected the cultural rights of minorities. We are 'beginning to realize that the racial problem is not a problem by itself but one which is a part of another, that of basic human rights,' Soper wrote ([55], p. 80). He urged American Christians to develop a social ethic in America to match the force of communism in the USSR.

At the very moment when Protestant leaders publically aligned themselves with human rights and antiracism, they were pushed further in these directions by their coreligionists from communist nations. In 1948, the long dream of a Protestant international came to life in the World Council of Churches' (WCC) inaugural gathering in Amsterdam. What should have been a celebratory moment of the work begun by Mott in Edinburgh in 1910 was clouded by deep divisions between American Protestants and those from communist East-Central Europe. The Czechoslovak theologian Josef Hromadka, in particular, became a spokesperson for communism at the meeting's discussion of economic affairs. The gathering tried to strike a middle way between capitalism and communism, which it called 'the Responsible Society,' but this was a perilous position for American representatives to take during the Red Scare ([5], pp. 124–53; [20], pp. 209–13).

At the 1948 Amsterdam assembly, the representatives elected T.C. Chao, a backer of Mao's communist government in China, as one of the WCC's co-presidents. Chao was forceful in his insistence that China has a distinctive history and its adoption of communism should come as no surprise. He pointed to the long history of imperialism in the country and praised Mao for liberating China from the West and from its feudal past. In the new era that was dawning, religion would no longer be the handmaiden of imperialism. The task now, in China and elsewhere, was for the Christianity to 'confess its sins and shortcomings in seeking to save its own life by occasionally siding with reactionary forces,' he wrote to American Protestants ([57], p. 1067). At a moment when American Protestants were uniting their coreligionists from many lands and translating their religious values into a purportedly universal system of human rights, Chao was insistent that China would go its own way and that Protestantism should accept, and even celebrate, national differences.

Tensions persisted in the ensuing decades as Protestant intellectuals returned to the question of Protestant universalism. The Harvard scholar Wilfred Cantwell Smith cited his experience teaching in India in the 1940s as an affirmation that 'man's life today is cast in a multicultural context. We live in a pluralistic world' ([58], p. 505). Smith was responding to the experience of living in a religiously-diverse city in India, where he regularly encountered Buddhists and Muslims in the Christian college where he worked. He would have also been familiar with Indian critics of Anglo-American supremacy, like Madathilparampil Mammen Thomas, who objected to the Protestant embrace of human rights on the grounds that 'the oneness and universality of the Church is not so manifest as to speak one word and to act in unison in this sphere, and the attempt to do so when we are not ready has only been done by the domination of a certain kind of politics, which may be called Anglo-American' ([20], p. 67). Smith thought of these experiences in 1960 as he explained to his coreligionists that they now lived in 'an age of minorities' and that they, too, needed to change the way they thought about their status. 'Christians have tended to think of themselves as secure in a position of authority,' especially in the countries where they predominate, where 'white men have assumed that they are dominant and Negroes, for instance, a minority to be dealt with in one way or another' ([58], pp. 505–6). Internationally, the 'West has built up a diplomatic and economic world order of its own pattern into which other groups have, with more or less success, gradually come to play a role; but the west remains Western' ([58], pp. 505–6). Smith's attack on religious chauvinism was bound together with antipathy for racism, colonialism, and economic inequality in a general criticism of Western domination.

In his critique of earlier efforts to create world unity in a way that had smuggled in Christian and Western supremacy, Smith held out hope for a form of universal brotherhood. His argument built on the works of Hocking, Soper, and other Protestant intellectuals of the 1930s and 1940s. But unlike Hocking and others who attempted to balance out pluralism and universalism, Smith placed all the emphasis on coming to terms with the world's diversity through the acceptance of difference. He explained that 'the whole of mankind with its radically different civilizations, religious traditions and value systems, its radically different economic and political statuses, should become one community, so that we should be loyal to each other across cultural and creedal as well as political frontiers, both in theory and in practice—this is quite a new challenge' ([58], p. 506). The challenge of diversity was so great for Smith that he predicted it would take an entire age to resolve. Making peace with ethno-national pluralism was akin to the challenge that Greek philosophy presented to early Christianity and that Darwinism presented to Christian orthodoxy in the late nineteenth and early twentieth centuries. Pluralism was the immediate goal now. The creation of a world community would come in some distant future. And this was not a uniquely Christian challenge, Smith observed; 'communists are a minority, and the world will have no peace until they abandon their explosive unwillingness to remain so' ([58], p. 506).

By the time of Smith's 1960 article, Protestant international thought had gone through three great stages in the quest to develop a world community. First, in 1900, Mott believed that the Christian Gospel must be brought to every corner of the world in order to create a more just international order. In 1932, Hocking insisted that the project of exporting Christianity and respecting cultural difference were one in the same. By 1960, Smith cast suspicion on any rendering of Christianity as a universal system, even in the guise of human rights or a Western economic and political order. Smith, like other Protestant intellectuals, was pushed in this direction by Marxist critics like Chao and Thomas in a post-WWII context of rapid decolonization and the ascension of communism. Without ever giving up on the notion that a universal international system was, in fact, possible, he placed all the emphasis on rooting out all pretense of universality.

Mott's ambition to spread Christianity throughout the world was taken up by evangelicals, who did not share the ecumenical Protestant concern for pluralism in the 1960s and 1970s [9,59–69]. Indeed, evangelicals did not just affirm the missionary project that Hocking had rejected in 1932. They explicitly defined their missionary work against the ideology Hocking, Smith, and others had laid out. In 1958, the evangelical intellectual Carl Henry chastised his liberal coreligionists for their 'naïve confidence... that recognition and admission into the family of nations has a reformatory effect' ([70], p. 23). Henry was writing about a recent pronouncement by the main ecumenical Protestant body that urged the United States to recognize 'Red' China and admit it into the United Nations. But Henry's point was broader: American Christians had little to gain in such dialogues and should instead focus on spreading the gospel, which was mankind's only hope. He was skeptical of the 'reformatory effect' that the world was having on ecumenical Protestant intellectuals, who had inherited Mott's institutions but had largely repudiated his vision.

The Protestant celebration of difference, which coincided with the election of John F. Kennedy as America's first Catholic president, is typically narrated as the end of Protestantism's propriety claim over the American nation [71–74]. The Protestant establishment, whose influence in the 1960s still dwarfed evangelical power, made more room for Jews and Catholics in public life and embraced church-state separation, a process that aided Protestant intellectuals' move toward pluralism. As Sydney Ahlstrom put it, 'the decade of the sixties seems in many ways to have marked a new stage in the long development of American religious history. Not only did this intense and fiercely lived span of years have a character of its own, but it may even have ended... a unified four-hundred year period... in the Anglo-American experience' of Protestant exclusivism ([75], p. 1079). Such narratives typically focus on the domestic advent of 'Tri-Faith' America, ignoring developments abroad. As this article has shown, pluralism came to the United States not only through Protestant interaction with American Jews and Catholics, but also through encounters with Hindus and Buddhists, socialists and nationalists in the Global South. Viewed from a more global vantage point, the 1960s marked an even more decisive break; intellectuals like Smith renounced Protestantism's proprietary claim over the entire globe.

That Smith believed communism must come to terms with its own particularity signals the importance of this secular other to the history of Protestant thought. The engagement of some American Protestants from the 1920s to the 1950s with communism moved them to increasingly make peace with secular ideas and pushed them toward antiracism and anti-colonialism. They kept thinking about what Christianity's relationship to international affairs should be, and they derived it from biblical exegeses, from denominational histories, from ethical investigations, and from the insights of ecumenical discussions with coreligionists from a diversity of nations and cultures. They did this with a new sense that there were other equally tenable traditions of international affairs and that they had to relinquish their universal claims. Human rights, to take one example, were no longer defended as a universal translation of Protestant values that could be adopted by everyone. Rather, they were reconceived as a neutral tradition with multiple interpretations and understandings, paving the way for a secularized revival of human rights in the 1970s.[5] Ecumenical Protestant intellectuals continued to relate to international affairs in distinctive ways, informed by theology and tradition, but they now did so without claiming that such understandings were for everyone.

Conflicts of Interest: The author declares no conflict of interest.

References

1. John R. Mott. *The Evangelization of the World in This Generation*. New York: Student Volunteer Movement for Foreign Missions, 1900.
2. Carlos M. N. Eire. *Reformations: The Early Modern World, 1450–1650*. New Haven: Yale University Press, 2016.
3. David D. Hall. *A Reforming People: Puritanism and the Transformation of Public Life in New England*. New York: Knopf, 2011.
4. Charles McCrary, and Jeffrey Wheatley. "The Protestant Secular in the Study of American Religion: Reappraisal and Suggestions." *Religion*. Published electronically 26 October 2016. [CrossRef]
5. Mark Thomas Edwards. *The Right of the Protestant Left: God's Totalitarianism*. New York: Palgrave Macmillan, 2012.
6. Justin Reynolds. "Against the World: International Protestantism and the Ecumenical Movement between Secularization and Politics, 1900–1952." Ph.D. Dissertation, Columbia University, New York, NY, USA, 2016.
7. Ernest Gellner. *Nations and Nationalism, Second Edition*. Ithaca: Cornell University Press, 2009.
8. William R. Hutchison, ed. *Between the Times: The Travail of the Protestant Establishment in America, 1900–1960*. New York: Cambridge University Press, 1989.
9. Molly Worthen. *Apostles of Reason: The Crisis of Authority in American Evangelicalism*. New York: Oxford University Press, 2014.
10. Elesha Coffman. *The Christian Century and the Rise of the Protestant Mainline*. New York: Oxford University Press, 2013.
11. Jonathan P. Herzog. *The Spiritual-Industrial Complex: America's Religious Battle against Communism in the Early Cold War*. New York: Oxford University Press, 2011.
12. William Inboden. *Religion and American Foreign Policy, 1945–1960: The Soul of Containment*. New York: Cambridge University Press, 2008.
13. Kevin M. Kruse. *One Nation Under God: How Corporate America Invented Christian America*. New York: Basic Books, 2015.
14. "Conference for Missions: Welcome to Delegates from All Parts of the World." *New York Times*, 21 April 1900.
15. "A Century of Mission Work: Reviewed at Carnegie Hall..." *New York Times*, 24 April 1900.
16. "Last Day of the Conference." *New York Times*, 2 May 1900.
17. Brian Stanley. *The World Missionary Conference, Edinburgh 1910*. Grand Rapids: William Eerdmans Publishing Company, 2009.
18. Samuel Moyn. *Christian Human Rights*. Philadelphia: University of Pennsylvania Press, 2015.
19. Michael G. Thompson. *For God and Globe: Christian Internationalism in the United States between the Great War and the Cold War*. Ithaca: Cornell University Press, 2015.

---

[5] As Barbara Keys argues, "Before the 1970s, women's, peace, labor, and religious groups with longstanding internationalist agendas were the main guardians of a discourse of international human rights. The achievement of human rights liberals in the 1970s was... to popularize for more secular audiences the human rights talk of religious groups" [76].

20. Gene Zubovich. "The Global Gospel: Protestant Internationalism and American Liberalism, 1940–1960." Ph.D. Dissertation, University of California, Berkeley, CA, USA, 2015.
21. Theodore Louis Trost. *Douglas Horton and the Ecumenical Impulse in American Religion*. Cambridge: Harvard University Press, 2002.
22. William Ernest Hocking. *Re-Thinking Missions: A Laymen's Inquiry after One Hundred Years*. New York: Harper & Brothers, 1932.
23. Mark Greif. *The Age of the Crisis of Man: Thought and Fiction in America, 1933–1973*. Princeton: Princeton University Press, 2015.
24. Amy Gutmann. *Identity in Democracy*. Princeton: Princeton University Press, 2003.
25. David Hollinger. *Postethnic America: Beyond Multiculturalism*. New York: Basic Books, 1995.
26. Will Kymlicka. *Multicultural Citizenship: A Liberal Theory of Minority Rights*. Oxford: Clarendon Press, 1995.
27. David Miller. *On Nationality*. Oxford: Clarendon Press, 1995.
28. Joseph Raz. *Ethics in the Public Domain: Essays in the Morality of Law and Politics*. Oxford: Clarendon Press, 1994.
29. Sarah Song. "What does it mean to be an American? " *Daedalus* 138 (2009): 31–40. [CrossRef]
30. Charles Taylor. "The Politics of Recognition." In *Multiculturalism: Examining the Politics of Recognition*. Edited by Amy Gutmann. Princeton: Princeton University Press, 1994, pp. 25–73.
31. Jeremy Waldron. "Minority Cultures and the Cosmopolitan Alternative." In *The Rights of Minority Cultures*. Edited by Will Kymlicka. New York: Oxford University Press, 1995.
32. Iris Young. *Justice and the Politics of Difference*. Princeton: Princeton University Press, 1990.
33. Odd Arne Westad. *The Global Cold War: Third World Interventions and the Making of Our Times*. New York: Cambridge University Press, 2007.
34. Francine Hirsch. *Empire of Nations: Ethnographic Knowledge & the Making of the Soviet Union*. Ithaca: Cornell University Press, 2005.
35. Terry Martin. *Affirmative Action Empire: Nations and Nationalism in the Soviet Union, 1923–1939*. Ithaca: Cornell University Press, 2001.
36. Susan Curtis. *A Consuming Faith: The Social Gospel and Modern American Culture*. Columbia: University of Missouri Press, 2001.
37. Martin E. Marty. *Modern American Religion, Volume 1: The Irony of It All, 1893–1919*. Chicago: University of Chicago Press, 1986, pp. 286–97.
38. Paul A. Carter. *The Decline and Revival of the Social Gospel*. Ithaca: Cornell University Press, 1956.
39. Gary Dorrien. *Social Ethics in the Making: Interpreting an American Tradition*. New York: Wiley-Blackwell, 2009.
40. Ralph E. Lucker. *The Social Gospel in Black and White: American Racial Reform, 1885–1912*. Chapel Hill: University of North Carolina Press, 1991.
41. Henry F. May. *Protestant Churches and Industrial America*. New York: Harper and Brothers, 1949.
42. Ronald C. White, Jr. *Liberty and Justice for All: Racial Reform and the Social Gospel, 1877–1925*. New York: Harper & Row, 1990.
43. William R. Hutchison. *The Modernist Impulse in American Protestantism*. Cambridge: Harvard University Press, 1976.
44. Edward J. Larson. *Summer for the Gods: The Scopes Trial and America's Continuing Debate over Science and Religion*. New York: Basic Books, 1997.
45. G. Bromley Oxnam. *Russian Impressions*. Los Angeles: self-published, 1927.
46. Robert Moats Miller. *Bishop G. Bromley Oxnam: Paladin of Liberal Protestantism*. Nashville: Abingdon Press, 1990.
47. Robert A. Divine. *Second Chance: The Triumph of Internationalism in America during World War II*. New York: Antheneum, 1967.
48. Francis J. McConnell, ed. *Christian Bases of World Order: The Merrick Lectures, 1943*. Nashville: Abingdon-Cokesbury, 1943.
49. Richard Fox. *Reinhold Niebuhr: A Biography*. New York: Harper & Row, 1987.
50. Heather A. Warren. *Theologians of a New World Order: Reinhold Niebuhr and the Christian Realists, 1920–1948*. New York: Oxford University Press, 1997.
51. David A. Hollinger. *After Cloven Tongues of Fire: Protestant Liberalism in Modern American History*. Princeton: Princeton University Press, 2015.
52. John Nurser. *For All Peoples and All Nations: The Ecumenical Church and Human Rights*. Washington: Georgetown University Press, 2005.

53. Karsten Lehmann. *Religious NGOs in International Relations: The Construction of "the Religious" and "the Secular".* New York: Routledge, 2016.
54. E. Stanley Jones. *The Christ of the American Road.* New York: Abingdon-Cokesbury Press, 1944.
55. Edmund D. Soper. *Racism: A World Issue.* New York: Abingdon-Cokesbury Press, 1947.
56. Yuri Slezkine. "The USSR as a Communal Apartment, or How a Socialist State Promoted Ethnic Particularism." *Slavic Review* 53 (1994): 414–52. [CrossRef]
57. T. C. Chao. "Red Peiping after Six Months." *The Christian Century,* 14 September 1949.
58. Wilfred Cantwell Smith. "Christianity's Third Great Challenge." *The Christian Century,* 27 April 1960.
59. Sara Diamond. *Spiritual Warfare: The Politics of the Christian Right.* Boston: South End Press, 1989.
60. Darren Dochuk. *From Bible Belt to Sunbelt: Plain-Folk Religion, Grassroots Politics, and the Rise of Evangelical Conservatism.* New York: W.W. Norton, 2012.
61. Robert Booth Fowler. *A New Engagement: Evangelical Political Thought, 1966–1976.* Grand Rapids: Eerdmans, 1982.
62. William R. Glass. *Strangers in Zion: Fundamentalists in the South, 1900–1950.* Macon: Mercer University Press, 2001.
63. R. Marie Griffith. *God's Daughters: Evangelical Women and the Power of Submission.* Berkeley: University of California Press, 1997.
64. Barry Hankins. *Uneasy in Babylon: Southern Baptist Conservatives and American Culture.* Tuscaloosa: University of Alabama Press, 2002.
65. Susan Friend Harding. *The Book of Jerry Falwell: Fundamentalist Language and Politics.* Princeton: Princeton University Press, 2000.
66. Darryl G. Hart. *That Old-Time Religion in Modern America: Evangelical Protestantism in the Twentieth Century.* Chicago: Ivan R. Dee, 2002.
67. Randall J. Stephens, and Karl Giberson. *The Anointed: Evangelical Truth in a Secular Age.* Cambridge: Belknap Press of Harvard University Press, 2011.
68. David R. Swartz. *Moral Minority: The Evangelical Left in an Age of Conservatism.* Philadelphia: University of Pennsylvania Press, 2012.
69. Daniel K. Williams. *God's Own Party: The Making of the Christian Right.* New York: Oxford University Press, 2010.
70. "NCC World Order Policy Softens on Red China." *Christianity Today,* 22 December 1958, pp. 23, 29.
71. Will Herberg. *Protestant—Catholic—Jew: An Essay in American Religious Sociology.* Chicago: University of Chicago Press, 1983.
72. Katherine Healan Gaston. "The Genesis of America's Judeo-Christian Moment: Secularism, Totalitarianism, and the Redefinition of Democracy." Ph.D. Dissertation, University of California, Berkeley, CA, USA, 2008.
73. Martin E. Marty. *Modern American Religion, Volume 3: Under God, Indivisible, 1941–1960.* Chicago: University of Chicago Press, 1996.
74. Kevin Schultz. *Tri-Faith America: How Postwar Catholics and Jews Held America to its Protestant Promise.* New York: Oxford University Press, 2011.
75. Sydney E. Ahlstrom. *A Religious History of the American People,* 2nd ed. New Haven: Yale University Press, 2004.
76. Barbara Keys. *Reclaiming American Virtue: The Human Rights Revolution of the 1970s.* Cambridge: Harvard University Press, 2014, vol. 12, pp. 28–30.

religions

MDPI

Article

"This World Is Not My Home": Richard Mouw and Christian Nationalism

Aaron Pattillo-Lunt

Spring Arbor University, Spring Arbor, MI 49283, USA; aaron.lunt@arbor.edu

Academic Editors: Mark T. Edwards and Christine A. James
Received: 6 November 2016; Accepted: 23 December 2016; Published: 27 December 2016

Abstract: American evangelicalism has often been punctuated by dual commitments to the United States and to God. Those commitments were strongest within politically conservative evangelicalism. Though representing a solid majority among professing evangelicals, conservatives could not speak for the movement as a whole. Politically progressive evangelicals, beginning in the 1960s, formed a dissenting opinion of the post-World War II revival of Christian nationalism. They dared to challenge American action abroad, noticeably during the Vietnam War. Their critique of Christian nationalism and conservative evangelicals' close ties to the Republican Party led them to seek refuge in either progressive policies or the Democratic Party. A third, underexplored subgroup of evangelicalism rooted in reformed theology becomes important to consider in this regard. These reformed evangelicals sought to contextualize nationalism in biblical rather than partisan or political terms. This goal is championed well by Richard Mouw, resulting in a nuanced look at evangelical Christians' difficult dual role as both citizens of the Kingdom of God and the United States.

Keywords: evangelicalism; nationalism; Mouw; reformed; Calvinism; Kuyper; Biblicism

1. Introduction

Evangelicalism is one of the most pervasive and dominant movements in United States' history. Yet it has no cut and paste definition. It is diverse and adaptive. Despite this changeability, evangelicals can be loosely defined by their theological views. They are religiously orthodox regardless of their political views. This belief is compounded by a staunch Biblicism, meaning evangelicals take the Bible as the highest authority over all of life. The difficulty of this approach lies in the protestant understanding of the priesthood of believers which affords endless interpretations of the sacred text ([1], p. 7). This informs the diversity within the movement. Different subgroups read the Bible differently and appropriate it as necessary. The consequence of this belief is a fractured movement, united by a firm belief that the Bible is supreme.

A close examination of American evangelicalism reveals that evangelicals do not have a unified approach to American history either. This essay seeks to explore just three such approaches. An acceptance of a Christian America is the dominant view in the movement and is perpetuated by politically conservative evangelicals, henceforth labeled conservative evangelicals. Politically progressive evangelicals, henceforth called progressive evangelicals, critique this view. They argue America cannot be considered uniquely Christian or chosen by God. The last view cannot be politically labeled. Its adherents reach across the aisle and are driven by reformed theology when approaching nationalism. These reformed evangelicals approach American Christianity with an integrationist viewpoint. They are more comfortable recognizing America as a chosen nation, though their understanding of chosen-ness differs from that of conservative evangelicalism. Reformed evangelicals are also critical of the United States' actions nationally and internationally. By injecting a third evangelical subgroup into a discussion on Christian nationalism, this paper intends to reinforce the reality of a diverse evangelicalism through the exploration of a thinker representative of reformed evangelicalism. Before considering these differing viewpoints, a brief understanding of how America can be considered a Christian nation must be discussed. Considering the important role that conservative evangelicals play in advancing this view of the past, they must be inserted into the narrative.

Conservative evangelicals' identity as citizens is rooted in their view of the past. Prominently, they identify their nation as firmly Christian, formed with biblical principles in mind. By doing so, conservative evangelicals find their identity as citizens in their nation's supposedly religious origins. This results in an understanding of history which promotes a distinctly Christian brand of nationalism and a belief that America is exceptional because it is chosen by God.

Proof-texting allows Christian nationalists to utilize documents from the colonial and founding period to support their claims. John Winthrop's "Citty [sic] upon a hill" statement is one key example ([2], p. 65). To the Christian nationalist, Winthrop employed these words to indicate that Puritan settlements in North America were intended by God to be a shining and exportable example to the rest of the world. This allows one to read a sense of divine calling into Winthrop's mission. As historians have pointed out, this reading of history is incomplete. Winthrop's words were meant to be internalized not externalized. Puritans were not to have an exceptional view of themselves. Rather, they were expected by Winthrop to behave themselves so their mission would not fail under the watchful "eies of all people [Puritans still in England] ([2], p. 65)". Winthrop worried moral failure would discredit the Puritans' mission. His words are, therefore, best seen as directed to a specific community for a specific purpose. He sought to build a local, religious, and guilt free community, not construct a national, Christian example.

Regardless of this historical corrective, conservative evangelicals tend to favor a providential viewing of history. A number of prominent evangelicals rise to the fore in this regard—Tim LaHaye (1926–2016), Peter Marshall (b. 1964), and, most recently, David Barton (b. 1954). These three men, and others like them, worked to ensure the myth of a Christian America, as historian Stephen Green titled it, is spread [2]. Marshall and Barton are popular evangelical authors specializing in writing revisionist histories which seek to irrevocably connect Christianity and the United States. Their success is evident when one looks at conservative evangelical circles. These evangelicals are more likely to see the United States' formative years, such as Peter Marshall who commonly asked rhetorically affirmative questions—"Wasn't Christopher Columbus inspired by the Holy Spirit as he sailed west? Weren't the pilgrims who landed on New England's rocky shores driven by divine purpose?"—to enforce this viewing of history ([3], p. 75). These perceptions are incredibly persistent, lasting into the twenty-first century. Conservative evangelical figures continue to comment on the seemingly providential rise to power of the United States, particularly as it pertains to the nation's special, or exceptional, role in God's plan.

This leaves conservative evangelicalism touting a triumphalist, providentially driven view of Christian nationalism. It is a perception that is advanced in this evangelical subgroup's approach to both politics and history. To be clear, a belief in Christian nationhood does not mean that conservative evangelicals trust or even support the government. Instead, they seek to return their nation to its Christian moorings, opposing secularism and progressivism as antithetical to Christianity. This goal led to an alliance with the Republican Party that became solidified in the 1980s.

Despite the power of this conservative line of thought, opposition to the myth of a Christian America can be found in works put forth by evangelical scholars, such as Mark Noll and John Fea, and progressive figures within the movement, such as Jim Wallis or Ronald Sider. This paper will first discuss how leading figures within conservative and progressive evangelicalism have tackled the issue of Christian nationalism. Then its focus will shift towards reformed evangelicalism and the works of Richard Mouw as an example of an evangelical who sidesteps progressive and conservative evangelical approaches to nationalism with an insider's perspective of the movement.

Mouw is a professor of philosophy who taught at both Wheaton and Fuller Theological Seminary—two of the most prominent evangelical schools in the United States. He also served as the president of Fuller from 1993 to 2013. He offers a corrective of Christian nationalism based within evangelicals' own conception of the authoritative role of the Bible and God. Of special importance is how Mouw challenges both progressive and conservative evangelicals to return to their Biblicist roots by using the Bible for its own purposes rather than appropriating it for political or national means. Through his argument, a nonpartisan, third way for evangelicals to approach the issue of nationalism becomes apparent.

2. Results

2.1. Belief: Christian Nationalism in the Conservative Evangelical Movement

Twentieth century evangelicalism descended from the late nineteenth and early twentieth centuries' fundamentalist movement. Fundamentalists were theologically orthodox, separated themselves from the dominant culture, and believed strongly in premillennial dispensationalism. Their beliefs did not include, at least inherently, a strongly nationalistic tendency. Rather, they built small citadels of the faith in every church body that could be viewed as holy amidst a culture and a nation too corrupt to save. From these fortresses, they could preach the end was nigh, hoping to save a final few before Armageddon. Indeed, social engagement was deemed foolish in such a climate ([4], p. 15). Therefore, while neo-evangelicals (referred to only as evangelicals in this paper as the evangelicals of the 19th century are not discussed) were theological descendants of the fundamentalists, their social engagement and their patriotism signified a distinct break from their parent movement. A look at conservative evangelicalism's rise to social prominence indicates how leaders within the movement reconciled fundamentalism's strict theological orthodoxy and deep concern for the prophetic with a strict nationalism.

This reconciliation began with the mid and post-World War II resurgence of evangelicalism. Carl Henry's 1947 jeremiad, *The Uneasy Conscience of Modern Fundamentalism*, signaled an increase in social engagement among evangelicalism as a whole ([5], p. 52). This book was, in many ways, a response to an opportunity which arose in World War II. By 1941, a number of marginalized groups in America found acceptance in the larger culture by supporting the United States' military conflicts ([6], pp. 217–18).[1] Evangelicals did likewise. In asserting their support for the war and its religious aims—defending religious liberty and thereby democracy—they overcame fundamentalism's extremist and detached reputation ([6], pp. 370–71). By doing so, evangelicals indicated that they could not be the same separatist group that *radically* stood against modernization and religious and political progressivism while still holding on to key tenets of fundamentalism. Simply put, the war allowed conservative evangelicals to market themselves as a deeply patriotic group committed to the political and social success of their nation.

For the post-war, conservative evangelical, this national outlook rooted itself in a deeply held belief that America was chosen by God, had a prophetic destiny, and was designed to be Christian. This myth did not originate after World War II. It extended back to revisionist histories written dating back to the 1790s and through the 1800s ([2], pp. 199–41). Regardless, conservative evangelicals had good reasons to contend that America was a Christian nation in the post-war years. An increase in civil religion made it easier for conservative evangelicals to build on the Christian America myth by looking at the past. Historian Kevin Kruse illustrated how a Christian America was reinforced beginning in the 1930s as a response to the New Deal rather than during the nation's formative years in the eighteenth century [7].

In an effort to regain their post-depression reputations, businesses around the country found an unlikely ally in American pastors ([7], p. 4). James W. Fifield Jr. served as the chief pastoral lobbyist for

---

[1] Preston's work details how a number of groups—Irish Americans, Catholics, and Mormons—all joined the military and supported actions abroad, such as the Spanish American War and the colonization of the Philippines to indicate their loyalty to the United States and overcome marginalization.

businesses and conservatism. (Fifield was not an evangelical, but his work did provide a foundation that conservative evangelicals utilized to advance their nationalistic beliefs.) He opposed the New Deal for its collectivistic tendencies, something he contended to be unbiblical and un-American, and he praised businesses and conservative values for their libertarian conceptions, something he contended to be deeply biblical ([7], pp. 6–7). Furthermore, Fifield was able to contrast conservatism and his vision for a Christian America with the collectivistic tendencies of America's enemies, such as Nazi Germany and, in time, Soviet Russia. He formed Spiritual Mobilization to champion his perception of the Bible and America, one rooted in individual liberty as opposed to "pagan statetism" ([7], p. 14). Spiritual Mobilization rallied pastors around the nation to this cause, forming the foundation of a nation that was perceived to be under God years before those words formed part of the United States' unofficial motto under President Eisenhower. Conservative evangelicals built upon this framework in the post-war years to defend the assertion that God stood with and for the United States ([8], pp. 76–96).[2] Despite these realities, there were few indications that conservative evangelicals would embrace Christian nationalism as fully as they have.

The evangelical elite began to organize even before Henry's jeremiad. Harold Ockenga (1905–1985) was important in this regard. He was very educated, an attendee of Princeton Theological Seminary, and he helped form the National Association of Evangelicals (NAE) in 1943 ([9], pp. 147–50). Additionally, Ockenga had strong conservative impulses. Therefore, his thoughts on America's role in the world require consideration due to their thoughtful nature.

Ockenga's deeply evangelical approach to America's divine role rooted itself in the belief that evangelicals, particularly American evangelicals, would play a vital role in halting the "disintegration of Christianity" and the "break-up of the moral fiber of the American people" ([9], p. 147). This was his prime impetus for beginning the NAE and accepting the presidential role in the organization. In one of his first addresses to the NAE, titled "Christ in America," Ockenga laid out his vision. He believed "the United States of America has been assigned a destiny comparable to that of ancient Israel" ([9], p. 149). Evangelicals were destined to lead the "rescue of western civilization . . . by a revival of evangelical Christianity" ([9], p. 149). Ockenga's address made sense in the post-war context. Indeed, as Joel Carpenter points out, "Ockenga was hopeful the trial of war would promote a fresh tide of 'common sense, faith [and] vision'" ([9], p. 149). To Ockenga then, America's post-war destiny was to lead a moral revolution against the idols of "blood, power, sex, money, hunger, strong men, and strong weapons" ([9], p. 149). Indeed, he felt America in general, and evangelicals in particular, were called by God to bring about this revival of western Christianity. Despite his many attempts to lead this revival, Ockenga was unable to capture the audience required to make his dream a reality. Somewhat reluctantly, he passed his vision on to a rising star in the movement ([9], p. 226). It is here that Billy Graham's role as a leader of the movement becomes important to consider.

After a 1949 rally, Graham became the rising star and the public face of the evangelical movement. His staunch opposition to communism, his belief in free enterprise, and his many connections to big business made him a powerful defender of American conservatism as well ([7], p. 37). By strengthening evangelicalism's affiliations with the presidency—Graham was a notable asset to the Eisenhower, Johnson, and Nixon administrations—he connected the religious movement to the White House like never before. Despite an extremely close relationship with Johnson and attempts to remain non-partisan, Graham's social conservatism connected him more closely with Republican policies. This was a mutually beneficial relationship. The party gained a massive constituency, and evangelicals gained a powerful ally, one they could partner with to champion America's exceptional nature.

One such example of this can be found in Graham's Honor America Day. This religious and political event, which doubled as a rally for Nixon, was held in Washington D.C. on July 4, 1970.

---

[2] Giberson and Stephens chronicle how Peter Marshall and David Manuel's *The Light and the Glory* and David Barton's organization Wallbuilders have disseminated this providential view of history. They argue evangelicals tend to care little that works by these men have often been debunked by professional historians.

The event's organizers intended to restore Americans' faith in their nation, despite its controversial actions abroad. Graham, in an attempt to invoke the memory of Martin Luther King Jr., titled his sermon "The Unfinished Dream" ([7], p. 268). He reminded his audience "The Bible says, 'Honor the nation.' As a Christian, or as a Jew, or as an atheist" ([7], p. 268). Graham was preaching to the choir. He urged his listeners to remember "The men who signed the Declaration of Independence were moved by a magnificent dream. This dream was rooted in a book called the Bible" ([7], p. 268). In essence, Graham spoke both to condemn the left-wing radicalism of the 1960s and to emphasize the United States' Christian origins. The conservative evangelical turnout to Honor America Day is difficult to gauge, but Graham's influence in the movement cannot be understated. Furthermore, the entire event was filmed and sold as a two-disc album narrated by Jimmy Stewart and titled *Proudly They Came . . . To Honor America* ([7], p. 278). It quickly sold out. As Graham aged and suffered through political errors, he stepped away from a staunch nationalism. When the Watergate scandal broke, Graham stepped away from politics, in no small part because Graham nearly endorsed Nixon in 1960 as the moral candidate ([10], p. 209).[3] Post-Watergate, Graham recognized his continual support for Nixon, and other politicians, had the potential to diminish his evangelistic efforts. This disengagement from politics allowed others to take his place ([10], p. 293).

Jerry Falwell stands as a prominent replacement to Graham. He rallied a significant number of evangelicals in the contemporary era through Moral Majority—a political action group he formed in 1979 ([11], p. 340). The group gained ecumenical support behind a pro-life and traditional family values platform. Throughout the 1980s, it primarily worked to shift elections in favor of conservative values and to champion a belief that America needed to be returned to its Christian roots. When it came to Christian nationalism, Falwell was a disciple of Francis Schaeffer (1912–1984). Schaeffer's belief in a Christian America was fleshed out in a yearlong debate with George Marsden and Mark Noll—evangelicals and professionally trained historians. Schaeffer set out to prove the founders' general ideas were biblical, even if their writings did not explicitly mention the Bible. He called for evangelicals to return to the methods the founders employed politically ([12], p. 212). Noll retorted by indicating the ambivalence and even distaste that some of the founders had for the Bible, particularly Jefferson and Madison. Noll's rebuke infuriated Schaeffer. He labeled Noll's approach to history as something common among "weak Christians" ([12], p. 215). Falwell, mimicked Schaeffer's view of the past. He put it succinctly when he said, "We [the religious right] believe our nation must come back to God or else" ([11], p. 554). While this statement can, and should, be understood as a call for religious revival, it cannot be divorced from evangelicals' commitment to emphasize the Christian nature of the United States. The very notion of "coming back to" implies a desire to return to something that tangibly existed. Falwell was, knowingly or unknowingly, making a historical statement cemented in the perception that the United States was losing its Christian grounding. (Schaeffer advanced this argument too.) A call for revival, therefore, can be seen as serving both a religious and historical purpose.

The intent of men such as Graham, Schaeffer, and Falwell to emphasize how Christianity was inherent to the United States' national course has been championed time and again by conservative evangelicalism's most notable figures and self-titled experts. For example, Tim LaHaye claimed "The history of America's . . . guiding political philosophy cannot be described without reference to its biblical roots" ([2], p. 5). The strongest contemporary, conservative evangelical champion of these views is David Barton. Barton goes so far as to rewrite history, ignoring facts and proper historical interpretation, in order to perpetuate the myth ([8], pp. 83–96). This leads him to conclude "virtually every one of the fifty-five founding fathers who framed the Constitution were members of orthodox Christian churches and that many were outspoken evangelicals" ([2], p. 137). Despite the numerous

---

[3] Graham went so far as to write an article for Time magazine in 1960 endorsing Nixon because of his "strength, knowledge, wisdom, and integrity as well as faith in God." Henry Luce pulled the article to protect Graham from partisanship.

historical errors in Barton's assertion, his opinion is respected among members of the evangelical movement. He has even gained a national audience, serving as an expert witness in Supreme Court cases, advising lawmakers, and having a regular slot on Glenn Beck's programs ([8], pp. 84, 87). Additionally, Barton and Peter Marshall were both instrumental advisers for the Texas State Board of Education's 2010 shift towards a conservative history curriculum. To name just one change in the curriculum, Thomas Jefferson was removed from the list of enlightenment thinkers ([8], p. 89). This fits into Barton's agenda to whitewash the founding era in such a way that it lacks any secular impetus. His views are generally accepted because they satisfy conservative evangelicals' presupposition that the United States has a Christian past and a God given destiny.

2.2. Critique: Progressive Evangelicals and Christian Nationalism

As David Swartz and Brantley Gasaway have chronicled, progressive evangelicals, along with their conservative brethren, emerged in the post-World War II climate [13,14]. Progressive evangelicalism grew slowly as a subgroup, emerging fully during the protest movements of the 1960s. In this rebellious decade, the subgroup mimicked the left-wing culture that conservative Americans detested. Its members adopted countercultural tactics, dressed like the new left and hippie movements, and modified the rhetoric of these secular youth movements for their Christian purpose. They even began their own publications—*The Other Side* (first known as *Freedom Now*) and the *Post American* (founded by Jim Wallis and eventually retitled *Sojourners*)—to disseminate their views. These publications championed progressive, Christian approaches to social justice and united the youthful subgroup ([14], p. 25). Progressive evangelicals also joined in anti-Vietnam protests and attacked unquestioning patriotism, pointing out the seeming hypocrisy conservative Christians evidenced by supporting war. They believed the United States' engaged in wars fought without regard for human life. This was a jab at the pro-life reputation of conservative evangelicals. As Charles Fager pointed out, no one could "weep for aborted fetuses" when they wanted to engage in unjust wars abroad ([14], p. 135). Progressive evangelicals could not idly sit by and watch the United States perpetrate violence without regard for the image of God in its foreign victims.

Both Gasaway and Swartz illustrate how progressive evangelicals sought to establish a political platform rooted in social justice. These left-leaning evangelicals intended to create a nonpartisan and biblically based approach to politics. The tangible example of this goal was the "Chicago Declaration of Evangelical Social Concern." This document, written in 1973, was signed by a number of prominent evangelicals from across the political spectrum, including Carl Henry, Jim Wallis, and Richard Mouw ([13], p. 181). The declaration affirmed evangelicals' commitment "to the Lord Jesus Christ and full authority of the Word of God" while denouncing the involvement of the "church in America with racism" and the United States' "pathology of war" ([13], pp. 267–68). The document explicitly stated that its signers endorsed "no political ideology or party" ([13], p. 268).

Of special importance to this paper is the ways progressive evangelicals have protested, and continue to protest, injustices committed by the nation they call home. While not always explicitly stated, hidden behind this willingness is a belief that the United States does not receive special favor by God. Even if the United States were given special favor by God, the nation and its governing bodies still needed to be corrected when national sins went unchallenged or were even supported by public policy. Progressive evangelicals' support for the Civil Rights Movement informs this point. Leading figures in the movement, such as Ronald Sider, spent time living among the marginalized in order to better understand their plight ([13], p. 155). Jim Wallis was influenced by the effects of racism and felt a desire to help the oppressed because of the brutality he witnessed in Detroit's 1967 race riots. Wallis credits the riots as his "baptism of fire," explaining the racism that they evidenced "betrayed the ideals I had been taught as a child" ([13], p. 50). As a result of these views, Wallis and Sider would find themselves outcasts from mainstream, conservative evangelicalism while becoming the rising stars of the progressive evangelical movement. While all evangelicals appealed to the same God and shared many religious beliefs, progressive and conservative evangelicals differed in their interpretation of the

United States' past and present role in the world. These differences were highlighted by Wallis's 2005 bestseller, *God's Politics. God's Politics* is a thorough critique of the United States' political atmosphere. It is equal parts admonition and instruction. In writing it, Wallis intended to reach across the aisle by forging a third way in American politics that is not partisan but godly [15]. Wallis also sought to combat the unbreakable alliance between conservative evangelicals and the Republican Party by connecting certain policy measures to biblical precepts.

Wallis spoke out heavily against conservative evangelicals' unquestioning support for George W. Bush and the Iraq War ([16], p. 196).[4] He did so by questioning the notion that God is on America's side, particularly as God would not stand by a war fought so unjustly. In one of his most poignant assaults on Christian nationalism, Wallis questioned whether "we [Christians] really believe that America and George W. Bush have been divinely appointed to root out evil in the world? That's bad theology and a very dangerous one" ([15], p. 119). He urged conservative evangelicals and politicians to reconsider their support for the war. Another notable critique of Christian nationalism can be found in Wallis's views on racism, especially his label for it, "America's original sin" ([15], pp. 307–8). By titling racism thus, Wallis is making an implicit argument that the United States and the will of God cannot be seen as linked due to the nation's sinful tendencies.

While Wallis builds an interesting political argument against the prominence of Christian nationalism in the evangelical movement, his argument lacks a distinctly biblical and non-partisan approach to Christian citizenship. He fails to adequately highlight the difficulty in managing one's earthly and heavenly nationalities. Instead, Wallis tends to speak in the language of the left, injecting the Bible as necessary in an effort to reach across the aisle. Wallis's approach also fails because of how similar it is to conservative evangelicalism's understanding of biblical citizenship. Both Wallis and his conservative evangelical counterparts tend to use the Bible as a political and rhetorical tool; they both impose particular visions of God's will on the United States' political situation. The only difference is that one vision is progressive and one is conservative. It is here that reformed evangelicalism, with Mouw as a standard bearer, sets itself apart. Reformed evangelicals distance the conception of nationalism from a partisan mindset, establishing theology as the arbiter of Christian political thought along the way. By exploring Mouw's works, reformed evangelicalism's third way for evangelicals to approach citizenship and Christian nationalism becomes evident.

2.3. Challenging a Partisan Consensus: Richard Mouw and the Search for a Homeland

Reformed evangelicalism is a small and a relatively unknown subgroup within the larger evangelical movement. It is defined by its approach to theology. Much like members of the larger movement, reformed evangelicals are theologically orthodox. What sets them apart is their attention to the works of reformed thinkers, prominently John Calvin (1509–1564) and Abraham Kuyper (1837–1920). A focus on these thinkers and reformed theology allows these evangelicals to engage uniquely with cultural and political issues. It also enables reformed evangelical scholars to attain a certain level of consistency and uniformity in their thinking. Whereas many evangelicals interpret the bible through a radical application of the priesthood of believers, resulting in Molly Worthen's "crisis of authority," reformed evangelicals have an established ecclesiology in which they can base their beliefs [1]. In essence, they have an authority to answer to. (In Mouw's own journey, the Canons of Dordt, the Belgic Confession, and the Heidelberg Catechism, along with the teachings of reformed scholars, serve this role [17], p. 21). Nicholas Wolterstorff (b. 1932), a philosopher and theologian, and Richard Mouw can be seen as leaders of the movement.

Mouw is a globally recognized leader of evangelicalism [18]. Indeed, he has gone out of his way to see evangelicals engage in interfaith dialogues—notably with Mormons [19,20]. Additionally, he has authored or served as an editor of over twenty books. His most recent book, *Adventures*

---

4   Luhr provides a breakdown of how evangelicals voted in 2004, indicating Wallis is correct in his claim.

in *Evangelical Civility*, has received praise from evangelical leaders and non-evangelical scholars alike [21].[5] Considering his life's work, a devotion to Christian higher education, it is important to mention the multitude of addresses that he has delivered at Christian colleges around the nation. A quick YouTube search reveals many of these talks. His influence is easier to understand when one considers these following thoughts from his former colleague and friend Nicholas Wolterstorff. Wolterstorff has praised Mouw for his "concrete" theology, "conversational style", and his mastery of the "illustrative anecdote" [22]. Additionally, Wolterstorff recognizes that even Mouw's whimsical thoughts serve a deeper purpose. He speaks in a language that the laity understands and values, never discounting the pietistic roots of evangelicalism. This makes Mouw well suited to address a movement that is rightly seen as anti-intellectual. This is not to say that Mouw is not an academic and a careful thinker. He is. In that regard, he is more comparable to Harold Ockenga than either Graham or Falwell as pastors and organizers or Wallis as an activist. However, Mouw is representative of how reformed evangelicals approach the world—much like Graham, Falwell, and Wallis are representative of how their evangelical subgroups engage with the culture. Additionally, in a movement where the intellect is often lambasted, the work of academic thinkers must be, at times, compared to the impact popular leaders have. Indeed, compared to figures such as Graham, Falwell, or Wallis, Mouw's influence is very limited and is difficult to discern. Regardless, his thinking further diversifies evangelical thought, deepening and widening it in the process.

Mouw's views on Christian nationalism are often implicit throughout his writings, offering insights that soften the hardline Christian nationalism of men such as Barton or Falwell. Mouw also stands apart from progressive evangelicals such as Wallis due to his Biblicist focus. He asks for the Bible to be used for the Bible's sake. Granted, Mouw does not solely focus on the Bible's advice for nationalism, but he also does not attempt to diminish the Bible's role as the ultimate truth for his worldview, one which bridles his extra-biblical conceptions. This means that Mouw offers general, not specific, cures for the faults that he sees in evangelicals' approach to citizenship. He uses the Bible to point out the extremes of thought, offering guidance when necessary. Ultimately, however, he urges the laity to develop their own public theology without stepping over certain biblical parameters ([23], pp. 123–42). Therefore, he does not advance a sole vision for America, rather, he delights in the diversity of thought allowed for in the created order. The outcome of this thinking is an insider's corrective to evangelicals' nationalistic tendencies, overcoming efforts by progressive and conservative evangelicals to politicize the Bible in specific ways. In an attempt to connect thoughts that are spread across his many writings, five key themes will be explored due to their prominence—commonness, exile, idolatry, "many-ism," and triumphalism ([24], p. 81). Each theme sheds light on Mouw's understanding of Christian nationalism and Christian citizenship. For the purpose of this essay, Mouw's books will be primarily explored. While he has published many essays and articles, his books are written for the largest audience and are often marketed to evangelical audiences by Christian publication companies such as William B. Eerdmans. As such, they are the most likely to be read by the ordinary evangelical.

By Mouw's own admission, he sees "commonness as the theme that has been informing the main intellectual endeavors" throughout his career ([21], p. xi). As a theme, commonness' centrality to Mouw's thought makes it relevant to consider before going further. As it concerns Christian nationalism, this theme is also much harder to flesh out than the others. Essentially, commonness takes many forms in Mouw's life—a belief in common grace, a recognition of a shared likeness of God among all of humanity, and desire to seek common ground [21]. These three branches of commonness reveal a good deal about why Mouw is concerned about how Christians approach nationalism. They also serve as a good introduction to the topic.

---

[5] The dust flap on this book reads like a who's who of Christian scholars and scholars on contemporary evangelicalism—this includes Russell Moore, Molly Worthen, and Grant Wacker. They have the highest of praise for the work Mouw has done over the years.

The reformed notion of common grace is "a kind of non-salvific attitude of divine favor toward all human beings" ([25], p. 9). It is also a belief that Mouw adheres to very closely, inspiring his desire to seek out the good things of Christ wherever this be found. Simply put, "Grace is everywhere" ([25], p. 45). In certain reformed circles, this notion is taken quite literally. "Abraham Kuyper, for example, saw grace not only as operating broadly in *human* affairs; he argued that it also abounds in nature in general" ([25], p. 45). Indeed, "creation would self-destruct" without Christ's continual outpouring of grace ([25], p. 45). In essence, grace not only falls on the saved and the unsaved, it falls on creation as a whole. This means that no part of creation is exempt from the workings of grace, including nations. They all serve a divine purpose, and are sustained through the workings of Christ. (A conception of multinational chosen-ness will be explored more adequately later in this essay.) This idea of multinational chosen-ness flows well into Mouw's understanding of the image of God.

Humankind is distinguished from the rest of creation through the image that they share with the creator. Commonly, the notion of imago Dei (the image of God) is applied only to individual humans. Mouw affirms Herman Bavinck's (1854–1921) understanding of a "collective possession of the *imago*" ([21], p. 31). Bavinck further declares "the image of God is much too rich for it to be fully realized in a single human being" ([21], p. 32). Mouw takes this understanding and asserts,

> we might think of the creator as having distributed different aspects of the divine likeness to different cultural groups, with each group receiving, as it were, a unique assignment for developing some aspect or another of the divine image. Thus, it will only be in the eschatological gathering-in of the people of the earth, when many tribes and tongues and nations will be displayed in their honor and glory in the new Jerusalem, that we will see the many-splendored *imago dei* in its fullness ([21], p. 32).

This too hearkens to an understanding of multinational chosen-ness and the diversity that Mouw adores in creation. Indeed, this passage indicates that national exceptionalism is only a reality if each nation is considered exceptional in its relation to Christ as lord.

Finally, in an effort to seek common ground, Mouw is affirming his belief in common grace and his communal vision of imago dei. He seeks out the image of Christ and truth, wherever they may be found, and he seeks to relate to God's likeness in the saved and unsaved alike. This has made him, in the words of George Marsden, "a builder of bridges," someone "who can find commonalities with just about anyone" [26]. Marsden's testimony illuminates Mouw's qualifications concerning the subject matter of this essay. It is in Mouw's nature to seek out that which is common among individuals and people groups rather than seeking out exceptions. This makes him a voice capable of toning down the American exceptionalism found in conservative evangelical circles by linking American Christianity to its global allies and even promoting a desire to see that which is good in its religious and international opponents. In turning to Mouw's more concrete advice concerning Christian nationalism, exile as a theme explores how Christianity supersedes earthly nationalities.

When considering exile, Mouw turns to the Puritan's view of exile, chronicling how Puritan settlers "thought of themselves as Israel wandering in the wilderness in search of a promised land" ([23], p. 47). He argues their rhetoric shifted shortly after settling in the New World. To Mouw, Puritans saw themselves as transitioning "from a wandering people to a 'Zion' people," creating a precedent for future Christian generations to do the same ([23], p. 43). From this position as the chosen people, triumphant Christian nationalism became justifiable. It is this shift in perception from exile to the chosen people Mouw seeks to combat. He believes the appropriate Christian perspective to citizenship is exile. Christians should not be at home in this world. They are exiles from their heavenly home. To cement this point, Mouw turns to 1 Peter. Here, Peter addresses "the New Testament church as a community of 'aliens and exiles'" ([23], p. 48) Mouw posits Peter was "making a theological point ... indicating how we are to understand the status of the church in the present age" ([23], p. 48). In this regard, Mouw would proudly sing along with fundamentalists that "This world is not my home, I'm just a passing through." After all, "Christians are first and foremost Christians, citizens of the theocratic commonwealth over which Jesus reigns as king" ([23], p. 48). Unlike a fundamentalist,

Mouw would not, however, argue for cultural disengagement and the hope of an imminent eschaton. Rather, he champions the theme of exile in a different light, choosing to focus on the book of Jeremiah as a platform for viewing exile, and thereby Christian nationalism. Several of these verses are listed here as they are vital to Mouw's argument.

> Thus says the LORD of hosts, the God of Israel, to all the exiles whom I have sent into exile from Jerusalem to Babylon: Build houses and live in them; plant gardens and eat their produce. Take wives and have sons and daughters; multiply there, and do not decrease. But seek the welfare of the city where I have sent you into exile, and pray to the LORD on its behalf, for in its welfare you will find your welfare (Jer. 29:4–7).

The theme of exile is obviously prominent in these verses. While Christians are exiles, they are not, in Mouw's opinion, to be culturally disengaged. They are also not forbidden from loving their country. In order to discern how one can love their country, yet avoid being a Christian nationalist, Mouw points to a word hidden in the translation. He explains the word for "welfare" in the Hebrew text is shalom. Mouw chronicles the "richer meaning" of the word, a meaning that goes beyond the common interpretation of peace and welfare ([24], p. 69). Shalom is rightly interpreted as justice and flourishing. As Mouw understands it, Jeremiah is telling the exiled Israelites "neither indifference nor hostility is a proper way of treating our pagan neighbors [or our fellow citizens]. We must seek their shalom" ([24], p. 70). By framing the debate over commitment to one's earthly home in the context of exile, Mouw does not demand Christians cease to love their earthly home, nor does he ask them to stop seeking its success. Rather, he modifies the aim. Christians are called to seek their nation's success without forgetting they are exiles, merely passing through to their true homeland, the one that demands their deepest affections.

Mouw's understanding of exile and its relation to Christian citizenship satisfies the intense Biblicism evidenced in the evangelical movement ([27], pp. 13–14).[6] However, unlike conservative and progressive evangelicals, Mouw does seem to use the Bible for its own sake [28].[7] He does not advance an explicit political agenda through the theme of exile. Nor does he outline exactly how Christian citizens should behave in any given nation. Rather, he quite simply states that Christians should seek the welfare of their nation without losing sight of their true home. The ambiguity of this theme should be striking considering how often evangelicals politicize the Bible to support policy measures. Mouw also chooses not to mention any modern nation by name while discussing exile. In doing so, he opens the door for Christians to seek the welfare of any earthly nation in which they reside. He further downplays the importance of worldly citizenship while emphasizing the national identity of the body of believers. In sum, Mouw declares Christians' only true nation is the kingdom of God. They must behave accordingly in their temporary homes, but they must never assume their earthly nations can represent the Kingdom of God. To quote Mouw, "Absolute loyalty is something that only God deserves from us [Christians]" ([29], p. 117).

This informs Mouw's attack on idolatrous Christian nationalism. In one of his more critical thoughts, Mouw recalls the post September 11 reaction of evangelicals. He found it similar to the "super-patriotic" attitude of evangelicals during the Vietnam War ([29], p. 116). He especially remembered the chants of "My country, right or wrong" evangelicals employed during that war ([29],

---

[6] It is worth noting that, while he does believe in Sola Scriptura, Mouw would not go so far as to say that the Bible alone holds all truth. Rather, it holds ultimate truth. He believes truth can be found through scientific exploration as just one example. He details these beliefs in his book *Called to the Life of the Mind*.

[7] This portion of the paper borrows from Mark Noll's *In the Beginning was the Word: The Bible in American Public Life*. Noll expertly illustrates how the Bible has oft been used by American Christians, particularly evangelicals in the colonial era, and I would contend beyond the colonial period, to advance agendas that are not biblical. Noll indicates how the Bible has been used to advance and contest Christendom, how the Bible has been thinned or absorbed into the sciences and political thought, and how it has been, at times, a Bible for the Bible's sake. A brief summation of this argument can be found on page 329 of *In the Beginning was the Word*.

p. 116). In both the Vietnam War and the post-9/11 climate, evangelicals had an unquestioning love of country. While Mouw affirms there is a place for proper patriotism, he does state "That kind of patriotism struck me as bordering on idolatry" ([29], p. 117).

Furthermore, in an essay exploring the role of national icons in church settings, he declares "Our [Christians'] worship services are gatherings in the divine throne-room, where we acknowledge that our true loyalties belong to God alone. Nothing in our liturgical content or setting should detract from this expression of fidelity" [30]. To be clear, Mouw is not expressing a desire to ban flags and the like from church services unless they are a distraction to the congregation. Apart from national symbols, Mouw also addresses the way Christians worship, particularly through song. He cites the "dangerous teachings" many patriotic songs convey [30]. For instance, "Themes that in the book of Revelation are used to describe the Holy City are here applied to the United States: 'alabaster cities,' 'undimmed by human tears,' the 'shining sea.' As if the United States will become the promised New Jerusalem! [30]". This attention to the content churchgoers often accept denotes his fear of the "very real threat" idolatry poses [30]. Mouw reaffirms the "multinational character of the body of Jesus Christ" [30]. He then shifts towards his views on healthy patriotism. Hearkening back to his understanding of exile. Mouw contends

> Christians need to work hard at keeping patriotic feelings within proper bounds. There is nothing wrong with loving my country . . . However, this does not put my country beyond criticism. To honor our nation in a godly manner is to want it to contribute to the cause of Christ's kingdom. To love our country with a Christian love is to want our nation to do justice and love mercy and walk in humility before the face of the Lord. [30]

His own understanding of idolatry is further informed by an exploration of his Kuyperian sensibilities.

Mouw borrows Kuyper's conception of sphere sovereignty when discussing idolatry. Boiled down, sphere sovereignty is a theological idea wherein each area of life—such as family, government, church, art, and the economy to name just a few—are relegated to separate spheres. Each sphere ultimately answers to God. However, apart from the government on a limited basis, spheres cannot infringe on other spheres ([31], pp. 33–34).[8] The blurring of boundaries is, in itself, a form of idolatry because, according to Kuyper, these spheres were mandated by God. Any attempt to infringe on these boundaries or to have one sphere subsume another sphere would be a deeply idolatrous action. Mouw offers a brief corrective to this Kuyperian conception without disregarding the notion of sphere sovereignty. He contends spheres can step in to supplement weaker spheres if necessary. For example, Mouw believes the church must step in to bolster the family sphere if it is not strong enough to thrive on its own. The church cannot become the family though. "While the two modes [spheres] may be combined, they must not be confused" ([32], p. 51). Therefore, while Mouw contests certain aspects of sphere sovereignty, he does believe each sphere has its own special role, and he does not object to Kuyper's conception of idolatry as the blurring of these boundaries.

Mouw's own view of idolatry is, therefore, rightly seen as an extension of Kuyper's. Idols are often made from "something that is a good part of Creation;" they come about from the worship or improper understanding of the relation between created and creator ([31], p. 21). Notably for evangelicals, Mouw believes "Political parties and movements are worthy of our respect when they are kept in their place—in their proper sphere of life" ([31], p. 21). It would not be improper, I believe, to claim that Mouw would express a similar belief for nations. If a nation is conceived of as more important than God intended and is heavily relied on to maintain a certain lifestyle, it too can be seen as an idol. Mouw once again emphasizes the created should worship and rely on the creator alone. The created should not elevate the importance of the political or the national in such a way that

---

8   The government is only allowed to interact across spheres out of necessity. It maintains boundaries, protects the weak from the strong in spheres, and allows spheres to run efficiently. Quite simply, all the spheres use roads. The government is in charge of infrastructure; therefore, the government interacts with all spheres.

God's role as king over all is diminished even slightly. Such an action would not only be dangerously idolatrous, it would also elevate one sphere above others in a way that downplays God's creational diversity. Here, Mouw's notion of many-ism comes to the fore.

Many-ism is more than a simple recognition and appreciation of diversity. It is fueled by a profound love of the created order. In this regard, it is connected to the idea of sphere sovereignty. Many-ism began with the cultural mandate. This mandate originated, according to Mouw, in the Garden of Eden ([33], p. 126). Intended by God to fill the earth, humanity was expected to do more than multiply. Men and women were also designed to be a lesser, co-creator. One of the more important tasks given to the co-creator was the development of cultures and, thereby, cultural diversity. Mouw contends that the God of the Bible strongly dislikes "deadly uniformity" ([24], p. 81).[9] He particularly cites the words of Genesis 1:20—"Let the waters bring forth swarms of living creatures" ([24], p. 82). The God that Mouw sees in the bible delights in these swarms. It is an almost childlike celebration of diversity. Mouw does not argue that God could not have created a uniform universe. Instead, he believes that God loves diversity. In a way, Mouw implies that "deadly uniformity" would simply not be as enjoyable to God ([24], p. 81).

There are several lessons that many-ism can teach Christian nationalists. In particular, it stands in stark contrast to the national exceptionalism that most evangelicals take. A short look at Mouw's interpretation of Isaiah 60 lends credence to this claim [34]. For those unfamiliar with this chapter of Isaiah, it is a prophetic passage focused on the restorative work of God over all of creation at the end of days. Notably, it is the moment when the nations of the earth, along with elements of nature, are called before the throne of God. A brief passage from Isaiah informs this point—"Your [the kingdom of God's] gates shall be open continually; day and night they shall not be shut; that men may bring to you the wealth of the nations, with their kings led in procession" (Isaiah 60:11). God calls the nations to him so that he may restore them. The plurality displayed by "nations" is telling. Isaiah does not single out a nation or a king. Obviously, the United States was not a nation during biblical times; therefore, it is not listed in Isaiah 60. Yet, many nations are listed in the chapter, and their cultural achievements are called before the throne of God to be restored and called good. In Mouw's own words, the act of assembling "kings together, then, was in an important sense to assemble their national cultures together" ([34], p. 50). Interestingly, and this is a pattern that can be found through all of his books, Mouw does not inject the United States into the biblical narrative. This may seem like a minor point, yet one does not need to dig deeply into evangelical history to find frequent attempts by evangelicals to place the United States biblically [4]. Rather, Mouw seeks to affirm something that can be seen as deeply biblical. All of creation is chosen and ordered by God. Therefore, each and every nation is chosen by God to some degree ([34], p. 57). They are all providentially guided, and they will all find themselves called to account before the throne of God to be restored to their created goodness.

To be sure, this interpretation of Isaiah 60 is informed heavily by Mouw's Calvinism and Kuyperiansim. His Calvinist sensibilities are satisfied by the sovereignty of God displayed in Isaiah 60, and his Kuyperian sensibilities are satisfied by the restoration of the created spheres to their proper order—God once more is recognized as ruler over them all. However, Mouw is also evincing a deeply evangelical reading of this passage. He takes the text, quite simply, at its word. God calls the nations and chooses to restore them all. This connotes a rejection of the exceptionalism or chosen-ness of one nation. They may be called for different purposes, but they are all chosen. For the nationalistic evangelical, this quells a recognition of America as exceptional. It places God firmly as king and ruler over all, in such a way that one nation does not come to the fore. To put it in Kuyperian terms, "There is not a square inch in the whole domain of our human existence [nations included] over which Christ,

---

[9] Mouw borrows this phrase from South African politician Nic Diedrich. While Diedrich used these words to defend apartheid's forced segregation. Mouw uses these words for a different purpose. He intends, in the original context, to illustrate how God's distaste for uniformity breathes life into a kind of godly, cultural pluralism.

who is sovereign over all, does not cry 'Mine!'" ([31], p. 4).[10] Despite the triumphant nature of this claim, Mouw urges his readers to balance this perspective, softening it in the process. It is here where Mouw's opinions on triumphalism become relevant.

The western world has, in Mouw's opinion, long worshipped a triumphant Christ. Japanese theologians have been particularly critical of this view. Mouw cites Kosuka Koyama to support this claim. "A strong Western civilization and the "weak" Christ cannot be reconciled harmoniously. Christ must become "strong." A strong United States and a strong Christ!" ([35], p. 3). Koyama contrasts this Western viewpoint with a depiction of Christ found in the "image of the same broken Christ who comes to us every time we approach the Lord's Supper" ([35], p. 3). Mouw does not challenge the triumphant image of Christ. He, in fact, affirms it in several ways. First, Christ is victorious over sin. He then extends that victory to his followers. Finally, Christians should be proud of this victory ([24], pp. 163–64). This is not, however, an excuse for Christians to claim "the spoils of Christ's victory" ([24], p. 165). In an effort to illustrate his point, Mouw offers Mother Teresa as an example of how a victorious Christ can be balanced by a suffering Christ.

The life of Mother Teresa cannot be fully understood without understanding her love for the broken Christ. The most prominent example, in Mouw's view, was her advice to nuns that aided her in Calcutta. She encouraged them to find Christ "in his dreadful disguise, among the poorest of the poor" ([31], p. 135). For Mouw, this is not a rejection of a triumphant Christ. Even on Calvary, at his most vulnerable, Christ stood triumphant. A recognition of the suffering Christ does, however, focus on an aspect of Jesus that is often overlooked, the one who suffered, and encouraged his followers to suffer with him.

Mouw argues that "the lack of earthly suffering in the lives of white American theologians" could have led to this dominant vision of a triumphant Christ ([35], p. 62). He contrasts this Caucasian understanding of Christ with that of slaves in the Western Hemisphere. Negro spirituals convey this point excellently. As just one example, "Nobody knows de trouble I see Lord, nobody knows like Jesus" ([35], p. 65). The suffering develops a Christology focused on a Christ who suffers rather than a triumphant Christ. Mouw contends that both views are theologically correct. This leads back to his main point. Christ is victorious even in his suffering, but he alone lays claim to that victory. The Christian cannot seize that right. What the Christian is left with, according to Mouw, is a Christ who still claims "Mine" over all of creation while still evincing an image of the Christ "whose 'footprints are splattered with blood'" ([31], pp. 132–33).

Mouw's Christological understanding of Christ is different than the savior conservative and progressive evangelicals serve. It highlights a Christ who does not serve political interests and one that does not necessarily support national triumphs. Instead, it is a Christ who stands above his creation with his arms outstretched, as they were on the cross, awaiting the day when he can once more joyfully say "'Mine!' over the creation that he has made new" ([31], p. 134).

3. Conclusions

The post-World War II re-awakening of evangelicalism deeply impacted the history of the United States. It led to a bolstering of conservatism in the nation advanced by a movement that predominantly believed God chose the United States for a great purpose. This belief manifested itself in a Christian nationalism wherein conservative evangelicals argued the nation was exceptional because it was chosen by God. More importantly though, this sense of chosen-ness, combined with an entrenched sense of Biblicism, gave right-wing evangelicals the perception that political compromise was dangerous and a lack of patriotism evinced a lack of faith in God's will. The result of this belief was an evangelicalism that often unquestioningly supported the national direction, particularly when the Republican Party sat in the halls of power.

---

[10] Mouw is quoting Abraham Kuyper.

Religions **2017**, *8*, 2

Focusing on this singular perception of evangelicalism ignores the reality of a movement better defined in terms of diversity. Competing attempts to interpret the Bible and determine its impact on the world left evangelicals with a "crisis of authority" ([1], p. 265). While conservative evangelicals held a lion's share of the movement's power, evangelical subgroups cultivated differing opinions. Within this context, certain figures were seen as authoritative. Conservative evangelicals see figures such as Graham and Falwell as anointed and progressives see Wallis in a similar light. However, to see any of these figures as the only ones worth listening to and studying overlooks important lines of thought.

Mouw is representative of one such alternate viewpoint—reformed evangelicalism. In his effort to defend the Bible's core message, he evinces a desire to appreciate the general will of God. He often shies away from particulars. While this can be contrived as a weakness in his line of thought, it does differentiate him from most evangelicals regardless of their political affiliation, highlighting his ability to rise above the "schisming and squabbling" common within the movement ([1], p. 7). Through his desire to build a Christian foundation to citizenship, rather than decorate the house as it were, Mouw also stands apart from conservative evangelicals such as David Barton. Barton's focus on particulars leaves little to the imagination. His only conception of citizenship for the evangelical is one of loyalty. This is because of America's supposedly chosen nature. To oppose what is chosen by God cannot be allowed in Barton's thinking. To this, Mouw would likely say God dislikes "deadly uniformity" ([24], p. 81).

Furthermore, Mouw delights in the diversity of creation, even if it is currently depraved, while never losing hope in its renewal. Behind this hope is an unquestioning belief that Jesus is Lord over all. All of creation is his; it has all been chosen for his purpose. This means God is not merely lord over the United States, nor has he chosen one nation to serve his purposes. He has, instead, chosen all nations in his eternal plan. Through this view of Christ and creation, Mouw restores the image of a Christ who deeply empathizes with and defends those who are suffering. Christ, though triumphant, does not bow to or serve the powers of this earth. To put it quite simply, Mouw's views on the God of the Bible and of Christians' earthly responsibilities contextualizes evangelicals' earthly role by reminding them who is triumphant, and they are "just a-passin' through." He urges their deepest affections to reflect that reality.

Conflicts of Interest: The author declares no conflict of interest.

References

1. Worthen, Molly. *Apostles of Reason: The Crisis of Authority in American Evangelicalism.* New York: Oxford University Press, 2014.
2. Green, Stephen K. *Inventing a Christian America: The Myth of the Religious Founding.* New York: Oxford University Press, 2015.
3. Stephens, Randall J., and Karl W. Giberson. *The Anointed: Evangelical Truth in a Secular Age.* Cambridge: Belknap Press, 2011.
4. Sutton, Matthew. *American Apocalypse: A History of Modern Evangelicalism.* Cambridge: Belknap Press, 2014.
5. Hart, Darryl G. *That Old Time Religion in Modern America: Evangelical Protestantism in the Twentieth Century.* Chicago: Ivan R. Dee Publishing, 2002.
6. Preston, Andrew. *Sword of the Spirit, Shield of Faith: Religion in American War and Diplomacy.* New York: Anchor Books, 2012.
7. Kruse, Kevin. *One Nation Under God: How Corporate America Invented Christian America.* New York: Basic Books, 2015.
8. Stephens, Randall J., and Karl W. Giberson. *The Anointed: Evangelical Truth in a Secular Age.* Cambridge: Belknap Press, 2011.
9. Carpenter, Joel. *Revive Us Again: The Reawakening of American Fundamentalism.* New York: Oxford University Press, 1997.
10. Wacker, Grant. *America's Pastor: Billy Graham and the Shaping of a Nation.* Cambridge: Belknap Press, 2014.

11. Self, Robert. *All in the Family: The Realignment of American Democracy since the 1960s.* New York: Hill and Wang, 2012.
12. Hankins, Barry. *Francis Schaeffer and the Shaping of Evangelical America.* Grand Rapids: William B. Eerdmans Publishing Company, 2008.
13. Swartz, David. *Moral Minority: The Evangelical Left in an Age of Conservatism.* Philadelphia: University of Pennsylvania Press, 2012.
14. Gasaway, Brantley. *Progressive Evangelicals and the Pursuit of Social Justice.* Chapel Hill: The University of North Carolina Press, 2014.
15. Wallis, Jim. *God's Politics: Why the Right Gets It Wrong and the Left Doesn't Get It.* New York: Harper One, 2005.
16. Luhr, Eileen. *Witnessing Suburbia: Conservatives and Christian Youth Culture.* Berkeley: University of California Press, 2009.
17. Mouw, Richard. *Calvinism in the Las Vegas Airport: Making Connections in Today's World.* Grand Rapids: Zondervan Press, 2004.
18. Fuller Theological Seminary. "Friends Pay Tribute to Dr. Mouw's Legacy." Available online: http://cms.fuller. edu/RJMouw/root/Home/Friends_Pay_Tribute_to_Dr__Mouw_s_Legacy/ (accessed on 21 December 2016).
19. Mouw, Richard. *Talking with Mormons: An Invitation to Evangelicals.* Grand Rapids: William B. Eerdmans Publishing Company, 2012.
20. Mouw, Richard, and Robert Millet, eds. *Talking Doctrine: Mormons and Evangelicals in Conversation.* Downers Grove: Intervarsity Press, 2015.
21. Mouw, Richard. *Adventures in Evangelical Civility: A Lifelong Quest for Common Ground.* Grand Rapids: Brazos Press, 2016.
22. Wolterstorff, Nicholas. "Richard Mouw: Reflections on His Writing." Available online: https://perspectivesjournal. org/blog/2013/07/01/richard-mouw-reflections-on-his-writing/ (accessed on 6 December 2016).
23. Mouw, Richard. *Called to Holy Worldliness.* Philadelphia: Fortress Press, 1980.
24. Mouw, Richard. *Uncommon Decency: Christian Civility in an Uncivil World.* Downers Grove: IVP Press, 2010.
25. Mouw, Richard. *He Shines in All That's Fair: Culture and Common Grace.* Grand Rapids: William B. Eerdmans Publishing Company, 2001.
26. Marsden, George. "Rich Mouw: A Fundamentalist with a Sense of Humor." Available online: https:// perspectivesjournal.org/blog/2013/07/01/rich-mouw-a-fundamentalist-with-a-sense-of-humor/ (accessed on 6 December 2016).
27. Mouw, Richard. *Called to the Life of the Mind: Some Advice for Evangelical Scholars.* Grand Rapids: William B. Eerdmans Publishing Company, 2014.
28. Noll, Mark. *In the Beginning Was the Word: The Bible in American Public Life, 1492–1793.* New York: Oxford University Press, 2016.
29. Mouw, Richard. *Praying at Burger King.* Grand Rapids: William B. Eerdmans Publishing Company, 2007.
30. Mouw, Richard. "The Danger of Alien Loyalties: Civic Symbols Present a Real Challenge to the Faithfulness of the Church's Worship." Available online: http://www.reformedworship.org/article/march-1990/danger-alien-loyalties-civic-symbols-present-real-challenge-faithfulness-churchs- (accessed on 6 December 2016).
31. Mouw, Richard. *Abraham Kuyper: A Short and Personal Introduction.* Grand Rapids: William B. Eerdmans Publishing Company, 2011.
32. Mouw, Richard. *The Challenges of Cultural Discipleship: Essays in the Line of Abraham Kuyper.* Grand Rapids: William B. Eerdmans Publishing Company, 2012.
33. Mouw, Richard, and Sander Griffoen. *Pluralisms and Horizons.* Grand Rapids: William B. Eerdmans Publishing Company, 1993.
34. Mouw, Richard. *When the Kings Come Marching In.* Grand Rapids: William B. Eerdmans Press, 2002.
35. Mouw, Richard, and Douglas A. Sweeney. *The Suffering and Victorious Christ: Toward a More Compassionate Christology.* Grand Rapids: Baker Publishing Group, 2013.

Article

Ambassadors for the Kingdom of God or for America? Christian Nationalism, the Christian Right, and the Contra War

Lauren Frances Turek

Department of History, Trinity University, 1 Trinity Pl, San Antonio, TX 78212, USA; lturek@trinity.edu

Academic Editor: Mark T. Edwards
Received: 3 October 2016; Accepted: 7 December 2016; Published: 18 December 2016

Abstract: This essay uses the concept of Christian nationalism to explore the religious dynamics of the Contra war and U.S.–Nicaraguan relations during Ronald Reagan's presidency. Religious organizations and individuals played crucial roles on both sides in the war in Nicaragua and in the debates in the United States over support for the Contras. Evangelistic work strengthened transnational ties between Christians, but also raised the stakes of the war; supporters of the Sandinistas and Contras alike alleged a victory by their adversary imperiled the future of Christianity in Nicaragua. Christian nationalism thus manifested itself and intertwined in both the United States and Nicaragua. Examining how evangelicals and Catholics in the United States and Nicaragua, as well as the Reagan administration, the Contras, and the Sandinistas, used Christian nationalism to build support for their policy objectives sheds light on both the malleability and the power of identifying faith with the state. Having assessed Christian nationalism as a tool and a locus of conflict in the Contra war, the essay then steps back and considers the larger methodological implications of using Christian nationalism as a category of analysis in U.S. foreign relations history.

Keywords: evangelicals; foreign policy; Reagan; U.S.-Nicaraguan relations; Christian internationalism; Christian nationalism

---

On 16 July 1974, Billy Graham addressed over two thousand evangelical Christian leaders who had gathered in the large assembly hall at the Palais de Beaulieu in Lausanne, Switzerland. Flags from each of the 150 nations that the members of the audience represented lined the stage. A massive screen hanging from the ceiling projected live video of Graham, who stood gripping the podium with one hand as he gestured toward the crowd with the other, so even those sitting far in the back of the hall could see his face as he spoke. He welcomed the men and women before him to the International Congress on World Evangelization, an unprecedented gathering he hoped would inspire Christians across the globe to rededicate themselves to the evangelistic mission of the church. In his plenary address, Graham highlighted the challenges that Christians faced as they worked toward their goal of spreading the Gospel to all people on earth. Significantly, he emphasized the threat that Christian nationalism posed to world evangelism ([1], p. 30).

With his voice rising, Graham condemned the impulse to conflate a particular culture, political system, or country with the Christian faith, and confessed that this tendency had even endangered the efficacy of his own ministry. In emphatic tones, he boomed: "when I go out to preach the Gospel now, I go as an ambassador for the Kingdom of God—and not America. To tie the Gospel to any political system, any secular program, or any society is dangerous and will only serve to divert the Gospel" [2]. As the translation of his words made its way to the audience members' headphones, applause erupted throughout the hall. Evangelical leaders from Latin America, Africa, and Asia welcomed his sentiment. Some of the speakers who hailed from these regions had incorporated strong critiques of American Christian nationalism or "American culture Christianity" in the papers they pre-circulated and then presented at the Congress ([3], p. 136; [4]). Yet despite Graham's entreaty, and the emphasis that the Congress participants and subsequent Lausanne movement placed on developing both indigenous and cross-cultural evangelism, nationalism and Christianity remained deeply entangled in the decades that followed.

Indeed, despite his intentions, Graham's insistence that he represented his faith rather than his country when he preached abroad only served to underscore the extent to which people living in other parts of the world viewed him and his fellow American evangelicals as representatives of the United States. In the paper he presented at the Congress, Latin American theologian C. René Padilla suggested that U.S. interventions abroad, not to mention the country's position as a world superpower, shaped how people who lived in nations that received American missionaries perceived Christianity ([3], p. 136). Padilla saw "American culture Christianity"—or the conceptual fusion of Christianity with American capitalism and "'socio-political conservatism'"—as a hindrance to evangelism and a reason to impose a moratorium on foreign missions ([3], pp. 125, 136; [5,6]; [7], pp. 36, 42). Graham and many other U.S. evangelical leaders opposed the suggested moratorium. Yet, tactical disagreement aside, both Graham and Padilla recognized the power that identifying Christianity with a particular nation held, not to mention the damage it wrought. For this reason, the debate over Christian missions and "culture Christianity" that unfolded at the Congress on World Evangelization revealed an important fault line that existed within the global evangelical community, and particularly between U.S. Christians and those they sought to evangelize. As American evangelicals grew more influential as a political bloc in the late 1970s and early 1980s, this disjuncture between how they and their brethren abroad understood the relationship between their faith and their nation became increasingly consequential for U.S. foreign relations.

For this reason, thinking about Christian nationalism in a global context holds great analytical value for historians. Christian nationalism, an ideology or worldview which merges religious and national identities, shapes the beliefs that individuals hold about the role their country should play in the world and how their country should interact with other nations. In the late twentieth century, many members of the Christian right believed that the United States was a Christian nation and that its culture as well as its laws, politics, and foreign policy should therefore embody the core religious values that they embraced. In this way, religious nationalism informed their views on international relations, contributing to the development of an American Christian internationalism that conflated Christianity with American political and economic principles, and sought to export these values globally.[1] Christian nationalism and internationalism are not exclusively American phenomena, though. Studying the relationship between Christian nationalism, domestic public opinion, and foreign relations in the United States as well as in other countries illuminates how ideology and religious beliefs influence political rhetoric as well as policy.

Even though Graham, Padilla, and the other evangelical leaders at the Congress did not use the term "Christian nationalism" in their debate over the future of world missions, their efforts to describe and grapple with the underlying issues that inspired the discussion illuminate key aspects of the concept. Unwittingly or not, many Christians and non-Christians in the mid-1970s did see a link

---

[1]   Over the past two decades, historians of modern U.S. foreign relations have become increasingly open to using religion as a means for analyzing or understanding policymaking and foreign affairs. More recently, scholars such as Andrew Preston and Melani McAlister have focused on evangelical Christians, examining how their religious beliefs blended with American politics, culture, and identity to shape the U.S. role in the world. For example, Preston argues that evangelicals in the mid-twentieth century acted as internationalist agents, "bring[ing] the world to Americans" as they spread their faith—and American culture—to the world ([8], pp. 190–91). McAlister brings this concept of "evangelical internationalism" into her work as well, as she explores American evangelicals' vision for and interest in global affairs, seeking to understand how their internationalist outlook shaped evangelical culture and political beliefs [9]. This essay builds on this concept of evangelical or Christian internationalism, but focuses more explicitly on the concept of Christian nationalism and the relationship between Christian missions and U.S. politics, policymaking, and diplomacy, including democracy promotion during the Reagan era. For other recent work on Christian internationalism, broadly defined, see: Thompson [10], Preston [11], Inboden [12], Herzog [13], and Thomas [14].

between the Christian faith and Western, specifically American, culture. Yet, as Padilla and Graham made clear in their Congress remarks, Christians throughout the world contested the identification of their faith with any one culture, country, or system of government. They and others committed to world evangelism sought to promote Christianity as a universal faith. Nevertheless, the link between Christianity and the nation persisted. Furthermore, religious and political leaders could (and did) operationalize this link, using it justify, impel, or promote national and international policies. Examining Christian nationalism as both an operational tool and a contested concept in U.S. foreign relations can help us better understand how religion shaped U.S. policy and the reception those policies enjoyed abroad.

To this end, this essay will use the concept of Christian nationalism to explore the religious dynamics of the Contra war and U.S.–Nicaraguan relations during Ronald Reagan's presidency. Religious organizations and individuals played crucial roles on both sides in the war in Nicaragua and in the debates in the United States over support for the Contras. Evangelistic work strengthened transnational ties between Christians, but also raised the stakes of the war; supporters of the Sandinistas and Contras alike alleged a victory by their adversary imperiled the future of Christianity in Nicaragua. Christian nationalism thus manifested itself and intertwined in both the United States and Nicaragua, due in part to the internal religious dynamics in each country that infused the rhetoric about the conflict. Examining how evangelicals and Catholics in the United States and Nicaragua, as well as the Reagan administration, the Contras, and the Sandinistas, used Christian nationalism to build support for their policy objectives sheds light on both the malleability and the power of identifying faith with the state. Having assessed Christian nationalism as a tool and a locus of conflict in the Contra war, this essay will then step back and consider the larger methodological implications of using Christian nationalism as a category of analysis in U.S. foreign relations history.

When the *Frente Sandinista de Liberación Nacional* (FSLN) overthrew the reviled dictator Anastasio Somoza DeBayle in July 1979 and established a revolutionary government, Nicaragua became a major flashpoint in the Cold War between the United States and the Soviet Union. U.S. leaders perceived the Nicaraguan revolution as evidence of Soviet and Cuban interference in Central America. Eager to counter communist incursions in the region, Ronald Reagan committed his administration to providing military aid to the nascent anti-Sandinista counterrevolutionary movement, known as the Contras, when he took office in 1981.[2] The ensuing war between the U.S.-backed Contras and the Sandinistas lasted until 1988. Tens of thousands of Nicaraguans died in the fighting and many more suffered atrocities ranging from torture, maiming, and rape to forcible relocation and the loss of their property. Christian groups within Nicaragua and the United States involved themselves in the conflict; Catholics and evangelicals in both countries found themselves divided over which side to support, and regardless of denomination or nationality, supporters of both the Contras and the Sandinistas claimed the mantle of Christianity and country.[3] Christian nationalist rhetoric infused the debate in the United States and in Nicaragua over the war, and proved particularly resonant with the public and with legislators in discussions about religious persecution and U.S. military aid for the Contra forces.

In Nicaragua, church-state relations and religious freedom lay at the heart of these intra-denominational political divisions among Christians. Though predominantly Catholic, Nicaragua had a small Jewish community as well as a Protestant population that began expanding rapidly in the

---

2   There is a wealth of scholarship on the Contra war and U.S.-Central American (and U.S.-Nicaraguan) relations during the Reagan administration. For background, see LeoGrande [15], LaFeber [16], Grandin [17], and McCormick [18].

3   Much of the existing literature on religion and the Contra war focuses either on denominational change and political involvement in Nicaragua itself, or on the Catholic and Protestant left's activism against Reagan's foreign policy. For the former, see Gooren [19], Smith and Haas [20]; for the latter, see Strauss [21], Smith [22], Nepstad [23], Peace [24], and Keeley [25]. Unlike these works, this article takes a different tack by examining the relationship between Christian nationalist rhetoric, public diplomacy, and policy among evangelical Protestants and Catholics across the political spectrum in both the United States and Nicaragua. Sara Diamond's work on the Christian right reflects some of these themes, and though she completed and published her research before the Contra war ended and only devotes part of a chapter to the conflict, her book remains a very useful primer. See Diamond [26].

1970s. The national constitution guaranteed religious freedom, yet for decades the Catholic Church had enjoyed special state privileges due to its close relationship with the Somoza regime. As the Catholic clergy and laity grew increasingly critical of the dictator's corruption and penchant for brutality during the 1960s and 1970s, the Church leadership tempered and then withdrew its support from Somoza [19,27,28]. By the time of the revolution, the vast majority of Catholics and Protestants in Nicaragua welcomed his ouster. That said, this did not mean they universally welcomed Sandinista leadership. In November 1979, just a few months after Somoza fled Managua and the FSLN claimed victory, the Catholic Nicaraguan Bishops' Conference released a pastoral letter that praised "the current revolutionary moment" as "a propitious occasion to make real the Church's option for the poor" ([29], p. 144). This phrasing alluded to Liberation Theology, a theological movement that emerged from the Catholic Church in Latin American during the 1950s and 1960s and continued to enjoy broad influence in the region [30,31]. Liberation theology promoted economic and social justice for oppressed peoples. Yet the Bishops' statement remained cautious and did not offer unreserved approval of the Sandinistas or their socialist political aims ([29], p. 144). This caution reflected internal tensions among the bishops about the relationship between the Catholic Church and the revolutionary government that only hardened as the FSLN consolidated power in 1981 and 1982.

Despite the hopeful if wary tone that the Bishops' pastoral letter struck about the possibilities for achieving social justice and the broad aims of Liberation Theology after Somoza's exile, the Catholic church found itself divided deeply over support for the FSLN. A delegation of U.S. evangelicals who visited Nicaragua in 1982 noted that while "large numbers of clergy and laity (the so-called 'popular' or 'people's church') are enthusiastic about the revolution," the church hierarchy had split: "four of the eight bishops are supportive and four are not" ([32], frame 294). When a number of revolutionary Catholic priests received appointments to important posts in the Sandinista government, including the Ministry of Culture and the Ministry of Education, the archbishop of Managua Miguel Obando y Bravo and other conservative members of the Catholic hierarchy attempted to discipline them for their involvement in the government ([19], p. 344; [32], frame 292). In his study of religious change in Nicaragua during the 1980s, anthropologist Henri Gooren noted that "the conflict was essentially a political power struggle over the control of the Roman Catholic believers," with the official church hierarchy retaining strong support from "rural and urban elites" while alienating the poorer sectors of Nicaraguan society, which tended to support the Sandinistas and the popular church ([19], p. 344).[4]

Similar divisions wracked the evangelical Protestant churches. Most evangelical denominations belonged to the Evangelical Committee for Aid Development (CEPAD), an organization that Gustavo Parajon, a Baptist medical doctor, founded in 1972 to assist in relief efforts after a devastating earthquake struck the country ([32], frame 295). In addition to spreading the Gospel, CEPAD promoted progressive causes and development projects, and received funding from the National Council of Churches and the World Council of Churches [33]. As investigative groups from the United States reported, CEPAD had a friendly though not totally uncritical relationship with the Sandinista government. According to one account, "about three months after the fall of Somoza, 500 evangelical pastors connected with CEPAD endorsed a document thanking God for the fall of the Somoza dictatorship and affirming the goals of the revolution," though they maintained the primacy of their commitment to Jesus Christ and the Gospel ([32], frame 295). A number of anti-Sandinista groups in the United States, including the Institute on Religion and Democracy, criticized Parajon and the members of CEPAD for their willingness to work with the Sandinista government, which they alleged suggested Parajon was "a loyal Sandinista" and a promoter of Liberation Theology [34].

Yet the CEPAD pastors noted that the evangelical community as a whole held mixed views. According to them, even though most evangelical denominations belonged to CEPAD, a slight majority

---

[4] Gooren also notes that this disillusionment with the Catholic church led some of the laity to convert to Protestantism (typically Pentecostalism); the Catholic church lost considerable market share to the Protestant churches during the 1980s ([19], p. 340).

of Nicaraguan evangelicals were actually "conservative, fearful of Communism and involved only with spiritual matters" ([32], frame 295). In 1980, a small group of conservative pastors who opposed the FSLN and its political aims joined together to form the National Council of Evangelical Pastors of Nicaragua (CNPEN) [35]. This organization developed close ties with political conservatives and evangelical groups in the United States, such as the National Association of Evangelicals and the World Evangelical Fellowship ([36], p. 2). Still, as the CEPAD pastors told the interviewers, a significant number of evangelicals, including the majority of young evangelicals, were "progressive moderates" who supported the Sandinistas with some reservations ([32], frame 295; [37]). Additionally, these pastors reported that a small number of evangelicals identified themselves as "radical revolutionaries strongly influenced by liberation theology" ([32], frame 295). Age played an important role in these ideological divisions within the evangelical churches. A group of Baptist seminary students related numerous examples of young Baptists, Pentecostals, and non-denominational evangelicals who worked actively for the revolution. They contrasted the beliefs these young evangelicals held with the views of older pastors and church members, who tended to embrace the same conservative ideological perspectives of their co-religionists in the United States and thus rejected revolutionary activity ([38], frames 245–48).

Meanwhile, those evangelicals and Catholics who had participated actively in the revolution shared a sense that the goals of the FSLN aligned with their Christian beliefs and the social teachings of the Bible. John Stam, a U.S. evangelical missionary based in Costa Rica who aided Sandinistas and refugees fleeing from Somoza's forces in 1978 and 1979, shared numerous accounts about revolutionaries at the Sandinista safe house he served who blended their faith with their fight for the FSLN ([39], p. 201). He reported to evangelicals in the United States that Christian themes infused the most popular revolutionary songs and that the Sandinista fighters he met and prayed with yearned to promote social justice and "full and responsible Christian participation in the birth of a really new Nicaragua" ([40], pp. 2–3). After Somoza's ouster, many of these Christian Sandinistas worked in the FSLN government or worked on its behalf through organizations they founded, such as the Protestant Commission for the Promotion of Social Responsibility (CEPRES) and the *Centro Ecumenico Antonio Valdivieso* (CAV) [41,42]. In one pastoral letter, CAV explained that it operated with the express aim of "proclaiming the Good News of the Kingdom" while "denouncing those ... that oppose the building of a New Society," much as the revolutionary Christians that Stam had encountered in his ministry hoped to do ([43], frames 75–76).

The FSLN leadership seized on these links that the Sandinista fighters drew between the revolution and their religious beliefs in their attempts to build broader support for their movement among Catholics and Protestants. To this end, in October 1980, the FSLN National Directorate released an official statement that praised the role Christians had played in the revolution and pledged that the new Sandinista government would protect the religious freedom of all Nicaraguans ([44], pp. 2, 20–31). The statement celebrated revolutionary priests—such as Gaspar García Laviana, who attributed his willingness to die for "the liberation of the people" to his belief that God desired freedom for all—for blending their "Christian vocation and the revolutionary conscience" ([44], p. 11). It also played up the relationship between the FSLN's political goals and the foundations of the Christian faith, incorporating Biblical verses about renewal and the command to care for all people as evidence that Christianity, the revolution, and Sandinista-style socialism went hand in hand ([44], pp. 4, 9; [45]). Yet these efforts to gain Catholic and Protestant support by relating the aims of the revolution to the Christian faith ultimately exacerbated the intra-denominational ideological divides discussed earlier.

Indeed, despite the promises the National Directorate made in its statement on religion, many conservative Catholics and evangelicals in Nicaragua and the United States doubted the sincerity of the FSLN's commitment to religious liberty. These doubts, coupled with their skeptical reading of the religious rhetoric the FSLN had attempted to adopt, sowed the seeds for Christian nationalist conflict as U.S.-backed anti-Sandinista forces began to coalesce in 1981 to 1982 and mount increasingly serious challenges to the Sandinistas' hold on power.[5]

Humberto Belli, a former Marxist and editor of the Nicaraguan newspaper *La Prensa*, became a particularly influential critic of the FSLN's religious policies. After the Sandinistas shuttered *La Prensa*, Belli moved to the United States and began publishing damning screeds against the Sandinistas, focusing in particular on their attempts to politicize Christianity. In several pieces, he recounted how he and his fellow *La Prensa* editors unearthed a secret FSLN memo that instructed all regional leaders to transform Christmas from a religious celebration to "a special day for the children, one 'with a different content, *fundamentally political*,'" to ensure that everything—including the Christian faith—remained "inside the revolution" [46]. Likewise, he argued that the Sandinista government's 1981 New Year's address, which "proclaimed that 'the true Christians, the sincere Christians, embrace the option of the Sandinista revolution, which in Nicaragua today is the road toward the option for the poor,'" made manifest the FSLN's intention to cast opponents of the revolution as opponents of Christianity ([47], p. 45). Belli opposed this form of Christian nationalism, stating that the FSLN's demands that "Christians give unconditional support to the revolution, not to the Church" and efforts to merge Christian beliefs with Marxist-Leninist principles perverted Christianity ([47], p. 46). He noted that these imperatives also opened those Christians who did not pledge their fealty to the state to reprisals.

Along with the Institute on Religion and Democracy (IRD) and other anti-Sandinista activists in the United States, Belli reported that such reprisals began in mid-1981 when the Sandinistas started harassing and marginalizing religious groups that did not lend their full support to the FSLN government. He argued that "the Sandinistas have achieved this partly by giving the revolutionary Christians exclusive access to the virtual state monopoly of the mass media," while preventing conservative Catholics and evangelicals from communicating with their followers through newspapers, radio, or television ([47], p. 47). In a booklet entitled "Nicaragua: A Revolution Against the Church?" the IRD stated that in July 1981, the Sandinistas barred the Catholic Archbishop of Managua from making his customary television broadcast of Sunday Mass because they wanted only "pro-Sandinista priests" on the air ([48], pp. 13–14). According to the IRD and Humberto Belli, this media blackout and new laws that forbade Nicaraguans from making negative statements about the regime to people abroad made it nearly impossible for these conservative Christians to share their plight with the rest of the world ([47], p. 48). Similarly, when the Sandinistas arrested and killed a number of Miskito Indians for engaging in guerilla warfare against the FSLN, and then forcibly relocated around 10,000 predominately Moravian Christian Miskitos to resettlement camps to contain them, Belli decried Sandinista efforts to isolate them and silence their protests ([32], frames 287–88; [47], p. 49).

According to U.S. evangelical observers, this pattern of harassment escalated further in 1982 when Sandinista organizations vandalized and seized a number of churches. These incidences occurred within the context of mounting counterrevolutionary pressures, which led the Sandinistas to impose a State of Emergency on the country in March 1982, restricting a number of civil liberties including freedom of speech and of the press. With this in mind, sympathetic observers described the attacks on the evangelical churches as a simple government misunderstanding, noting that after CEPAD complained, FSLN leader Daniel Ortega returned the church buildings, "apologized for the mistake and repeated the government's clear commitment to religious liberty" ([32], frame 290). Yet FSLN distrust of the conservative evangelical groups persisted, particularly as U.S.-based counterrevolutionary forces—which had ties to some of these Nicaraguan church groups—intensified their media and international public opinion campaign against the Sandinistas.

---

[5] As historian Greg Grandin recounts, in these years the C.I.A. and some members of Reagan's National Security Council began providing covert aid to former members of Somoza's National Guardsmen, as well as to the anti-FSLN Nicaraguan Democratic Union, to help them form a counterrevolutionary movement that would oppose and seek to overthrow the Sandinista government ([17], pp. 113–14).

U.S. interventions aimed at undermining the Sandinista government raised the stakes considerably. In 1981, members of the State Department and Reagan's national security advisors were divided over how to best respond to the revolution in Nicaragua as well as to the civil war unfolding in El Salvador, which they viewed as connected developments and as evidence of Soviet and Cuban efforts to seize control of Central America ([18], pp. 75, 77). During a meeting of National Security Council (NSC) on 16 November 1981, the Reagan administration worked to come to an agreement on an appropriate policy response. Through these discussions, the president and the NSC developed National Security Decision Directive 17 (NSDD 17), which Reagan signed on 4 January 1982. NSDD 17 affirmed U.S. "support for those nations which embrace the principles of democracy and freedom for their people," and as such declared that the Reagan administration would "support democratic forces in Nicaragua" as well as lend assistance to anti-insurgency groups throughout Central America [49]. To this end, in April 1981, the Reagan administration suspended U.S. economic assistance to Nicaragua and, later that year, authorized the CIA to train and arm the Contras, a group of counterrevolutionaries which included former members of Somoza's National Guard. As historian David Painter notes, although Reagan claimed that the goal of these polices was to halt Sandinista aid to the growing insurgency in El Salvador, "[their] main objective quickly became the overthrow of the Nicaraguan government" ([50], p. 99). By 1982, Contra forces had begun to launch attacks in Nicaragua, leading the FSLN to seek support from the Soviet Union and Cuba to shore up its defenses and to declare an official State of Emergency.

In addition to laying the groundwork for the covert counterinsurgency war against the Sandinistas, NSDD 17 also set the stage for a pro-Contra public relations campaign in the United States, a campaign that would ultimately draw heavily on Christian nationalist themes. Reflecting Reagan administration concern about congressional and public opinion against lending support to counterrevolutionary groups, NSDD 17 placed the NSC's plan to "create a public information task force to inform the public and Congress of the critical situation in the area" first in its enumerated list of decisions [49]. The passage of the first Boland Amendment in December 1982, which prohibited the use of congressionally-appropriated funds to "furnish military equipment, military training or advice, or other support for military activities ... for the purpose of overthrowing the government of Nicaragua," bore out the Reagan administration's concerns about congressional resistance to its policy agenda [51]. When Congress passed a second Boland Amendment in late 1983 prohibiting "covert assistance for military operations in Nicaragua," and then banned aid for military and paramilitary operations in Nicaragua entirely in 1984, the administration launched a concerted effort to bring congressional and public opinion around to supporting to the Contras [52,53].

Allegations that the Sandinistas violated the human rights of their political opponents and persecuted non-revolutionary Christians formed the centerpiece of White House outreach on behalf of the Contras. Faith Ryan Whittlesey, the director of the Office of Public Liaison, discussed this strategy to mobilize public opinion explicitly as she and her staff considered how to best communicate the president's aims in Central America. Department memoranda called for a strategy that would "trigger humanitarian emotions," by sharing the details of "the utter inhumanity and unspeakable cruelties of Marxist guerillas in Central America" through "case studies, documentation," and the like [54]. They also proposed religious theme lines, such as emphasizing the incompatibility of revolutionary activities and Christianity ([54], p. 5). The Office of Public Liaison noted that "nongovernment support must be recruited and prepositioned for activation," by inviting key groups to the White House for foreign policy seminars and following up with regular policy updates, which would provide them with information to incorporate into letter writing and lobbying campaigns ([54], pp. 12, 15, 18). The memo recommended that the White House look to conservative Protestant and Catholic religious organizations in the United States in particular to participate in these activities.

In May 1983, the Office of Public Liaison began holding weekly briefings on U.S.–Central American relations for political, business, and religious leaders from all denominations and political perspectives [55]. For a seminar on religious persecution in Nicaragua, Whittlesey invited a number of "eyewitnesses" to share their experiences, including the former *La Prensa* editor Humberto Belli, a self-described Pentecostal preacher and Sandinista torture victim named Prudencio de Jesus Baltodano, and Geraldine O'Leary Macías, a former Maryknoll nun. When introducing the speakers, Whittlesey addressed the ideological divisions within the Nicaraguan churches and argued that "the Sandinista leadership is following a two-track policy of persecution and subversion" designed to weaken conservative Christian churches, especially Protestant denominations, while cultivating ties with more sympathetic churches ([56], p. 2). She also stated that "believers have been harassed, arrested, and even tortured," by the Sandinistas, allegations that her guest speakers elaborated on in detail ([56], p. 2). Baltodano, for example, described Sandinistas tying him to a tree, torturing him, cutting his ears off, and leaving him for dead because they suspected him of supporting the Contras ([56], p. 7; [57]). Whittlesey invited Baltodano to speak at the briefings often because, as she wrote to U.S. Ambassador Terence A. Todman, his testimony about this experience "unfailingly effects a dramatic change in the attitude in the audience" [58].

To expand the reach of their messaging beyond the weekly briefings, the Office of Public Liaison sent speakers out to events across the country, began publishing and distributing a special series of White House *Digests* on the situation in Central America, and sent out targeted mailings to religious groups ([55], pp. 1, 3). Some of the speakers, including Geraldine O'Leary Macías, also traveled abroad under the auspices of the U.S. Information Agency to share their testimony with foreign political leaders, religious organizations, and journalists in an effort to sway international public opinion [59]. The mailings and White House *Digests* suggested that the Sandinistas persecuted both Catholics and Protestants, prevented Christians from evangelizing "within Sandinista organizations," and only allowed revolutionary Christians to participate in civic life [60]. They also included statements from Belli, Baltodano, and other Nicaraguan evangelicals.

Evangelical organizations in the United States, already publishing actively about religious persecution throughout the world and in Central America, amplified these messages from the Reagan White House. Christian news services that focused on religious freedom, such as *Jesus to the Communist World* and the *Open Doors News Service*, shared regular updates with their readers about evangelicals who faced arrest and torture at the hands of the Sandinistas [61–63]. The Institute on Religion and Democracy and other Christian organizations incorporated reports about Sandinista attacks on religious liberty into their fundraising campaigns [64]. In all cases, these groups conveyed the impression that the Sandinistas engaged in widespread yet selective religious repression, targeting only those "true" Christians who rejected Marxism and the FSLN. In this way, they attacked the Sandinista nationalism of revolutionary Christians in Nicaragua, while promoting their own version of Christian nationalism—an American Christian nationalism rooted in democratic and liberal capitalist principles.

Yet despite the allegations that the Reagan administration and its religious surrogates made about Sandinista religious persecution, U.S.-backed Contra forces committed extensive and appalling human rights abuses, which opponents of Reagan's policies publicized extensively.[6] Politically progressive and moderate Catholics, Mainline Protestants, and evangelicals spoke out against the war in Nicaragua through pamphlets, newspaper editorials, letter writing campaigns to their representatives, and testimony before Congress. These religious leaders focused on the Contras' poor human rights record and questioned the Reagan administration's foreign policy objectives in Central America. One brochure from the Inter-Religious Task Force, an interdenominational activist organization, compiled statements from a wide range of religious leaders who argued that the firsthand experiences of their missionaries and sister churches in Nicaragua made clear "that poverty, oppression and injustice are the primary causes of unrest in the region," not "Soviet and Cuban-directed agitation and aggression," as the Reagan administration claimed [65]. The prominent evangelical social justice activist Jim Wallis also

---

[6] As Greg Grandin recounts, the Contras killed, kidnapped, and tortured thousands of civilians. He quotes one advisor to the Joint Chiefs of Staff describing them as "just a bunch of killers," and notes the Contras themselves admitted to vast atrocities ([17], p. 115).

drew on firsthand experience in a searing piece in *Sojourners* about his trip to Nicaragua with the anti-Contra organization Witness for Peace, in which he recounted:

> I will not easily forget another mother who tearfully told us how her 13-year-old daughter was decapitated by a *contra* mortar, or the Baptist pastor who could not understand the brutality of the *contras* who hacked to death with machetes a whole group of evangelical teenagers who were simply teaching campesinos how to read ... Every Witness for Peace volunteer can tell stories of terror, torture, rape, pillage, and murder carried out by the *contras* ([66], p. 4).

Such essays aimed to counter the narratives of Sandinista brutality against Christians that conservative organizations shared, seeking to undermine their portrayal of the contras as defenders of religious liberty and American political values.

The fierce disagreements among and within Christian denominations over U.S. policy in Nicaragua greatly intensified the debates in Congress over Reagan administration requests for contra funding in 1985 and 1986. As historian Theresa Keeley has shown, the testimony of Catholic anti-contra activists, including Maryknoll nuns and Jesuit priests, played a significant role in shaping congressional attitudes against contra funding, yet also pushed the Reagan administration to recruit conservative Catholic allies to lend moral support to his cause ([25], pp. 548, 554). These allies, along with conservative Protestant and evangelical activists, proved effective at softening congressional resistance, particularly after FSLN leader Daniel Ortega sought direct aid from the Soviet Union and extended the State of Emergency, further restricting civil liberties, which bolstered contra supporters' negative claims about the Sandinistas ([25], p. 548; [67], p. 226; [68]). Evangelical and Christian fundamentalist media personalities such as Jerry Falwell and Pat Robertson, whom the White House invited to receive special briefings from Oliver North on U.S.–Nicaraguan relations, urged their followers to contact Congress in advance of pending votes on contra funding [69]. The Reagan administration's public relations efforts to undermine its liberal adversaries bore fruit in June 1985, when Congress passed a measure to extend humanitarian aid to the Contras. This aid did not include any funds for military purposes, however, so the White House shifted its religious outreach and lobbying efforts into high gear in advance of a March 1986 congressional vote over military funding.

Christian nationalist rhetoric took center stage in this campaign as Reagan pressured Congress to extend an additional $100 million in aid to contra forces, most of it expressly intended for military purposes. In early 1986, the White House made a five-minute long videotape of President Reagan discussing the conflict in Nicaragua for the Christian media to air on its networks. In the tape, Reagan implored American Christians to contact their congressmen and tell them to support the contra "Freedom Fighters" in the vote on military aid [70]. He blended national and religious ideals as he castigated Sandinista restrictions on civil liberties, particularly religious freedom, and connected the Christian faith with American democracy and anti-communism explicitly in his closing words when he intoned:

> In this time when freedom has flashed out like a great astonishing light in the most surprising places;—in this time when democracy is new again, and communism is more and more revealed as an old idea that's as tired as tyranny;—in this time it is nothing less than a sin to see Central America fall to darkness. Let's not let it happen. It won't if we work together. We can save Central America, with the help of your senators and representatives. Please let them know how you feel. Thank you ... and God bless you all [71].

These media pieces mobilized evangelical Christians, many of whom had already donated money directly to the contras through fundraising campaigns that Pat Robertson coordinated through his aid organization Operation Blessing, and advertised on his television show *The 700 Club* [72–75]. In addition to the videotape, which the White House sent to Jerry Falwell, Pat Robertson and the Christian Broadcasting Network, the Trinity Broadcasting Network, and other major Christian television outlets, Reagan also recorded a 60-second long audio message that went out to over 1500 Christian radio stations across the country [76,77]. These messages included instructions for listeners to call a 1–800 number, which would connect them with the contact information for their congressional representatives so that viewers and listeners could call or write letters urging them to support the president's policies [76,77]. These constituent letters and phone calls poured in to congress, providing additional moral backing to legislators who supported White House policy on Central America.

Reagan's approach of conflating Sandinista victory with "sin" and "darkness" in contrast to American democracy and freedom also proved effective in the congressional debate that followed. Senators and representatives who supported the president's foreign policy agenda in Nicaragua reiterated these points, sharing details on Sandinista persecution of Catholics and Protestants; some even participated in hearings on the threats that communism and Liberation Theology posed to the survival of the Church in Central America [78]. Opponents of the military aid measure also appealed to religious themes, marshaling evidence of contra human rights violations and religious persecution, and incorporating statements and testimony from anti-contra Catholic and Protestant leaders into the proceedings [79,80]. In the end though, the contra supporters edged out their opponents. Congress approved the $100 million spending measure.

This military support for the contras did not end the religious controversy over the conflict in Nicaragua, of course, which continued throughout the rest of the contra war and only intensified as the details of the Iran-Contra scandal emerged. Still, in 1987, evangelical news sources reported that "the Sandinista government has recently adopted a more relaxed approach toward the Church and that evangelistic activities within the country are at an all-time high" ([81], p. 9). Yet they also noted that the National Association of Evangelicals had announced its intention to participate in a worldwide prayer campaign to protest Sandinista religious repression, including the closure of religious radio stations and limitations on church publications, which they argued made evangelism "extremely difficult" ([81], p. 10). Conflicting reports about the extent of ongoing Sandinista persecution abounded. After the Sandinistas signed the Esquipulas Peace Agreement in 1987, in which they and the other Central American leaders committed to pursue economic cooperation, democratic reforms, and conflict resolution, they loosened some restrictions on internal opposition groups. By January 1988, the FSLN had ended the six-year long state of emergency, a move that conservative Christians in the United States and Nicaragua welcomed, though with some skepticism [82]. The democratic elections that followed in 1990 ousted the Sandinistas from power.

The ideological divisions that emerged during the revolution and the contra war continued to rive Nicaraguan Christian groups after the election and well into the 1990s. As Henri Gooren notes in his anthropological study of the post-Sandinista religious marketplace in Nicaragua, in the early 1990s "the Roman Catholic Church remain[ed] divided between a conservative hierarchy and a sizeable minority, made up of the so-called 'popular church'" ([19], p. 354). Evangelical church members also seemed to vary in their political views; many worshippers who belonged to indigenous churches (a significant proportion of the evangelical population) continued to support the FSLN, while those belonging to churches with stronger ties to U.S. denominations tended to have more negative views of the Sandinistas ([19], p. 353). That said, some revolutionary evangelical organizations, such as the *Comisión Evangélica de Promoción de La Responsabilidad Social*, worked to strengthen their relations with liberal Protestant churches in the United States in the late 1980s and early 1990s [83].

Thus although to some extent the contra war compromised evangelistic efforts by U.S. churches due to the associations that Nicaraguans drew between them, the United States, and the contras—just as Billy Graham and C. René Padilla had warned decade earlier at the Congress on World Evangelization—the evangelical churches and organizations that cooperated with the Sandinistas experienced tremendous growth during the 1980s.[7] The Sandinistas had tended to brand their more conservative brethren, those with ties to U.S. churches and evangelists such as Pat Robertson, as imperialists, which somewhat dampened their appeal. In some ways, the evangelical experience in Nicaragua bore out C. René Padilla's vision: rejecting "American culture Christianity" and moving toward indigenous evangelism models enabled them to flourish. Their growth put the Roman Catholic Church in Nicaragua on the defensive, contributing to ongoing interdenominational conflict in addition to the intra-denominational ideological conflicts that affected both Protestants and Catholics.

Christian nationalism did not cause the contra war, obviously, but the rhetoric of Christian nationalism raised the stakes for all concerned. Religious beliefs, commingled with ideas about freedom and democracy, formed part of the ideological prism through which Reagan viewed U.S. interests in Central America. Operationalized Christian nationalism encouraged U.S. conservative Christians to rally around the president and promote his policy agenda. It also led revolutionary Christians in Nicaragua to lend their support to the Sandinistas, with some even opting to serve in the FSLN government. Nicaraguan Christians, emboldened by the Sandinista vision for a new nation which seemed to embrace their religious commitments to social justice, went to war to fight for the FSLN. Likewise, the contras and their U.S. supporters fought (or funded the effort) to "save" Nicaragua from the "sin" of communism, with its attendant state-sanctioned atheism and religious persecution. That both combatants adopted the mantle of Christian nationalism, and operationalized the concept, demonstrates just how malleable the concept was—but also how powerful. The tactic of conflating faith and nation, or national political principles, proved exceedingly effective in mobilizing people to take political and military action.

For this reason, using the lens of Christian nationalism to examine a conflict between two deeply Christian nations illuminates how ideology, core national values, and religious beliefs shape foreign policy. The belief that there was an enduring relationship between Christianity and American principles influenced how U.S. evangelicals defined their foreign policy objectives and shaped their success in projecting them abroad. When U.S. evangelicals lobbied their congressional representatives to fund the contras in order to protect religious liberty and prevent anti-religious totalitarian forces from gaining a foothold in Nicaragua, they brought American Christian nationalism to the global arena. From their perspective, threats to religious liberty posed a grave threat to their ability to spread the Gospel throughout the entire world and "make disciples of all nations" [84,85]. Regimes that repressed Christians also imperiled the advance of democracy throughout the world. Evangelicals viewed religious liberty as the foundation of human rights—and of democracy. Accordingly, states that denied religious liberty were undemocratic—and, in the context of the Cold War, a danger to American national interests as well as evangelical objectives. The United States, as a bastion of religious freedom and democracy, stood in stark contrast to such regimes [86].

Using Christian nationalism as an analytic concept thus allows us to sharpen our understanding of the essential ideas that motivated U.S. evangelical policy opinion and activism in the late twentieth century. It also allows us to better appreciate how Christians and non-Christians in other countries contested, rejected, and adapted this concept to suit their local contexts. The language that Reagan, evangelical leaders, and allies in Congress used to discuss the contra war reflected the intertwinement of spiritual beliefs with American values and democratic principles that constitute American Christian nationalism. Christian nationalism (and internationalism) ultimately complemented the ideology and foreign policy objectives of the Ronald Reagan administration in Central America. Yet the deep divisions that Christian nationalist rhetoric drove into religious life in Nicaragua highlights why Graham and Padilla spoke about this concept with such anxiety and existential foreboding at the Congress on World Evangelism in 1974.

---

[7] Gooren notes that the evangelical churches gained considerable market share between 1980 and 1989, with the evangelical population nearly doubling (from about 8% of the population to roughly 15% and continuing to grow) ([19], p 348).

Conflicts of Interest: The author declares no conflict of interest.

References

1. Billy Graham. "Why Lausanne? " In *Let the Earth Hear His Voice: International Congress on World Evangelization, Lausanne, Switzerland Official Reference Volume*. Edited by James Dixon Douglas. Minneapolis: World Wide Publications, 1975.
2. Billy Graham. "Why Lausanne." Available online: https://www.lausanne.org/content/why-lausanne [starts 41:46] (accessed on 17 September 2016).
3. C. René Padilla. "Evangelism and the World." In *Let the Earth Hear His Voice: International Congress on World Evangelization, Lausanne, Switzerland Official Reference Volume*. Edited by James Dixon Douglas. Minneapolis: World Wide Publications, 1975, pp. 116–44.
4. Samuel Escobar. "Evangelism and Man's Search for Freedom, Justice and Fulfillment." In *Let the Earth Hear His Voice: International Congress on World Evangelization, Lausanne, Switzerland*. Edited by James Dixon Douglas. Minneapolis: World Wide Publications, 1975, Official Reference Volume, pp. 303–26.
5. In the paper, Padilla derives the quote "sociopolitical conservatism" from David Moberg. *The Great Reversal: Reconciling Evangelism and Social Concern*. Philadelphia: Lippincott, 1977, p. 42.
6. See also *Let the Earth Hear His Voice: International Congress on World Evangelization, Lausanne, Switzerland*. Edited by James Dixon Douglas. Minneapolis: World Wide Publications, 1975, Official Reference Volume.
7. International Congress on World Evangelization. "1974: The Lausanne Covenant, with an exposition and commentary." In *Making Christ Known: Historic Mission Documents from the Lausanne Movement 1974–1989*. Edited by John Stott. Carlisle: Paternoster Publishing, 1996.
8. Andrew Preston. *Sword of the Spirit; Shield of Faith: Religion in American War and Diplomacy*. New York: Alfred A. Knopf, 2012.
9. Melani McAlister. "What is Your Heart For? Affect and Internationalism in the Evangelical Public Sphere." *American Literary History* 20 (2008): 870–95. [CrossRef]
10. Michael G. Thompson. *For God and Globe: Christian Internationalism in the United States between the Great War and the Cold War*. New York: Cornell University Press, 2015.
11. Andrew Preston. "Evangelical Internationalism: A Conservative Worldview for the Age of Globalization." In *The Right Side of the Sixties: Reexamining Conservatism's Decade of Transformation*. Edited by Laura Jane Gifford and Daniel K. Williams. New York: Palgrave Macmillan, 2012.
12. William Inboden. *Religion and American Foreign Policy, 1945–1960: The Soul of Containment*. Cambridge: Cambridge University Press, 2008.
13. Jonathan P. Herzog. *The Spiritual-Industrial Complex: America's Religious Battle against Communism in the Early Cold War*. New York: Oxford University Press, 2011.
14. Scott M. Thomas. *The Global Resurgence of Religion and the Transformation of International Relations. The Struggle for the Soul of the Twenty-first Century*. New York: Palgrave Macmillan, 2005.
15. William M. LeoGrande. *Our Own Backyard: The United States in Central America, 1977–1992*. Chapel Hill: University of North Carolina Press, 1998.
16. Walter LaFeber. *Inevitable Revolutions: The United States in Central America*. New York: W. W. Norton & Company, Inc., 1993.
17. Greg Grandin. *Empire's Workshop: Latin America, the United States, and the Rise of the New Imperialism*. New York: Metropolitan Books, 2006.
18. Evan McCormick. "Freedom Tide? Ideology, Politics, and the Origins of Democracy Promotion in U.S. Central American Policy, 1980–1984." *Journal of Cold War Studies* 16 (2014): 60–109. [CrossRef]
19. Henri Gooren. "The Religious Market in Nicaragua: The Paradoxes of Catholicism and Protestantism." *Exchange* 32 (2003): 340–60. [CrossRef]
20. Christian Smith, and Liesl Ann Haas. "Revolutionary Evangelicals in Nicaragua: Political Opportunity, Class Interests, and Religious Identity." *Journal for the Scientific Study of Religion* 36 (1997): 440–54. [CrossRef]
21. Charles T. Strauss. "Quest for the Holy Grail: Central American War, Catholic Internationalism, and United States Public Diplomacy in Reagan's America." *U.S. Catholic Historian* 33 (2015): 163–97. [CrossRef]

22. Christian Smith. *Resisting Reagan: The U.S. Central American Peace Movement.* Chicago: University of Chicago, 1996.

23. Sharon Erickson Nepstad. *Convictions of the Soul: Religion, Culture, and Agency in the Central America Solidarity Movement.* New York: Oxford University Press, 2004.

24. Roger Peace. *A Call to Conscience: The Anti-Contra War Campaign.* Amherst: University of Massachusetts Press, 2012.

25. Theresa Keeley. "Reagan's Real Catholics vs. Tip O'Neill's Maryknoll Nuns: Gender, Intra-Catholic Conflict, and the Contras." *Diplomatic History* 40 (2016): 530–58. [CrossRef]

26. Sara Diamond. *Spiritual Warfare: The Politics of the Christian Right.* London: Pluto, 1989.

27. Philip J. Williams. "The Catholic Hierarchy in the Nicaraguan Revolution." *Journal of Latin American Studies* 17 (1985): 341–69. [CrossRef]

28. Dana Sawchuk. "The Catholic Church and the Nicaraguan Revolution: A Gramscian Analysis." *Sociology of Religion* 58 (1997): 39–51. [CrossRef]

29. "Compromiso Cristiano Para una Nicaragua Nueva (Carta Pastoral del Episcopado Nicaragüense)." *Mensaje*, 1980. Available online: http://biblioteca.uahurtado.cl/ujah/msj/docs/1980/n287_143.pdf (accessed on 20 September 2016).

30. The pastoral letter makes a direct reference to the writings of Gustavo Gutiérrez, one of the intellectual fathers of Liberation Theology, and to his contributions at the Latin American Episcopal Council meetings held in 1968 in Medellín, Colombia and in 1979 in Puebla, Mexico. See Gustavo Gutiérrez. *A Theology of Liberation: History, Politics, and Salvation.* Maryknoll: Orbis Books, 1973.

31. Christian Smith. *The Emergence of Liberation Theology: Radical Religion and the Social Movement Theory.* Chicago: University of Chicago Press, 1991.

32. Ronald J. Sider. "Evangelicals for Social Action news release (22 December 1982)." In *Nicaragua in The North American Congress on Latin America (NACLA) Archive on Latin Americana.* Wilmington: Scholarly Resources Inc., 1998, roll 19, file 124.

33. The Caribbean Commission. "The Tragedy of Nicaragua: Report of the Caribbean Commission Investigative Team." (New Orleans, LA: The Caribbean Commission, 1986): 12, Intercessors for the Suffering Church Collection, 1971–1997, SC #79 Box 1, Folder 14: The Caribbean Commission. "Dead Missing Imprisoned: The Tragedy of Nicaragua" (1986?) "Central America: The Cancer Within" (1986), Wheaton College Special Collections, Buswell Library, Wheaton College, IL (hereafter WCSC).

34. The Institute on Religion and Democracy. Briefing paper. "The Subversion of the Church in Nicaragua: an interview with Miguel Bolanos Hunter." no. 1 (December 1983), BGC Collection 459, Fellowship Foundation; 1935– ; Records; 1937–1988; N.D., Box 537, Folder 7: Central America Trip; 1984, Billy Graham Center Archives, Wheaton, IL (hereafter BGC).

35. John Gordon Melton, and Martin Baumann. *Religions of the World: A Comprehensive Encyclopedia of Beliefs and Practices.* Santa Barbara: ABC-CLIO, 2010, The authors note that CNPEN was "composed of individual pastors and not associations of churches (denominations) like CEPAD." Some of the churches/denominations that CNPEN members belonged to were part of CEPAD.

36. "Nicaraguan Church Reacts to Central American Peace Plan." *Open Doors News Service*, 9 November 1987. Intercessors for the Suffering Church Collection, 1971–1997, SC #79, Box 6, Folder 9: Open Door News Service 8/87-6/88, WCSC.

37. They also suggested that this moderate population was growing and might soon catch up to and overtake the conservative population.

38. "Notes from a meeting at the Seminario Teologico Bautista de Nicaragua, 23 June 1983." In *Nicaragua in the North American Congress on Latin America (NACLA) Archive on Latin Americana.* Wilmington: Scholarly Resources Inc., 1998, roll 19, file 124, frames 245–48.

39. For background on Stam's activities, see John Stam. "My Pilgrimage in Mission." *International Bulletin of Missionary Research* 38 (2014): 198–201.

40. John Stam. "Nicaragua Sandinistas: My Brothers and Sisters in Christ." October 1979, BGC Collection 459, Fellowship Foundation, Box 519, Folder 6: Miscellaneous Correspondence; 1960–1983, BGC.

41. Protestant Commission for the Promotion of Social Responsibility. "A Pastoral Letter from CEPRES to the Nicaraguan People and Churches." In *Nicaragua in the North American Congress on Latin America (NACLA) Archive on Latin Americana.* Wilmington: Scholarly Resources Inc., 1998, roll 18, file 120, frame 1016.

42. Centro Ecumenico Antonio Valdiviso. *"Informes*, no. 3 (June 1981)." In *Nicaragua in The North American Congress on Latin America (NACLA) Archive on Latin Americana.* Wilmington: Scholarly Resources Inc., 1998, roll 19, file 122, frames 55–58.

43. Sister Luz Beatriz Arellano. "Carta del CAV: Monthly Information Bulleting from the Area of Solidarity." In *Nicaragua in The North American Congress on Latin America (NACLA) Archive on Latin Americana.* Wilmington: Scholarly Resources Inc., 1998, roll 19, file 122, frames 75–76.

44. Frente Sandinista de Liberación Nacional. "Los Cristianos en la Revolucion Popular Sandinista: Comunicado Oficial de la Direccion nacional del F.S.L.N. Sobre la Religion." In *Nicaragua in The North American Congress on Latin America (NACLA) Archive on Latin Americana.* Wilmington: Scholarly Resources Inc., 1998, roll 19, file 126, frames 411–35.

45. The document quotes or paraphrases selective parts of Romans 12:2 ("Do not be conformed to this world, but be transformed by the renewing of your minds"), Colossians 3:9–10 ("you strip off the old self and his way of life to put on the new self"), and 1 John 4:20 ("How can you love a God whom you do not see, if you do not love your brother who you have seen?").

46. Humberto Belli. "Central American Policy." *Imprimis.* June 1984. Available online: https://imprimis. hillsdale.edu/central-american-policy/ (accessed on 17 September 2016).

47. Humberto Belli. "The Church in Nicaragua: Under Attack from Within and Without." *Religion in Communist Dominated Lands* 12 (1984): 42–54. [CrossRef]

48. Kerry Ptacek. "Nicaragua: A Revolution against the Church? " Washington: The Institute on Religion and Democracy, 1981, pp. 13–14."Nicaragua." In *The North American Congress on Latin America (NACLA) Archive on Latin Americana.* Wilmington: Scholarly Resources Inc., 1998, roll 19, file 126, frames 444–45.

49. National Security Council. "National Security Decision Directive on Cuba and Central America." National Security Decision Directive Number 17. 4 January 1982. Available from the Ronald Reagan Library.

50. David S. Painter. *The Cold War: An International History.* New York: Routledge, 1999.

51. "Amendment Offered by Mr. Boland." Congressional Record, 97th Cong., 2nd sess., 8 December 1982. Vol. 12, pt. 21: H 29468-69.

52. "Amendment Offered by Mr. Boland." Congressional Record, 98th Cong., 1st sess., 20 October 1983. Vol. 129, pt. 20: H 28560, H 28572.

53. Continuing Appropriations for the Fiscal Year 1985, P.L. 98-473, Stat. 1935–1937, sec. 8066 (12 October 1984).

54. "Mobilizing Public Opinion." ca. 1983, 4, folder "Central America: Responses from Ambassadors." Whittlesey, Faith Ryan: Records, 1983–1985 Series III: Subject File, Box 36, Ronald Reagan Library, Simi Valley. Underlining in the original.

55. "The Central American Outreach Effort." ca. 1984, 1, folder "Central America: Materials (1 of 7)." Whittlesey, Faith Ryan: Records, 1983–1985 Series III: Subject File, Box 34, Ronald Reagan Library.

56. Outreach Working Group on Central America. "Religious Persecution in Nicaragua." transcript (4 May 1984), 2, folder "Central America: Materials (3 of 7)." Whittlesey, Faith Ryan: Records, 1983–1985 Series III: Subject File, Box 34, Ronald Reagan Library.

57. Some critics questioned whether Baltodano was actually a minister or even a lay preacher; John Stam reported that when he confronted Baltodano, the man confessed that at the time the Sandinistas tortured him, he had only just converted to Pentecostalism. See Barbara Thompson to Doug Coe, Interview with John Stam, 7 January 1987, BGC Collection 459, Fellowship Foundation; Box 245, Folder 61: Nicaragua 1984, BGC.

58. Faith Ryan Whittlesey to Terence A. Todman. 7 August 1984, folder "Central America: Responses from Ambassadors," Whittlesey, Faith Ryan: Records, 1983–1985 Series III: Subject File, Box 36, Ronald Reagan Library.

59. Terence A. Todman to Faith Ryan Whittlesey. 23 July 1984, folder "Central America: Responses from Ambassadors," Whittlesey, Faith Ryan: Records, 1983–1985 Series III: Subject File, Box 36, Ronald Reagan Library.

60. Edward A. Lynch to Faith Ryan Whittlesey. "DIGEST Paper on Persecution of Christians." memorandum (19 January 1984), 2, folder "Persecution of Christians (2 of 5)," Lynch, Edward: Files, 1983–84, Box 1, Ronald Reagan Library.

61. "Entire Churches Jailed in Nicaragua." *Jesus to the Communist World, Inc.*, newsletter (December 1984): 1. Intercessors for the Suffering Church Collection, 1971–1997, SC #79, Box 4, Folder 12: Jesus to the Communist World "The Voice of the Martyrs" 6/82-10/93, WCSC.

62. Dan Wooding, and Kate Rafferty. "'Only Contras are preventing shut-down of Nicaraguan Church,' Claim Fleeing Refugees Now in Guatemala." *Open Doors News Service*, 28 June 1985, Intercessors for the Suffering Church Collection, 1971–1997, SC #79, Box 6, Folder 7: Open Doors News Service 9/84-8/86, WCSC.

63. Dan Wooding. "Nicaraguan Evangelical Leaders Arrested in Sandinista Crackdown." *Open Doors News Service*, 24 December 1985, Intercessors for the Suffering Church Collection, 1971–1997, SC #79, Box 6, Folder 7: Open Doors News Service 9/84-8/86, WCSC.

64. The Institute on Religion and Democracy to Doug Coe, Fundraising letter, July 1984, BGC Collection 459, Fellowship Foundation; Box 245, Folder 61: Nicaragua 1984, BGC.

65. Inter-Religious Task Force. "Different Convictions: What the Religious Community is Saying about Central America." Chicago: Inter-Religious Task Force, ca. 1984–85. Chicago Religious Task Force on Central America Records, 1982–1992, M93-153; M2004-170, Box 2, Folder: Interreligious Task Force, Wisconsin Historical Society, Madison, WI (hereafter WHS).

66. Jim Wallis. "Christians and Contras." *Sojourners*, October 1985.

67. Joe Renouard. *Human Rights in American Foreign Policy: From the 1960s to the Soviet Collapse*. Philadelphia: University of Pennsylvania Press, 2016.

68. Margaret Hornblower. "Ortega, in N.Y., Defends State of Emergency." *New York Times*, 21 October 1985.

69. J. Douglas Holladay to Oliver North, 3 May 1985, memorandum, folder: "Evangelical Press on Freedom Fighters and Budget, 04/19/1985." J. Douglas Holladay: Files, Series V: Events OA 12267, Box 13, Ronald Reagan Library.

70. Pat Buchanan, and Peter Waldron, 6 March 1986, folder "OA 17967: RR/Nicaragua Videotape for Christian Media 03/05/1986." Carl Anderson: Files, Series III: Events, Box 10, Ronald Reagan Library.

71. Ronald Reagan. "Taping: Message on Contra Aid for Religious Programs." *Transcript, 5 March 1986, folder "OA 17967: RR/Nicaragua Videotape for Christian Media 03/05/1986." Carl Anderson: Files, Series III: Events, Box 10, Ronald Reagan Library.*

72. Much to the great dismay of liberal, anti-contra evangelicals.

73. See "Christians Oppose TV Evangelist's Aid to Right-Wing Groups in Central America." *Synapses* press release (13 April 1985). Chicago Religious Task Force on Central America Records, 1982–1992, M93-153; M2004-170, Box 1, Folder: Christian Broadcasting Network (1/7), WHS.

74. "The Christian Broadcasting Network: Unholy Alliances." Memorandum (ca. 1985). Chicago Religious Task Force on Central America Records, 1982–1992, M93-153; M2004-170, Box 1, Folder: Christian Broadcasting Network (1/7), WHS.

75. "Pat Robertson Publicly Questioned on Operation Blessing Aid to Contras." *Synapses* press release (27 June 1985). Chicago Religious Task Force on Central America Records, 1982–1992, M93-153; M2004-170, Box 1, Folder: Christian Broadcasting Network (1/7), WHS.

76. Pat Youstra to Linas Kojelis. "Central America Support Checkup." 12 March 1986, memorandum, folder "OA 17967: RR/Nicaragua Videotape for Christian Media 03/05/1986." Carl Anderson: Files, Series III: Events, Box 10, Ronald Reagan Library.

77. Carl Anderson to William B. Lacy. "Christian Media Coverage for Central America." 5 March 1986, memorandum, folder "OA 17967: RR/Nicaragua Videotape for Christian Media 03/05/1986," Carl Anderson: Files, Series III: Events, Box 10, Ronald Reagan Library.

78. Senator Jeremiah Andrew Denton, Jr. "Sandinista Religious Oppression." Congressional Record, 99th Cong., 2nd sess., 18 March 1986, Vol. 132, pt. 33: S 2970.

79. Barbara Mikulski. "Opposing Aid to the Contras." Congressional Record, 99th Cong., 2nd sess., 18 March 1986, Vol. 132, pt. 35: E 919.

80. Barney Frank. "Nicaragua." Congressional Record, 99th Cong., 2nd sess., 10 April 1986, Vol. 132, pt. 43: H 1765.

81. Chris Woerh. "NAE Rallies Behind Nicaragua's Evangelicals." *Open Doors News Service* (1 April 1987): 9–10, Intercessors for the Suffering Church Collection, 1971–1997, SC #79, Box 6, Folder 8: Open Door News Service 7/86-7/87, WCSC.

82. Representative Jim Lightfoot to Mary Ann Gilbert, 15 April 1988, Intercessors for the Suffering Church Collection, 1971–1997, SC #79, Box 5: Serials Correspondence Liv-Ni, Folder 16: Nicaraguan Refugees, WCSC.
83. Reverend Miguel Angel Casco. "'CEPRES' and 'U.S.-Nicaragua Sister Protestant Church Project'." In *Nicaragua in The North American Congress on Latin America (NACLA) Archive on Latin Americana*. Wilmington: Scholarly Resources Inc., 1998, roll 18, file 120, frames 1029–33.
84. Mk. 16:15 (New Revised Standard Version).
85. Mt. 28:19 (NRSV), "the great commission."
86. Lauren Turek. "To Bring the Good News to All Nations: Evangelicals, Human Rights, and U.S. Foreign Policy, 1969–1994." Ph.D. Dissertation, University of Virginia, Charlottesville, VA, USA, 2015; pp. 14–16.

religions

MDPI

Article

Revivalist Nationalism since World War II: From "Wake up, America!" to "Make America Great Again"

Daniel Hummel

Ash Center for Democratic Governance and Innovation, Harvard Kennedy School, Harvard University, 79 John F. Kennedy Street, Mailbox 74, Cambridge, MA 02138, USA; daniel_hummel@hks.harvard.edu

Academic Editor: Mark T. Edwards
Received: 30 September 2016; Accepted: 24 October 2016; Published: 1 November 2016

Abstract: Between 1945 and 1980, evangelicals emerged as a key political constituency in American politics, helping to form the Religious Right and work for the election of Ronald Reagan and other conservative Republicans. This article argues that they embraced a distinctive type of revivalist nationalism, centered around the mass revival. Case studies of Billy Graham, Bill Bright, Jerry Falwell, and Ronald Reagan offer a narrative of postwar revivalist nationalism and demonstrate that evangelicals renegotiated the relationship between personal salvation and national renewal during this period, facilitating their mass entry into partisan politics. Billy Graham presented in his early crusades an unsophisticated assumption that mass conversion would lead to national renewal. Later revivalists such as Bill Bright, founder of Campus Crusade for Christ, sought to reorient revivalism toward directed political organization, leading in the 1970s to decreasing emphasis on personal conversion and increasing focus on the political process. By the 1980 presidential election, the Religious Right had completely abandoned the priority of personal conversion and sought instead to revive the "principles" of a Christian America. Ronald Reagan embodied this principle-oriented revival, and helped crystalize a revivalist nationalism that remains embedded in contemporary evangelical politics.

Keywords: Protestant revivalism; evangelicalism; Religious Right; Billy Graham; Harold Ockenga; Bill Bright; Jerry Falwell; Francis Schaeffer; Ronald Reagan; 1980 election

1. Introduction

"Wake up, America! Stir thyself!" The fiery words of a young Billy Graham in 1947 poured forth to an audience of thousands, pleading to each person, and to a nation: "God help us to return before it is too late" ([1], p. 27)! Graham was preaching revival—revival of the soul and the nation. Revival of souls *for* the revival of the nation. His theory of political change was straightforward: saved souls lead to a saved nation. In his Los Angeles crusade of 1949, which launched him into national fame, Graham warned that the fate of the City of Angels hinged on the spiritual lives of his listeners. "In this moment I can see the judgment hand of God over Los Angeles," he cried. "I can see judgment about to fall. If we repent, if we believe, if we turn to Christ in faith and hope, the judgment of God can be stopped" ([2], p. 57). Graham's language traveled fluidly, unhindered between individual salvation and national renewal. His words provided his audience with a politics that emphasized personal morality and individual responsibility.

Thirty years later, a call for revival, in a similarly spectacular setting, came from a man in many ways the opposite of Graham. While the evangelist preached against the apostasy of Los Angeles, Ronald Reagan made his name and his early career in Hollywood. Graham preached spiritual conversion above all else; Reagan's theory of political change had no explicit mention of Jesus Christ. Graham crusaded for souls; Reagan crusaded for principles. In his 1980 acceptance speech for the

Republican party nomination for president in Detroit, Reagan outlined his own revivalist agenda expressed through his revivalist campaign slogan, "Let's Make America Great Again." "For those who've abandoned hope, we'll restore hope and we'll welcome them into a great national crusade to make America great again" [3]. To revive hope was Reagan's primary passion; to "renew our compact of freedom", the principles of small government and American exceptionalism. Through restoring this compact, through voting out the Democrats and even those Republicans who violated American freedoms, Reagan offered his thousands of listeners, and millions of voters—many of whom also cherished Graham's revivalism—another kind of crusade.

The blurring of revival, politics, and nationalism that both Graham and Reagan embodied points to two understudied and misunderstood aspects of how evangelicals became part of a discrete political movement after World War II. Graham's religious revivalism and Reagan's political revivalism highlight how broad and malleable the practice of revival remained in postwar America, and yet also how distinct different types could be. "Revivalist nationalism"—this fusion of revivalist form, practice, and language with national concern and nationalistic politics—deserves attention in the postwar period for two reasons best illustrated by sketching the changing role of revivalism in American evangelicalism from Graham to Reagan [4–6].

First, revival as a political practice has been virtually ignored by historians of postwar evangelicalism or nationalism [7–13]. Its presence, however, is constant throughout the postwar era and offers a distinctive angle into growing mass political participation by evangelicals. Revival is an inherently political practice, including, as historian Bernard Weisberger noted, both a call for a previous, purer form of religion and a rebuke of the present ([14], p. vii). Taking place in the American context after World War II, revivalism fused with nationalism in new ways. George Mosse, the historian of European culture, wrote of the "nationalization of the masses" through public festivals, monuments, and mass gatherings in nineteenth century Germany [15]. In the same vein, revivalism contributed to the politicization of evangelical masses after World War II. In the American religious context, William McLoughlin argued more than forty years ago that revivals "are essentially folk movements, the means by which a people or a nation reshapes its identity, transforms its patterns of thought and action, and sustains a healthy relationship with environmental and social change" ([16], p. 2). McLoughlin sought to generalize revivals and awakenings across cultures; here we seek to understand how revivalist nationalism as a populist "folk movement" helped to bring millions of evangelicals into the political process. Historians have documented the decisive role of revivalism in nineteenth century America through the decline of revivalism in the 1920s ([17], pp. 180–89). Less studied has been the continuing relevance of this practice.

Second, while revival has remained a consistent practice of evangelicals over the postwar period, its relationship to politics has changed. That is because the goals of revival have changed. Certainly, there remain revivals in the twenty-first century that look strikingly similar to Graham's crusades in the 1940s, calling for individual salvation, the atonement of sin, and assuming a direct connection between individual and national revival [18]. However, in the main, American evangelical leaders marshalled the means of revival to different ends. While the practice and form of revival—of "crusading"—provides a through line to this story, evangelicals themselves redeployed revivalism toward different political ends. Jerry Falwell, who succeeded Graham as the unofficial spokesman for evangelicalism in the 1970s, articulated a new theory of revival and its relationship to politics: to win divine blessing God cared less about individual souls and more about the principles that society was based upon. A nation may be full of unregenerate sinners, he explained in 1981, but if it upheld biblical principles it could remain in God's graces. "He'll still go to hell a tither," Falwell remarked on the unsaved American who remained biblically moral, "but God blesses the principle" ([19], p. 22).

Since World War II, revivalist nationalism has maintained a central place in evangelical Christian nationalism. At the same time, revival has undergone a massive conceptual shift, making it more conducive to nationalist politics. There are at least three phases in this outline of revivalist nationalism worth exploring in more detail. Graham's revivalism, expressed in his crusades after World War II, offered an idealistic conception of politics and nationalism, what historian Steven Miller has termed "evangelical universalism", believing in a social ethic centered on the individual soul and free will, and predicated on the universal commonality of divinely created humans ([13], pp. 44–50). By the 1960s, this idealism gave way to a realism that "old fashioned" revival could not alone renew the nation. Bill Bright, the founder of Campus Crusade for Christ, promoted more explicitly and directly a political message in his massive revival campaigns of the 1970s. Bright added to his revivalist nationalism a concern for party politics and the political process and the Christian injunction to "help elect men and women of God in every position of influence" [20]. Finally, Falwell took revivalist nationalism in a new direction by reducing focus on the eternal fate of individual souls—the singular focus of Graham's early crusades. While Falwell remained concerned for individual salvation, he drew a stark line between individual and national revival. As the leader of the Moral Majority, he welcomed Catholics, Jews, and Mormons, whose eternal fate he regarded with grave concern, but whose role in national revival—in the crusade to make America great again—was essential.

There was no single cause for the shift in revivalist emphasis, but a number of developments deserve attention as contributing factors. First, as time went on, evangelical revivalists were less and less directly connected to fundamentalism's commitment, however perfunctory, to a separation between political and religious language. Scholars have shown this separatism to be mostly non-existent, especially when it came to national politics, but in the language and theology of revivalism, there remained a strong distaste for explicitly political discussion. This would fade over the postwar period until the trappings of revival were conscripted in the direct service of political rallies. A second factor shifting the goals of revival were the realities of expanding religious and ethnic pluralism in America. To put it bluntly, the early postwar expectations of an old fashioned, largely white, evangelical revival became impractical. Even accounting for the power of the Holy Spirit, evangelicals in 1980 did not exhibit the same confidence as their forbearers in 1950 that a national awakening could occur. A third factor was ideological: the concurrent rise of the conservative movement and the threat, both real and imagined, of "secular humanism". Billy Graham's unsophisticated embrace of revivalist individualism appeared quaint to 1970s evangelicals, who spoke of biblical presuppositions, secular humanism, and conservatism as concepts rooted in a "biblical worldview". "Old-fashioned" revivalism was concerned with morals, manners, and clear threats to Christianity like communism. The revivalist nationalism of the late 1970s embedded morality in more expansive arguments about values and developed an interpretation of secular humanism that made sense of the drift of American politics, the judiciary, and culture.

Throughout the postwar period, however, the outward trappings of revival remained as central to Falwell and Reagan as they were to Graham: the large crowds and the charismatic leader; the call to repent and the call to action; the return to apostolic faith and the rebuke of modern religion. Revival has become an innate pattern and ideological blueprint for evangelical politics. The progression from Graham to Reagan illustrates not only the centrality of revival to evangelical conceptions of politics and the changing relations of revivalism to Christian nationalism, but reveals a subtle and pervasive shift in evangelical concerns. By 1980, the chief purveyors of America as a "Christian nation" in fact had less interest in making new Christians of the nation's citizens. Theirs was a revival of principles, not souls.

2. Revival and the Nation

Though evangelicals believed that conversion ultimately depended upon the working of the Holy Spirit, they had immense faith and expectation that God dependably worked in history through mass revival. Joel Carpenter has called this faith an "evangelical Whig" tradition of political thinking, "which by means of revivalism and voluntary reform sought to provide the virtuous political culture that would keep the American republic true to its covenant" ([21], p. 117). The sawdust trails and big tent gatherings struck many Americans in the twentieth century as anti-modern [22]. Not so for postwar evangelicals who, while updating the forms and practices, saw in the content of revivalism the divine process for spiritual and national renewal. This was always paired with an intense apocalyptic expectation that revival, which witnessed the temporal being invaded by the eternal in the setting of a mass gathering, presaged the imminent return of Christ [23]. As much as evangelicals and fundamentalists believed in discernable, material, and historical fulfillment of prophecy, they also enumerated "conditions", "results", "consequences", and "implications" of revival with the same certainty. This science of revival was the backbone of revivalist nationalism, revealing with exactitude the ways that revivals would come about and renew souls, and through souls, the nation.

In Graham's commitment to his crusades, we can see that more than anything else he sought to convert the masses to Christ. However, he was also concerned with the social, cultural, and political changes roiling American society. The science of revival established that the relationship between revival, personal salvation, and national glory was spelled out clearly in the Bible; it was as ironclad as the laws of physics [24,25]. "I believe that God is true to His Word, and that He must rain righteousness upon us if we meet his conditions," he confessed ([1], p. 59). Graham saw the individual and the political as inextricable. His idealistic expectation of revival redeeming the nation comprised the primary theme of his early crusade messages. God's judgment was awaiting America "unless people repent and believe—unless God sends an old-fashioned, heaven-sent, Holy Ghost revival" ([2], p. 52).

Graham followed in the revivalist tradition of Dwight Moody and Billy Sunday, who made similar calls for individual souls to accept Christ on the way to national renewal. The same energy, militancy, and confidence animated Graham as it had his forbearers, though the form of Graham's revivals evidenced a fusion of "old-fashioned" revivalism and new technologies and organization. Speaking of his early work for Youth for Christ in 1945–1948, Graham recalled, "We used every modern means to catch the ear of unconverted young people and then punched them straight between the eyes with the gospel" ([26], p. 488). In the late 1940s, a typical Graham revival lasted ten to twenty-one days and claimed five hundred to fourteen hundred converts. As Graham focused on urban areas like Charlotte, Miami, and Baltimore, his revivals took place either in buildings meant to accommodate mass meetings (large churches, auditoriums, and stadiums) or, as in the case of Los Angeles in 1949, a massive tent on a vacant lot with seating for thousands. Graham's sermons were the top-billed events, but revivals also featured music (Graham preferred solemn hymns), guest speakers (often other evangelists or celebrities connected to Graham), and the all-important alter call to visually capture the "decisions for Christ". Seeking to improve upon his predecessors, Graham invested in follow-up counseling programs meant to integrate new converts into church life. Pervading the entire revival, at each stage and in each organizational decision, was the priority to reach the most people possible with the gospel message.

By the 1930s, national spiritual renewal had lost its distinctly Protestant evangelistic edge and become part of the developing civil religion of America [27]. The belief in a need for national "awakening" was shared by none other than President Roosevelt, who uttered a succinct summary of the concept in a 1936 radio address: "I doubt if there is any problem—social, political or economic—that would not melt away before the fire of such a spiritual awakening" [28]. However, Roosevelt's spiritual awakening was non-sectarian, a recognition of the "brotherhood of man" and a call to national unity in the face of global threats. Harry Truman and Dwight Eisenhower uttered similar hopes for "moral and spiritual reawakening", but these, too, elevated a tri-faith "Judeo-Christian" spirituality foreign to the pew benches of old-fashioned revivalism [29,30]. For Billy Sunday, and indeed for Billy Graham, spiritual awakening only came from on the saving grace of Jesus Christ. This was a theological necessity, as the Holy Spirit, the agent of renewal, only fell upon those who had accepted Jesus as their Savior [31]. Graham's revivalism, part of the new public religiosity in the postwar period, differed in that his remained exclusivist and centered on the saving power of Jesus Christ. While Graham readily associated his revivals with national political leaders including Eisenhower and Nixon, his language from the pulpit remained rooted in the "revivalist individualism" of fundamentalism, which prioritized individual spiritual regeneration over political actions to bring about social reform ([21], p. 118).

A faith in the power of spiritual revival pervaded American society in the 1930s and 1940s, though Graham's revivals were distinctive for retaining the particularistic goal of Protestant Christian conversions. This was in part a function of Graham's own fundamentalist upbringing, which he only slowly distanced himself from until separatists openly charged Graham with being too ecumenical in his 1957 crusade in New York City [32]. Another explanation for Graham's emphasis on old-fashioned revival points to the financial backing he received from Christian businessmen beginning in the 1940s. Like one of his most pivotal backers, business executive Herbert J. Taylor, Graham believed that social change came primarily through individual souls being transformed. This same emphasis on individual choice and freedom appealed to Taylor in the realm of business, as Darren Grem has shown. Taylor's turnaround of his own companies in the midst of the Great Depression "reassured him of the applicability of religion in the work place and the nation at large. If his faith, duly believed, resulted in his company's success, then Taylor reasoned that God would bless any other endeavor, whether in private enterprise or not, if it followed a few guidelines" ([33], p. 33). The alliance between old-fashioned revival and free enterprise gave Graham the resources and justification for continuing to insist that salvation through faith in Christ alone would bring about change.

With the gospel as the key ingredient in revival, Graham and other evangelical leaders took great pains to enumerate—for themselves and for their audiences—the conditions, consequences, and results of revival. Harold Ockenga, the longtime pastor at Park Street Church in Boston (1936–1969), was, like Graham, a student of the revival. Though he ultimately credited the Holy Spirit with the fruits of revival, Ockenga also insisted the practice itself was structured through discernable processes—there was a science to revivals, a pattern outlined in the Bible and detectable in church history. All revivals were patterned from the apostolic work detailed in the New Testament. The Holy Spirit-driven mass conversions recorded in the book of Acts set the template for modern revival. Ockenga's revivalist outlook was further shaped by his Methodist upbringing. Moreover, he and many other evangelicals also relied on the early twentieth-century work of James Burns, whose *Revivals: Their Laws and Leaders* (1909) became a guidebook [34]. Together, the New Testament, the history of American revivalism, and the enumerated "laws" of revivalism shaped the goals and expectations of Graham's crusades.

According to Ockenga, revivals followed an "ebb and flow" historical trajectory, reaching fruition with the confluence of a united confession by listeners, ecclesiastical cooperation, and visionary leadership. At such moments the Holy Spirit would take hold. Ockenga counted three major revivals in American history, the First and Second Great Awakenings and Dwight Moody's ministry in the late 19th century; Graham was content to note that "after every great crisis in American history we have always had a revival" ([1], p. 18). Ockenga described the "flow" of revival in broader historical language. "The powerful awakening resulting from the combination of these circumstances is like a mighty billow which rolls irresistibly over the land. Vast energies and new forces long in preparation now burst into being," he explained. "[T]here is a regrouping of forces for a new advance. In the ebb there is always the gathering of the swell before moving forward, and that swell is gathering now," he prophesied in 1947 ([35], p. 229).

Just as in revivals of the past, the most important transformation to occur in the midcentury revival would be in the individual sinner. "What is God's work which is to be revived?" Ockenga asked. "First, it is God's work to forgive sin." The message that "Christ Jesus came to save sinners" led to "the reconciliation of rebellious men with their sovereign God" ([35], p. 224). Graham's famous call, in virtually every one of his sermons, for each individual to "turn to Jesus" was the coda and the basis for his crusades. "What can you do? Right now you can turn to Jesus," he pleaded with his listeners. "Let Christ come into your heart and cleanse you from sin, and He can give you the assurance that if you died tonight, you would go to heaven" ([2], p. 62).

In the same way that revivals facilitated the coming of the Holy Spirit on individuals, they also, through their salvific power, could safeguard American society. Here the direct linkage between personal and national revival found its purest expression. In 1949, Graham assured his listeners that "revival brings tremendous social implications". Past revivals, he explained, had brought about the abolishment of slavery and child labor. Moreover, when "the Wesleys preached in England, people were working ninety hours a week! As a result of that revival, sixty hours became standard, and our great trade unions were organized" ([2], p. 61; [36]). More directly relevant after World War II, Graham regarded revival as the best, and the only legitimate, response to national threats like communism and materialism. "To safeguard our democracy and preserve the true American way of life," he concluded one sermon, "we need, we must have, a revival of genuine, old-fashioned Christianity, deep, widespread, in the power of the Holy Spirit." The corporate response that Graham had in mind mirrored the response of the individual to the alter call: "May God forgive our sins, change our stupidity, help us to repent, turn and pray, and turn us into the spiritual conflict! *Our only hope is revival*" ([2], p. 29).

Ockenga similarly understood revival to have social implications. The revival's "manifold effect upon society is just what men are seeking to promote by all other means, namely, to curb sin, to restrain evil, to promote righteousness, and to elevate mankind". In addition to the individual, the church and society would benefit. Revival aimed to "rebuild and strengthen the church as His witness in the world" through acting as "the custodian of the truth, the guardian of moral standards, the minister of mercy" and through receiving "thousands of new members, born-again ones". Revival could reform society and reorder the procedures of government. "There would be no need to resort to all the legislating processes to force men into these channels if a revival should occur, for then they would be moved from within to follow these channels." In other words, social revival flowed through personal redemption. Ockenga insisted, "It is obvious to us all that Christ is the solution. Let men acknowledge His authority, let them come to know Him as Saviour, let them love Him in life, and they will act accordingly" ([35], p. 226). This idealistic approach to the nature of politics underpinned both Graham's and Ockenga's embrace of revival as a process to spur mass politics.

A final component of the science of revival was the singular figure of the revivalist, the individual through which God worked and through which the work of the Holy Spirit would reach the masses. "When a revival is about to come a person is discovered who incarnates in his message and life the inmost need of the times," Ockenga explained, ecumenically citing Francis of Assisi, Savonarola, Luther, Wesley, and Moody as examples. "He is more sensitive to the longings of men, the ideas of his day, the whisperings of the Spirit of God, until in what he does and says he becomes the symbol of the revival movement and the interpreter of the revival message" ([35], p. 227). Writing of the Los Angeles crusade, Mel Larson waxed that "Revival flowed through Billy Graham during that time until the entire world was conscious of it" ([37], p. 9). Graham's rocket into national fame in 1949–1950 gave evangelicals like Ockenga and Larson confidence that Graham would fulfill the role of Holy Spirit-powered revivalist. Charismatic leadership was an essential and defining component to reaching the masses.

On the heels of his success in Los Angeles, at which he spoke to more than 350,000 people, Graham traveled to Boston on the invitation of Ockenga. Hoping for a repeat success, Ockenga scheduled Graham for a New Year's Eve service in the nearby town of Worcester. With expectations "surprisingly moderate and publicity ... sparse," Graham managed to draw 6000 people to the first night ([38], p. 132). He then did so again every night for the next eighteen days. Speaking on that first evening, Ockenga belted, "The hour for revival has struck. New England is ripe for evangelism. The same yearning which is seen over the land is experienced here" ([38], p. 133). The hope of revival overflowed naturally into the political sphere. Observing a litany of national and international problems, Ockenga assured that "millions and millions of Americans believe an old-fashioned spiritual revival could preserve our God-given freedoms and way of life" ([38], p. 134). If through Graham God converted the masses, and reawakened Christians, then the spiritual and social renewal of revival for the nation—"like a mighty billow which rolls irresistibly over the land"—had a vital place in the very fabric of the American century ([35], p. 227).

We can see in the work of Ockenga and success of Graham a deep-seated conviction in the "laws" of revival to improve the nation. Like many revivalists before them, including Charles Finney,

Dwight Moody, and Billy Sunday, their sermons preached against personal vices—drunkenness, sexual immorality, and laziness—and drew straight conclusions between these practices and the dire state of the nation. Conversely, the key to reviving the nation resided in turning from sin and receiving the blessing of the Holy Spirit through repentance. This theory of political change was immensely attractive to evangelicals after World War II and compelled hundreds of revivalists, Graham only the most prominent, to engage political questions through revivalism. Likewise, thousands of visitors to tent chapels and baseball stadiums in the 1940s and 1950s heard a clear and confident explanation of the challenges facing America, from communism to poor child rearing. Revivalism, more than virtually any other sphere of evangelical activity, brought evangelical religion and politics together to the masses.

3. Revivalist Nationalism and the Political Process

Graham's astronomical success with his crusades created a template and a network of institutions to perpetuate and expand revivalism. Most of the programming of the Billy Graham Evangelistic Association in the 1950s and 1960s worked off the model of an idealistic personal and national revival that animated Graham's early ministry. As late as 1973, with the national program of "Key '73" aiming to "evangelize the continent for Christ" in a single year, personal conversion still remained the primary process through which many evangelical leaders believed true political change could occur [39].

But the idealistic expectation of mass revival to spontaneously produce better government and a stronger America held less sway over a younger generation of revivalists, less submerged in fundamentalism and more concerned with accumulating cultural and political capital. For these evangelicals, including Bill Bright, the founder of Campus Crusade for Christ in 1951, evangelistic revival as the sole means to national reform was insufficient. Soul revival remained the crucial starting point, but it had to be paired with a more realistic understanding American politics that took into account the rough-and-tumble processes of democracy. To be sure, Bright remained fervently committed to the goals of personal spiritual revival and remained convinced that this was the bedrock of national renewal. From the 1950s until his death in 2003, Bright promoted his soul-focused "Four Spiritual Laws" literature with consistent verve and conviction. However, Bright's increasingly direct political engagement, especially in the 1970s, complicated the hitherto straightforward relationship between personal and national revival. Bright's fusion of soul revival and political engagement as two distinct steps in the process of national renewal fueled a more overt revivalist nationalism.

Graham himself presaged the changing role of revival in American political life. As he became close confidants of Presidents Eisenhower, Johnson, and Nixon, Graham's crusades and public utterances became more explicitly political. He held revivalist-type political rallies through Nixon's time in office, such as when Nixon spoke at a crusade event in Knoxville, Tennessee in May 1970, or when Graham helped organize "Honor America Day" for Fourth of July celebrations the same year. With close collaboration between Nixon and Graham, these rallies and crusades often played to Nixon's political advantage ([8], pp. 242–72).

This growing political valence could appear deceptively apolitical. At the 4 July rally he pleaded with the crowd of more than 300,000, "Let's sing a little, let's wave the flag, let's rejoice in all that's best in our country. We know America has its faults. But there are good things about America. It has not gone to the dogs. Let's be happy on our birthday" [40]. As part of an older of generation of revivalists who remained committed to evangelization as not only a necessary, but a sufficient force for social transformation, Graham remained hesitant, even with the president sharing the stage, to wade into full-fledged partisan politics. In public, Graham projected a more detached political engagement that could survive transitions of power from one party to another, such as from Johnson to Nixon. In Grant Wacker's words, Graham "seemed both confident and proud that he had addressed those issues in terms of wide moral principles, not Democratic or Republican agendas" ([41], p. 222) Graham was also a man easily tempted by power and a seemingly unbreakable loyalty to Nixon until the final hours of Watergate. As with previous presidents, Graham's certainty in each man's personal piety made him perhaps too endeared to personal persuasion. He was driven by the conviction that good leaders inevitably produced good policy, much as his revivalism was built on the conviction that revived citizens inevitably produced a good nation.

This would begin to change in the 1970s. One of the central agents of change was Bill Bright, who, more than any other evangelical, intensified the call for national revival in the early part of the decade. In his highly successful Campus Crusade for Christ student ministry, Bright had sizeable resources and opportunity to launch a national—even global—campaign for revival. In addition to constantly expanding its ministry (to almost 4000 employees in 1975), Campus Crusade organized some of the largest revivals of the postwar period. In one of the most successful spectacles, Explo '72 (short for "spiritual explosion") at the Cotton Bowl in Dallas, Bright, Graham, and other revivalists reached more than 80,000 students. Graham spoke in Dallas, but the target audience was much younger than Graham's aging generation. The vast majority of attendees were between the ages of 15 and 30 [42]. Another 100,000 attended the "Christian Woodstock" music festival that ended Explo '72, featuring musicians from Randy Matthews to Johnny Cash. This event, along with Graham's increasingly large crusades, including speaking to more than 500,000 people in Seoul, South Korea, in 1973, dwarfed most other as mass gatherings of any type [43]. They were also the lead up to Bright's more explicit political work.

Bright's fervor for a national revival climaxed in 1976 with the celebration of the nation's bicentennial, in a presidential election year no less [44]. Bright put in place a new program, Countdown to '76, as a lead up to this momentous year. Writing in late 1975, Bright warned, "The next 16 months will, in my opinion, likely determine the destiny of our nation and the future course of history." In language striving to capture the biblical immensity of the task before him, he explained, "We are in a battle with Satan and a race against time. Our present involvement as Christians is not enough. We must do more—yes, many times more. At present, we are losing the battle." The initial goal, he explained to supporters, was for "tens of millions of Americans [to] be reached for Christ in this country before we end our bicentennial celebrations, 31 December 1976" [45].

But this was only the first phase. While this evangelism may have satisfied Graham, Bright wanted a foothold in the American political process, too. He gave a number of reasons for expanding his interest into the realm of formal politics, including the rising threat of "secular humanism" evident in Supreme Court cases banning prayer and Bibles in school and the erosion of traditional Christian morality in culture. These were pertinent issues, but they were part of a more fundamental shift that concerned Bright and other evangelicals who continued to promote revival: the increasingly pluralistic beliefs and attitudes of Americans. The rise of constant polling and survey data in the 1970s laid bare that more Americans than ever did not agree some of the basic religious values that evangelicals considered essential. Moreover, the Hart-Cellar Act in 1965 abolished the immigration quota system based on national origin, which led to increasing numbers of non-Protestants settling in the country. Bright could point to some new statistical findings to encourage revivalism—in 1975 he cited "hundreds of thousands of surveys taken at random across the United States [that] indicate that one out of two unbelievers in certain parts of the nation to one out of four generally will receive Christ the first time they hear the gospel" [45]. However, these stats could easily be countered with survey after survey indicating increased religious pluralism across the nation [46]. For revival to achieve national renewal in this new context, it had to be directed and channeled.

As one part of this realization, Campus Crusade, which had evolved from a campus ministry into an organization with its hands in all sorts of social and political issues, embarked on a massive campaign in 1976 branded "Here's Life, America!" It was a combination of local church outreach, training, and evangelism, supported by a multi-million-dollar marketing budget, merchandise, and media coverage. By most accounts, the immediate goal of sharing the gospel with every American in 1976 came up short, and the church growth as a result of the campaign was modest. However, as historian John Turner has shown, the campaign helped bring Bright and evangelicals as a political demographic into the political light in 1976. It was coupled with other political efforts meant to build off of Here's Life, America, including a Washington D.C. based center, the Christian Embassy, which aimed to be a spiritual center for lawmakers. As an emerging religious identity, "evangelical" had yet to ally itself openly or exclusively with conservative and Republican Party politics. Indeed, a vocal minority of liberal-leaning evangelicals, the so-called evangelical left, vied for popular attention. Bright's efforts, however, had helped make "evangelical" a political as well as religious identity.

Like other evangelical leaders who recognized the limitations of personal salvation to directly affect the political process, Bright sought to politicize politically inactive Christians. He eagerly endorsed a new "Citizen's Guide to Politics" written especially to this group, titled *In the Spirt of '76* [47]. Published by Third Century Publishers in Washington D.C., which Bright and Arizona Congressman John Conlan founded in 1974, the book displayed a granular understanding of American political organizing. It made more complex the idealistic revivalist relationship between personal salvation and "good government", offering itself as "a 'how to' handbook on winning elections" and urging Christians that "taking part in the political processes of civil government" was biblically warranted. The bulk of the book took readers through a detailed outline of selecting candidates, building campaign teams, and organizing at the precinct level. The book featured a quotation by Billy Graham about the role of Christians in good government, but this offered a far more detailed theory of how being a Christian influenced the political process than Graham's revivalist messages.

Graham's prominent place on the cover of *In the Spirit of '76* was misleading for another reason. Through the mid-1970s, especially since Bright's decision during Explo' 74 to praise the regime of Park Chung Hee for allowing Christianity to be taught in Korean schools, Graham began to distance himself from his longtime associate. "When I read what Bright said over there [in South Korea], it sickened me," Graham told *Newsweek* in 1976 [48]. Part of Graham's concern over Bright's attempt to merge revivalism and political activism was because Graham was still reeling from the aftermath of Watergate, a searing experience that chastened, though did not eradicate, his public identification with any single politician [49]. Graham's unusually close relationship to Nixon had discredited him in the eyes of many Americans. "I learned my lesson the hard way," he reflected [48].

But there was an ever deeper chasm between Graham and Bright that revealed their different approaches to revival, salvation, and politics. One particular issue that angered Graham, according to *Newsweek*, was that he had come across "evidence of attempts by representatives of Campus Crusade to organize politically the hundreds of prayer and Bible-study groups spawned by [Graham's] crusades" [48]. This brazenly calculating intervention in the process between the revival (the crusade) and improving government struck at the most basic understanding that Graham's revivalism was built upon. Bright rejected the idealistic link between personal salvation and national renewal, recognizing instead the need to organize and place Christians in positions of power before national renewal could. "Bright has been using me and my name for twenty years," Graham complained. "But now I'm concerned about the political direction he seems to be taking" [48].

Bright himself did not take his more engaged political philosophy to its logical conclusion. John Conlan, Bright's partner at Third Century Publishers, began to use the organization and its literature to endorse specific Republican candidates and create an index of members of congress rating their conservative ratings. This was a bridge too far for Bright who remained foremost committed to the evangelistic work of the ostensibly non-partisan Campus Crusade. After a searing expose by the evangelical left magazine *Sojourners*, Bright reduced his official political activism even further ([12], pp. 120–22).

But while Bright retained a primacy on the revival as site for personal conversion, other evangelicals, similarly stoked into nationalistic celebration by the bicentennial, were willing to press forward and further utilize the methods of revival toward engaging in the political process. Jerry Falwell, an obscure Independent Baptist pastor from Lynchburg, Virginia, used the bicentennial celebrations as a coming out party for nationalizing his socially conservative message. In 1976 he endorsed Gerald Ford over the self-identified evangelical Jimmy Carter. In addition, the founder of Lynchburg Baptist College, Falwell brought a choir to Washington D.C. to sing in the bicentennial

"I Love America" celebrations ([12], p. 171–72). The performance, which Falwell turned into a television special, evidenced a mix of revival themes and Falwell's trademark deftness for electronic media and showmanship. The opening scene included, in the words of one reporter, "the singers stepping smartly in time up and down the steps [of Capitol Hill], smiling and singing 'I Love America' to upbeat, pre-recorded and fully orchestrated music." The song lyrics rang out: "Free to worship as we please ... that's why I love America ... America, America, the land I love" [50]. These types of events weren't explicitly partisan—they in fact echoed the form of old-fashioned revivals with choirs, praise music, and revivalist speakers. In his early efforts, Falwell hit on the same evangelical themes that had animated revivalism since World War II: moral decline, coming judgment, the unlimited potential of redemption for both the individual and the nation. However, one glaring omission to the revival formula was the alter call. Bright had tried to bridge the alter call and partisan politics and made modest headway. It would be left to Falwell, who had no intention of using events like "I Love America" to call sinners to Christ, to further develop revivalist nationalism.

4. "Pro-Principle" Revivalist Nationalism

By 1980, the Religious Right had assumed the mantel of leadership in the evangelical world—both spiritually and politically [51,52]. This reality underlay the shifting meaning of revival and the developing nationalism of the Religious Right. The often-weekly televangelist revival episodes of Jerry Falwell, Pat Robertson, Jack Hayford, and Jimmy Swaggart reached millions of Americans in their homes, while these same ministers laced their sermons with implicit and explicit political messages about what it would take for national revival. In form and style, there was a great continuity in postwar revivalism. However, the sawdust trails and big tents were much too small for the American Century. Massive buildings—stadiums, megachurches, theaters—required microphones, speakers, and lighting to best present the revivalist's message to audiences of thousands. Music, skits, and auxiliary ministers conveyed messages consonant with the central, charismatic revivalist, while a variety of books, tapes, programs, and bumper stickers supported both the believer and revivalist. Even in message many themes remained consistent. The judgment of God, the promise of salvation, the everlasting faithfulness of the Word echoed in cavernous halls and living rooms alike. The Religious Right inherited and leveraged revival with one major exception: it dropped the evangelism. It adopted the form of revival but shifted the emphasis. The result was a more political, less evangelistic, but equally urgent and populist revival suitable to the demands of grassroots, local, and culture wars politics.

One way to see this shift is in Jerry Falwell's reformulation of the relationship between personal salvation and national renewal alluded to earlier. In 1981, Falwell was interviewed by the evangelical magazine *Christianity Today* and asked about the rationale for his entrance into politics and, essentially, his entire ministry apparatus that included the Thomas Road Baptist Church, the Moral Majority, his *Old Time Gospel Hour* television program, and Lynchburg Baptist College (renamed Liberty University in 1984). Falwell's response was telling. The editors of *Christianity Today*, still operating in Graham's model of revivalism, were concerned that Falwell was mistaking politics for spirituality. They presented Falwell with a hypothetical:

> Say that in Salt Lake City they took the Moral Majority position right down the line, but because of false doctrine, they would not ultimately go to heaven. New York City has a reputation for the very things Moral Majority is against. Yet there is a possibility that some of those people in the corrupt society in New York City, in spite of their immorality, might be converted and wind up in heaven. Which would you rather see? I'm concerned that we could get the country morally straight and people would still go to hell [19].

This question got at the heart of the diverging purposes of revivalist nationalism. Did the saving of souls lead to the saving of the nation? Or did the underlying morality of society require the evangelist's primary attention? In response, Falwell emphasized a clear delineation between the spiritual and the political. "America has become the greatest nation on earth," he explained, not because it was full of Christians, but "because of what Solomon said in Proverbs 14 (in paraphrase): 'Living by God's principles promotes a nation to greatness; violating God's principles brings a nation to shame.'" He continued, "If a nation or a society lives by divine principles, even though the people personally don't know the One who taught and lived those principles, that society will be blessed. An unsaved person in business will be blessed by tithing to the work of God. He'll still go to hell a tither, but God blesses the principle." Here Falwell reversed the evangelical priority of personal salvation to save the nation. Instead, he sought to save the nation first, which would protect the needed political freedoms with which to save souls. *Christianity Today* asked for a clear statement on this reversal: "So then you can justify Moral Majority by this rather distinct, clear delineation between the political and the spiritual and say that in the long run Moral Majority contributes to the preaching of the gospel and the saving of souls?" Falwell responded, "Yes, because it creates and preserves freedom" ([19], pp. 22–23).

The Religious Right's priority of principles over souls was fashioned, delivered, and even embedded in the form of revival. Falwell and other leaders of the Religious Right fused revivalism with their overarching goal to preserve and revive the principles of America they felt to be in peril. One of Falwell's intellectual influences, Francis Schaeffer, relied on national revival as the primary frame within which to promote mass political action in the 1980s. Schaeffer and Falwell worked closely to promote a more theologically Christian understanding of "Judeo-Christian values", especially on the issue of abortion, and while Falwell, the longtime host of the *Old Fashioned Revival Hour*, played the role of revivalist, Schaeffer assumed the mantel of the Religious Right's theologian [53]. A broad set of concerns animated the more philosophically-minded Schaeffer, who could trace his rise as a popular conservative Christian intellectual to his attacks on modern Western thought formulated at his Swiss evangelistic center, L'Abri, and his well-attended speaking tours through college campuses in Europe and North America [54]. Schaeffer provided the Religious Right with another argument for the importance of revival in renewing the nation—one rooted almost entirely in the principles on which American society rested.

Schaeffer's philosophical approach reveals one of the additional shifts that was taking place in evangelical thinking and transforming the role of revival in the process. The overarching concern that Schaeffer displayed for principles could be traced to the presuppositionalist school of apologetics popular among Reformed theologians in the 1930s and 1940 ([55], pp. 220–24). Gordon Clark and Cornelius Van Til were two of the most prominent presuppositionalists and teachers of Schaeffer at Faith Theological Seminary. They focused on the most basic epistemological and ethical claims (presuppositions) as the basis for a Christian worldview. Without a Christian worldview, Christianity, morality, and Western civilization would collapse. These theologians had little affinity for revivalism or apocalypticism and emphasized a cerebral, philosophical, and systematic form of Christianity. Schaeffer's innovation was to marry the presuppositionalism with revivalism. Through the politics of the Religious Right, Schaeffer believed Christians could revive the worldview out of which evangelicalism had sprung. Along with Falwell, who featured him in his Lynchburg pulpit, Schaeffer saw revival as the vehicle to national salvation.

To that end, Schaeffer spoke out less against personal vices and trained his sights on the ideology of secular humanism. Bright anticipated the fixation on this newly defined enemy. In 1975 he charged that "the United States is being poisoned by a relatively small handful of people. They are the purveyors of pornographic filth, the writers of lewd plays and the producers of film. They are the ones who control the mass media and who pour atheistic humanism into the university classrooms." Bright numbered the culprits at "not more than one thousand individuals" [45]. The philosophical villain in Schaeffer's writings of the 1970s was "humanism", by which he meant "Any philosophy or system of thought that begins with man alone, in order to try to find a unified meaning to life" ([56], p. 200). He positioned the Christian worldview against humanism, and interpreted the rise of abortion rights and the looming threat of legal euthanasia as products of a "culture of death" rooted in humanism [57]. Popular evangelical writers like Tim LaHaye were equally charged against humanism and secularism. In his *Battle for the Mind* (1980), LaHaye outlined the sources, motivations, and arguments of humanism, a force which he aligned with political liberalism, public education, and the popular culture. This looming threat would decide the next decade, "a decade of destiny for America", LaHaye warned, "which will become increasingly humanistic or Christian in its philosophy" ([58], p. 46). In contrast to early postwar revivalism, the secular humanist threat of the 1970s removed from the center of concern the individual. The menace of humanism took precedence for the Religious Right, which worried that the very foundations of religious freedom and Christian society were eroding.

Thus, Falwell and Schaeffer were more concerned with the principles on which American society stood than the spiritual state of individual Americans. For example, in trying to revise the memory of revivalism, Schaeffer wrote in his call to political action, *A Christian Manifesto* (1982): "The old revivals are spoken about so warmly by the evangelical leadership. Yet they seem to have forgotten what those revivals were. Yes ... without any question and with tremendous clarity, [they called] for personal salvation. But they also called for a resulting social action. Read the history of the old revivals" ([59], p. 64). In fact, Graham rarely called for specific social action—he simply assumed it would follow. His idealistic notion that personal renewal would inevitably better the nation seemed naïve to Schaeffer. Schaeffer was calling for a revivalism even more politicized than Bright, who remained chiefly committed to "personal salvation" with an additional step of politicization.

Schaeffer had not rejected the importance of personal salvation, but he found less promise in the traditional revivalist emphasis. Moreover, he drew a more tenuous connection between personal and social salvation than had earlier evangelicals. While Graham traced the linkages between the personal forgiveness of sin and the elevation of mankind, Schaeffer only referred to the "resulting blessings" of "the gospel". His concern was more fundamental and more abstract than personal regeneration. "We have forgotten why we have a high view of life, and why we have a positive balance between form and freedom in government, and the fact that we have such tremendous freedoms without these freedoms leading to chaos." These deep cultural values were not the products of sinners turned saints, but "based on the fact that the consensus was the biblical consensus" in America ([59]. pp. 70–71). Here Schaeffer revealed that his ideas were not only informed by the tradition of revivalist nationalism, but also by the ideological conservatism then ascendant in the Republican Party. The same was true of Falwell and the majority of the Religious Right, which provided a pronounced difference to the new nationalist revivalism in comparison to its early postwar ancestor. Graham, Ockenga, and many other postwar evangelical leaders were conservatives by temperament and preference, but they did not possess a robust conservative worldview framed in terms of political philosophy. One of the achievements of the postwar conservative intellectual movement, as George Nash showed in the build up to the Religious Right's national prominence in the late 1970s, was supplying a comprehensive conservative worldview [60]. In the end, national revival for Falwell and Schaeffer was about restoring the principles of Christianity into the highest echelons of the American mind. Schaeffer cited the historical scholarship of Perry Miller to make the conservative case that behind the genesis of these deep cultural values—the American Revolution—a similar process had been at work [61].

5. "Make America Great Again"

The revivalist nationalism of Falwell and Schaeffer not only supported the Reagan Revolution, but Reagan himself fashioned his campaign as a revival to "make American great again". On Labor Day 1980, mere weeks before Americans cast their ballots, Reagan clearly defined what needed to be revived. "This country needs a new administration, with a renewed dedication to the dream of America—an administration that will give that dream new life and make America great again" [62]. A growing economy and American exceptionalism—"this last best hope of man on earth, this nation under God"—were two key components of this dream. These principles, Reagan prophesied, would find a revival of spirit and practice in his new administration.

Reagan playing the role of revivalist was in many ways unprecedented in modern American politics, which was peopled with presidents unsuitable or unwilling to borrow so liberally from the forms, themes, and language of evangelical revivalism. Most postwar presidents spoke of the need for a national "spiritual awakening", but few placed the theme at the center of their campaign. Most postwar presidents sought to stir the masses with speeches that evoked urgency and calls to action, but few had the Hollywood training to make such appeals resonate. Most postwar presidents associated with Billy Graham—the "Pastor to Presidents"—and gave tacit approval to improving the nation's civic religiosity, but few "endorsed" the work of conservative religious leaders, as Reagan did in a 1980 rally, and so closely allied themselves in public to the revivalists.

Like past presidents, Reagan had called for spiritual renewal in times of national upheaval. As early as 1972, at a Governor's Prayer Breakfast, he theologized, "I think our nation and the world need a spiritual revival as it has never been needed before . . . a simple answer . . . a profound and complete solution to all the trouble we face." But Reagan's conception of spiritual revival was narrower and more explicitly Christian than the civil religion of postwar America. In speaking to Pope Paul VI, Reagan especially praised the Jesus People movement of the late 1960s and "how so many young people had simply turned from drugs to faith in Jesus" ([63], p. 154). Moreover, during his presidency, Reagan received media scrutiny more than once for speaking too much in the vein of Protestant theology to a nation with vast religious pluralism. To the National Religious Broadcasters meeting in 1984, Reagan spoke of "a promise from Jesus to soothe our sorrows . . . He promised if our hearts are true, His love will be as sure as sunshine. And by dying for us, Jesus showed how far his love will go: all the way." This evangelism from the nation's bully pulpit had crossed the line for the *New York Times*, which took offense at Reagan's "private piety" made public in an official capacity as president ([64], pp. 157–70).

Both before and during his presidency, Reagan's overt religious language gave his campaigns an especially revivalist flavor that was apparent to reporters. For example, in a single story during Reagan's unsuccessful 1975–76 campaign to unseat Gerald Ford for the Republican nomination, *Newsweek* described him as "a missionary to the aggrieved" who ignited "visceral fire" in his fellow conservatives. "He's a man with a message who wants to make converts," one campaign staffer remarked. *Newsweek* observed that even though in March 1975 Reagan refused to make his campaign official, "the Reagan non-campaign still carries about it more nearly the aura of a Billy Graham crusade than of a classic political canvas." Reagan's anger against Ford was righteousness—the President "had fallen prey to the heresies of deficit spending and ecumenical politics" and Reagan aimed to "punish him for his apostasy". In all, while Reagan's language never reached this revivalist caricature, the form that Reagan had assumed was clearly, to reporters, an aping of the "old-fashioned" revival. Similar religious language to describe Reagan's campaigning could be found in 1980 and 1984. More than any other modern president—more even than the pious Jimmy Carter—Reagan utilized the trappings of revival and evoked its aura on the campaign trail [65].

However, being ecumenical by nature and surrounding himself especially with Catholic advisors, Reagan's revivalism was not about the alter call. Not only did evangelicals understand this, but they, too, had reconceived of their action in line with the revival of principle that Reagan espoused. Writing in 1982, Schaeffer described "a unique window open in the United States" following the 1980 elections. "It is unique because it is a long, long time since that window has been open as it is now . . . we should be struggling and praying that this whole other total entity—the material energy, chance worldview—can be rolled back with all its results across all of life" ([59], pp. 73–74). The "worldview" of the nation needed saving, and Reagan was the man through whom the revival would pour forth.

So dramatically had the priorities of evangelicals shifted that the eternal status of Reagan's soul was largely irrelevant to the Religious Right—a surprising development given revivalism's historical focus on personal salvation and piety. Certainly, evangelicals preferred leaders who were led by the Holy Spirit, but Jimmy Carter's unceremonious rejection by evangelical leadership showed that being saved was not everything. More to the point, Reagan was the candidate of the Religious Right because he held the principles evangelicals found most important. A final campaign episode evidences this point. In August 1980, a young Mike Huckabee, a future presidential candidate himself (who also attended Explo '72 as a high school student), helped organize the political rally in which Reagan said to evangelical ministers, "I know you can't endorse me. But I endorse you, and what you are doing" ([66], pp. 61–62). At the time Huckabee was an understudy of evangelist and revivalist James Robison. Huckabee's biographer recounted the final words that Robison imparted to Reagan that day:

> I looked at Mr. Reagan and I said, 'We really like you; we really like you. We like the principles that you espouse. But you need to understand something about the nature of this group that you'll speak to tonight and those of us in this room. We're not partisan; we're not pro-party; we're not pro-personality. We're pro-principle. If you stand by the principles that you say you believe, we'll be the greatest friends you'll ever have.' But I said, 'If you turn against those principles, we'll be your worst nightmare.' ([67], p. 143)

Robison captured the shifting priorities of American evangelicalism as it became more identified with the Religious Right. A receptive Reagan, if he reflected on Robison's caution, would have seen a clear picture of the scope and nature of what evangelical leaders expected spiritual revival to attain in the 1980s. Sawdust trails and alter calls—once the best hope of American national renewal—had been replaced by an entire set of principles related to family values, biblical morals, and political conservatism. The change in priorities is what allowed Robison, Falwell, and other evangelicals to cooperate with non-evangelicals and exert influence in national politics. The change was undoubtedly a response to the growing religious pluralism in America: with a Graham-like mass revival less and less likely, it made sense to resort to more universal principles of freedom and liberty. That this effort, like the "old fashioned" call for sinners to repent, was carried out through the practice of revival is a testament to how malleable and indispensable revivalist nationalism had become to American politics after World War II.

6. Conclusions

Insofar as evangelicals in the 1940s had a theory of political change, it was idealistic, straightforward, and direct: saving the nation came down to saving souls. "Our only hope is revival", Graham told his audiences. The dependability of God's promises and the laws of revivals dictated that through sinners coming to Christ, the nation could avert disaster and live up to its potential. This belief in the political and social power of revivals made mass revivalism central to the process of politicizing evangelicals. To the extent we can discuss a distinct nationalism among evangelicals, as opposed to mainline Protestants, Catholics, Jews, or other religious communities, it was a revivalism that interpreted global and national events in terms of sin, repentance, and salvation.

Revival remained central to evangelical politics throughout the postwar period, as the efforts of Bright and Falwell make clear. Even with the world of political organizing, campaigning, and fundraising knocking down the door to mobilize evangelicals, the allure of "Here's Life, America" and the *Old Fashioned Revival Hour* still remained strong. Reagan's revivalist-themed campaign to "Make America Great Again", which attracted lopsided numbers of evangelicals to the Republican ticket in 1980, evidenced the continuing endurance of revivalist motifs. And yet, Reagan's gospel was not about the fires of hell and Christ's saving grace. As president, perhaps, this was an impossible language with which to speak to such a diverse electorate. However, regardless, even among the 1970s revivalists and leaders of the Religious Right, revival had come to connote the biblically-based principles of America—wholly detached from the eternal status of individual souls. These principles needed to be revived against the onslaught of secular humanism. What principles did Reagan stand for? This, more than his personal faith, concerned the Religious Right.

By tracing revivalist nationalism through the postwar period, at least three points are worth summarizing. First, the centrality of revivalism to American evangelical nationalism reshapes how scholars should understand postwar evangelicalism, the rise of the Religious Right, and postwar conservatism. Revivalism has played a consistently disruptive role in American political culture. This did not change in the twentieth century, and in certain decades, like the 1970s, revivalism channeled, organized, and fueled a significant amount of political activity, especially in the fledgling conservative movement.

Second, revivalist nationalism is both an ideology and a process that contributed to the politicization of postwar evangelicals. Many evangelicals, from Mike Huckabee on, experienced decisive spiritual and political awakenings in the context of revival. Many of the most successful evangelical leaders, from Graham to Falwell to Pat Robertson, had deep ties to revivalism that deserve more exploration and contextualization.

Finally, because of revivalist nationalism's changing objectives over time—from winning individual souls to renewing the principles of the nation—we can observe a gradual secularization of revivalist nationalism, one that could even accommodate a non-evangelical figure like Donald Trump, so long as this figure was suitably "pro-principle". Indeed, this line of argument has pervaded evangelical discussions of the 2016 election and Trump's campaign to, once again, "Make American Great Again" [68]. Trump is the most recent in a long line of deft leaders—media savvy, charismatic, at home in front of a crowded stadium—who have continued to rely on revivalist forms to shape and share their message [69,70]. It would be too much to conclude that Trump's urgent message of recent national decline is merely an expression of a secularized revivalism, but it would be too little to ignore how this form, and its brand of nationalism, have shaped how millions of Americans understand the nation.

Conflicts of Interest: The author declares no conflict of interest.

References

1. Billy Graham. *Calling Youth to Christ*. Grand Rapids: Zondervan, 1947.
2. Billy Graham, ed. *Revival in Our Time: The Story of the Billy Graham Evangelistic Campaigns*. Wheaton: Van Kampen Press, 1950.
3. Ronald Reagan. "Republican National Convention." 17 July 1980. Available online: http://millercenter.org/president/speeches/speech-3406 (accessed on 29 September 2016).
4. Matthew Bowman. *The Urban Pulpit: New York City and the Fate of Liberal Evangelicalism*. Chapel Hill: University of North Carolina Press, 2014.
5. Margaret Bendroth. "Why Women Loved Billy Sunday: Urban Revivalism and Popular Entertainment in Early Twentieth-Century American Culture." *Religion and American Culture* 14 (2004): 251–71. [CrossRef]
6. Philip Goff, and Alan Heimert. "Revivals and Revolution: Historiographic Turns since Alan Heimert's 'Religion and the American Mind'." *Church History* 67 (1998): 695–721. [CrossRef]
7. The most recent studies of postwar evangelicalism have included revival settings, but have not systematically examined this particular form of participation even as they have emphasized relevant aspects to revivalism including apocalypticism, corporate funding of revivals, and the social networks built around revivalism.
8. Kevin M. Kruse. *One Nation under God: How Corporate America Invented Christian America*. New York: Basic Books, 2015.
9. Neil J. Young. *We Gather Together: The Religious Right and the Problem of Interfaith Politics*. New York: Oxford University Press, 2015.
10. Matthew Avery Sutton. *American Apocalypse: A History of Modern Evangelicalism*. Cambridge: Belknap Press, 2014.
11. Darren Dochuk. *From Bible Belt to Sunbelt: Plain-Folk Religion, Grassroots Politics, and the Rise of Evangelical Conservatism*. New York: W. W. Norton & Company, 2010.
12. Daniel Williams. *God's Own Party: The Making of the Christian Right*. New York: Oxford University Press, 2010.
13. Steven P. Miller. *Billy Graham and the Rise of the Republican South*. Philadelphia: University of Pennsylvania Press, 2009.
14. Bernard A. Weisberger. *They Gathered at the River: The Story of the Great Revivalists and Their Impact upon Religion in America*. Boston: Little, Brown and Company, 1958.
15. George L. Mosse. *The Nationalization of the Masses: Political Symbolism and Mass Movements in Germany from the Napoleonic Wars through the Third Reich*. New York: H. Fertig, 1975.

16. William McLoughlin. *Revivals, Awakenings, and Reform: An Essay on Religion and Social Change in America, 1607–1977*. Chicago: University of Chicago Press, 1978.

17. Josh McMullen. *Under the Big Top: Big Tent Revivalism and American Culture, 1885–1925*. New York: Oxford University Press, 2015.

18. For example, the "Together" revival held at Washington Mall on 12 July 2016. Michelle Boorstein. "'Together' is a modern-day evangelical revival, complete with TED Talks, hip-hop and no politics." *Washington Post*, 13 July 2016. Available online: https://www.washingtonpost.com/news/acts-of-faith/wp/2016/07/13/together-is-a-modern-day-evangelical-revival-complete-with-ted-talks-hip-hop-and-no-politics/ (accessed on 29 September 2016).

19. Jerry Falwell. "An Interview with the Lone Ranger of American Fundamentalism." *Christianity Today*, 4 September 1981, pp. 22–27.

20. William Bright to Wilbur M. Smith, letter, 17 November 1975, Wilber M. Smith papers, Archer Archives, Trinity Evangelical Divinity School, Deerfield, IL.

21. Joel A. Carpenter. *Revive Us Again: The Reawakening of American Fundamentalism*. New York: Oxford University Press, 1999.

22. T. J. Jackson Lears. *No Place of Grace: Antimodernism and the Transformation of American Culture, 1880–1920*. Chicago: University of Chicago Press, 1994.

23. Angela M. Lahr. *Millennial Dreams and Apocalyptic Nightmares: The Cold War Origins of Political Evangelicalism*. New York: Oxford University Press, 2007.

24. Timothy Gloege, and Guaranteed Pure. *The Moody Bible Institute, Business, and the Making of Modern Evangelicalism*. Chapel Hill: The University of North Carolina Press, 2015, pp. 76–84.

25. Branden Pietsch. *Dispensational Modernism*. New York: Oxford University Press, 2015, pp. 73–95.

26. Quoted in William McLoughlin. *Modern Revivalism: Charles Grandison Finney to Billy Graham*. New York: Ronald Press, 1959.

27. For the development of civil religion after World War II see Raymond J. Haberski. *God and War: American Civil Religion since 1945*. New Brunswick: Rutgers University Press, 2012.

28. "Radio Address on Brotherhood Day." 23 February 1936. Available online: http://www.presidency.ucsb.edu/ws/?pid=15250 (accessed on 29 September 2016).

29. "Address in Columbus at a Conference of the Federal Council of Churches." 6 March 1946. Available online: http://www.trumanlibrary.org/publicpapers/index.php?pid=1494 (accessed on 29 September 2016).

30. On "Judeo-Christianity" as a form of consensus liberalism, see Wendy Wall. *Inventing the "American Way": The Politics of Consensus from the New Deal to the Civil Rights Movement*. Oxford: Oxford University Press, 2008, pp. 143–48.

31. See, for example, Graham's sermon on "The Resurrection of Jesus Christ." In *Revival in Our Time: The Story of the Billy Graham Evangelistic Campaigns*. Edited by Billy Graham. Wheaton: Van Kampen Press, 1950, pp. 108–24.

32. William C. Martin. *A Prophet with Honor: The Billy Graham Story*. New York: Quill, 1991, pp. 204–24.

33. Darren E. Grem. *The Blessings of Business: How Corporations Shaped Conservative Christianity*. New York: Oxford University Press, 2016.

34. James Burns. *Revivals: Their Laws and Leaders*. London: Hodder and Stoughton, 1909.

35. Harold Ockenga. "The Great Revival." *Bibliotheca Sacra* 104 (1947): 224–35.

36. Graham's positive view of trade unions in this example is intriguing given his largely conservative approach to politics. Graham's support of Lyndon Johnson further establishes that another distinction between Graham and later revivalists was his lack of a detailed ideological conservatism.

37. Mel Larson. "Tasting Revival—at Los Angeles." In *Revival in Our Time: The Story of the Billy Graham Evangelistic Campaigns*. Edited by Billy Graham. Wheaton: Van Kampen Press, 1950.

38. Garth M. Rosell. *The Surprising Work of God: Harold John Ockenga, Billy Graham, and the Rebirth of Evangelicalism*. Grand Rapids: Baker Academic, 2008.

39. Carl F. H. Henry. "Looking Back at Key 73: A Weathervane of American Protestantism." *Reformed Journal* 24 (1974): 6–12.

40. "Gathering in Praise of America." *Time*, 13 July 1970, p. 15.

41. Grant Wacker. *America's Pastor: Billy Graham and the Shaping of a Nation*. Cambridge: Belknap Press, 2014.

42. Kenneth L. Woodward. "The Christian Woodstock." *Newsweek*, 26 June 1972, p. 52.

43. Graham and Bright, both international revivalists, were able to translate their revivalist individualism into a universal call for spiritual salvation largely by framing it in the context of the Cold War confrontation. They both remained American exceptionalists and regarded democracy, capitalism, and religious freedom as God-ordained norms.

44. Natasha Zaretsky. *No Direction Home: The American Family and the Fear of National Decline, 1968–1980*. Chapell Hill: University of North Carolina Press, 2007, pp. 143–82.

45. Bill Bright. "Countdown to '76." September 1976, box 1, folder 24, Wilber M. Smith papers, Archer Archives, Trinity Evangelical Divinity School, Deerfield, IL.

46. Gallup polling, for example, showed for the first time in 1979 that less than 60% of Americans identified as Protestant. The high-mark of Gallup's polling (dating back to 1948) was in 1956, when 71% identified as Protestant. By the same time in 1979, Catholic identification increased to 29% and "None" increased to 7%, from a low of 1% in 1956. Available online: http://www.gallup.com/poll/1690/religion.aspx (accessed on 29 September 2016).

47. *In the Spirit of '76: The Citizen's Guide to Politics*. Washington: Third Century, 1975.

48. Kenneth L. Woodward. "Politics from the Pulpit." *Newsweek*, 9 June 1976, p. 49.

49. For example, Graham endorsed John Conlan in his Arizona senate race in 1976 (Conlan lost in the Republican primary).

50. Megan Rosenfeld. "The Evangelist and His Empire: Cleaning up America with Jerry Falwell." *Washington Post*, 28 April 1978, B2.

51. David Swartz. *Moral Minority: The Evangelical Left in an Age of Conservatism*. Philadelphia: University of Pennsylvania Press, 2012, pp. 213–32.

52. J. Brooks Flippen. *Jimmy Carter, the Politics of Family, and the Rise of the Religious Right*. Athens: University of Georgia Press, 2011.

53. For a discussion of how the Religious Right of the 1980s re-appropriated "Judeo-Christianity" from its interfaith and ecumenical valences at mid-century, see Kevin M. Schultz. *Tri-Faith America: How Catholics and Jews Held Postwar America to Its Protestant Promise*. New York: Oxford University Press, 2011, pp. 198–210.

54. Barry Hankins. *Francis Schaeffer and the Shaping of Evangelical America*. Grand Rapids: W. B. Eerdmans, 2008.

55. Molly Worthen. *Apostles of Reason: The Crisis of Authority in American Evangelicalism*. New York: Oxford University Press, 2013.

56. Francis A. Schaeffer. *The God Who Is There*. Downers Grove: InterVarsity Press, 1968.

57. Francis A. Schaeffer. *How Should We Then Live? The Rise and Decline of Western Thought and Culture*. Old Tappan: Fleming H. Revell Co., 1976.

58. Tim F. LaHaye. *The Battle for the Mind*. Old Tappan: Revell, 1980.

59. Francis Schaeffer. *A Christian Manifesto*, Rev. ed. Westchester: Crossway Books, 1982.

60. George Nash. *The Conservative Intellectual Movement in America Since 1945*, 2nd ed. Wilmington: Intercollegiate Studies Institute, 2006. The first edition was published in 1976.

61. Schaeffer quoted Perry Miller's *Nature's Nation*. Cambridge: Harvard-Belknap, 1967, p. 110.: "'Rationalism' was never so widespread as liberal historians, or those fascinated by Jefferson, have imagined. The basic fact is that the Revolution had been preached to the masses as a religious revival, and had the astounding fortune to succeed."

62. Ronald Reagan. "Labor Day Speech at Liberty State Park, Jersey City, New Jersey." 1 September 1980. Available online: https://reaganlibrary.archives.gov/archives/reference/9.1.80.html (accessed on 29 September 2016).

63. Bob Slosser. *Reagan Inside out*. Waco: Word Books, 1984.

64. Paul Kengor. *God and Ronald Reagan: A Spiritual Life*. New York: Regan Books, 2004.

65. Jan Hanska. *Reagan's Mythical America: Storytelling as Political Leadership*. New York: Palgrave Macmillan, 2012, pp. 75–134.

66. Steven P. Miller. *The Age of Evangelicalism: America's Born-Again Years*. New York: Oxford University Press, 2014.

67. Scott Lamb. *Huckabee: The Authorized Biography*. Nashville: Thomas Nelson Inc., 2015.

68. For an example of this principle argument, see Jerry Falwell, Jr.'s endorsement of Donald Trump. Jerry Falwell Jr. "Trump is the Churchillian Leader We Need." *Washington Post*, 19 August 2016. Available online: https://www.washingtonpost.com/opinions/jerry-falwell-jr-trump-is-the-churchillian-leader-we-need/2016/08/19/b1ff79e0--64b1--11e6-be4e-23fc4d4d12b4_story.html?utm_term=.29636a6520e0 (accessed on 29 September 2016).

69. Michael Grunwald. "Trump's High Energy War on American Politics." *Politico*, 26 September 2016. Available online: http://www.politico.com/magazine/story/2016/09/2016-trump-clinton-rallies-debate-politics-214290 (accessed on 29 September 2016).

70. Mark Silk. "Trump's Tent Revival." *Religion News Service*, 22 March 2016. Available online: http://religionnews.com/2016/03/22/trumps-tent-revival/ (accessed on 29 September 2016).

MDPI AG

St. Alban-Anlage 66

4052 Basel, Switzerland

Tel. +41 61 683 77 34

Fax +41 61 302 89 18

http://www.mdpi.com

Religions Editorial Office

E-mail: religions@mdpi.com

http://www.mdpi.com/journal/religions

www.ingramcontent.com/pod-product-compliance
Lightning Source LLC
Chambersburg PA
CBHW051316020426
42333CB00028B/3360